MW01195778

SAY HELLO
TO THE BAD
GUYS

HOW PROFESSIONAL WRESTLING'S
NEW WORLD ORDER
CHANGED AMERICA

MARC RAIMONDI

Simon & Schuster

NEW YORK   AMSTERDAM/ANTWERP   LONDON
TORONTO   SYDNEY/MELBOURNE   NEW DELHI

Simon & Schuster
1230 Avenue of the Americas
New York, NY 10020

Copyright © 2025 by Marc Raimondi

For more than 100 years, Simon & Schuster has championed authors and the stories they create. By respecting the copyright of an author's intellectual property, you enable Simon & Schuster and the author to continue publishing exceptional books for years to come. We thank you for supporting the author's copyright by purchasing an authorized edition of this book.

No amount of this book may be reproduced or stored in any format, nor may it be uploaded to any website, database, language-learning model, or other repository, retrieval, or artificial intelligence system without express permission.

All rights reserved, including the right to reproduce this book or portions thereof in any form whatsoever. For information, address Simon & Schuster Subsidiary Rights Department, 1230 Avenue of the Americas, New York, NY 10020.

First Simon & Schuster hardcover edition June 2025

SIMON & SCHUSTER and colophon are registered trademarks
of Simon & Schuster, LLC

Simon & Schuster strongly believes in freedom of expression and stands against censorship in all its forms. For more information, visit BooksBelong.com.

For information about special discounts for bulk purchases, please contact Simon & Schuster Special Sales at 1-866-506-1949 or business@simonandschuster.com.

The Simon & Schuster Speakers Bureau can bring authors to your live event. For more information or to book an event, contact the Simon & Schuster Speakers Bureau at 1-866-248-3049 or visit our website at www.simonspeakers.com.

Manufactured in the United States of America

1   3   5   7   9   10   8   6   4   2

Library of Congress Cataloging-in-Publication Data has been applied for.

ISBN 978-1-6680-1375-5
ISBN 978-1-6680-1377-9 (ebook)

"The world is fake, and wrestling is real."
—Rick Rubin

CONTENTS

INTRODUCTION

The sun hadn't come up yet when I got to Los Angeles International Airport. It was May 2, 2023, and I had arrived about ninety minutes early for a 6 a.m. flight to Newark, New Jersey.

Another UFC fight week was awaiting me on the other side of the cross-country trek. I had already been covering combat sports for a decade. And sometimes, in that fast-moving world, it feels like a decade can go by in a month. So I was already tired.

I checked in my bag, walked through the TSA PreCheck line to security, and put my backpack and belongings on the conveyor belt. As I passed through the metal detector, I could hear the TSA agent humming a familiar, twangy tune.

I looked down and realized I was wearing a black hoodie with the white New World Order logo on the chest. The agent was, evidently, giving me my own entrance music to Terminal 4: the nWo theme. On the other side of the metal detector, he flashed me the signature nWo Wolfpac hand gesture and I reciprocated.

No words were exchanged. None were needed.

After I started working on this book in 2021, I flew down to Florida, visited Hulk Hogan's Beach Shop in Clearwater, and picked up the hoodie. I wore it on just about every work trip I made thereafter for the next few years. More than half the time, someone either commented on it or flashed the Wolfpac sign. One time, in Toronto, a gentleman waiting for his bags pulled up his sweater and showed me a giant tattoo of WWE legend Shawn Michaels on his rib cage.

Millions of wrestling fans are walking among us, even if we don't realize it. Some of them stopped watching at a certain age, but it still left an indelible impact on them from their childhood—enough of one, in some cases, to permanently put a reference to it on their bodies.

I moved to Atlanta in 2024 to cover the NFL's Falcons for ESPN. While getting a haircut in my new neighborhood, I struck up a conversation with the barbers, which inevitably led to the topic of pro wrestling. One of them pivoted his leg to show me a tattoo on his calf. It was the nWo Wolfpac hand gesture accompanied with the words "Too Sweet."

It's everywhere if your antennas are up to receive it.

All of these occurrences only underscored to me how important this book would be to many, not to mention how significant it could be to those who haven't quite understood just how much professional wrestling has penetrated the American psyche.

I couldn't help but laugh when, in 2024, there was controversy surrounding a photo of Republican vice-presidential candidate (and Donald Trump's running mate) JD Vance. In the picture, which surfaced on X (formerly Twitter) and appeared to be taken sometime in the 2000s, Vance was wearing a red shirt adorned with a Soviet hammer and sickle.

Was Vance a supporter of communism as a youth? Hardly. Just one look at the other people posing with him—three of whom were wearing nWo shirts—and that theory would easily be disproven. Any wrestling fan could have pointed out that it was probably Halloween and Vance's buddies were dressed as Scott Hall, Sting, and "Macho Man" Randy Savage. Fitting with the motif, Vance was confirmed by his representatives as wearing a costume inspired by wrestler Nikolai Volkoff, who played a Russian character during the Cold War.

It has become a prerequisite to understand pro wrestling in order to wrap your head around United States politics in this era. How else can you explain the rise of Trump, a WWE Hall of Famer who has hosted *WrestleMania* events and once shaved WWE owner Vince McMahon's head in the ring during a storyline? In 2025, Trump nominated McMahon's wife, Linda, the former WWE CEO, for U.S. Secretary of Education. Naturally.

The influence of wrestling goes far beyond politics. Dwayne "The Rock" Johnson is the world's highest-paid actor and one of the most recognizable people in the world. He got his start in his family business: professional wrestling. Johnson's grandfather and father were wrestlers, his grandmother was a wrestling promoter, and his daughter is now in WWE.

Music? You'd have to look pretty hard to find a hip-hop artist who has never rapped a lyric about pro wrestling. Latin reggaetonero Bad Bunny grew up watching wrestling in his native Puerto Rico, has titled songs after wrestlers, and has even gotten into the ring himself several times in WWE. He said, with complete sincerity, that his *WrestleMania* match made for the best day of his life. Hell, Taylor Swift used to babysit the kids of wrestling legend Jeff Jarrett, and Kendrick Lamar used the line "sweet chin music," Michaels's finishing move, in his definitive Drake diss track "Not Like Us."

Sports? San Francisco 49ers tight end George Kittle uses pro-wrestling taunts when he gets first downs and touchdowns. New York Knicks star Jalen Brunson and Indiana Pacers standout Tyrese Haliburton are huge wrestling fans and have actually faced off against each other in a WWE segment. Just about every major UFC headliner has some kind of connection with pro wrestling, including former champions Ronda Rousey and Brock Lesnar, who have both performed extensively for WWE. Legendary boxers Muhammad Ali, Mike Tyson, and Floyd Mayweather have all been involved with wrestling.

It goes on and on. To understand pro wrestling is to understand America itself. It's capitalism, it's materialism. It's bombast. A wrestling program is like a TikTok algorithm come to life.

But it's also something that has a certain set of rules and a belief system, not unlike religion. Pro wrestling's faith is called "kayfabe," the idea that everything that happens in the art—and it is a performance art—is completely real. Almost everyone has been aware for decades that pro wrestling isn't a legitimate sports competition, but Robert Downey Jr. isn't actually Iron Man, either.

Modern-day wrestling lives on the razor's edge of kayfabe, with elements of reality and fiction blended together as part of the show and on social media. Characters are like your favorite influencer. There's no telling where the real person ends and the persona begins. It's no wonder that Logan Paul has become a regular in WWE. Pro wrestling is a living, breathing meme.

Professional wrestling is fake, though the "f" word is a dirty one in the industry, understandably. The athleticism is real. The risks are real. The workload and travel are real. Surely, the injuries are very real. But pro wrestling is not a real sport. It's a simulated sport with melodramatic storylines and at-times ridiculous characters.

Some critics have called it lowbrow entertainment; others have questioned why anyone would watch pro wrestling rather than an actual sport. *You know it's fake, right?* The UFC has real fights, after all. But people saying those things are missing the entire point. Pro wrestling is a niche, albeit unconventional, medium of entertainment, like many others. Movies and television series aren't "real," either. They're made up of actors on sets reading scripts written by writers. I regret to inform you that Luke Skywalker isn't more real than The Undertaker, a six-foot-seven wrestling dead man. They're both characters played by men named Mark.

The biggest difference between wrestling and those other genres is that in wrestling, they're doing it live. It's one take, whether it be a match or acting out an interview, in front of a real crowd. No canned applause (most of the time) or laugh track.

So maybe in that way wrestling *feels* more real, even if it's not. Or maybe it is. That's the idea Eric Bischoff became obsessed with in the mid-to-late 1990s as the senior vice president of World Championship Wrestling (WCW). If everyone knows pro wrestling is a show—and by that time it was no longer a well-kept secret—how do you elicit an emotional reaction from the crowd? Bischoff's answer to that question was simply: manipulate people into thinking certain things they are seeing are indeed real, even if wrestling itself is not. Bischoff wanted to blend reality and fiction until he found what he refers to as a "sweet spot" where fans were entertained but also curious about the authenticity of what was happening.

That's where the nWo was born, at the intersection of genuine and phony. Lines became blurred. The antiheroes became the main characters. And pro wrestling was never the same again.

The nWo—the brainchild of Bischoff that came to life through the performances of Hogan, Hall, and Kevin Nash—was the catalyst for a wrestling boom period that was watched by millions, mostly young men. The kids, teens, and young adults who grew up watching the nWo in WCW from 1996 to 1999—and there were millions—are now leaders of industry, politicians, writers, producers, entertainers, musicians, and professional athletes, all of whom are helping to shape American culture right now. Many, like Trump, have learned from pro wrestling.

In 2022, I was wearing my nWo hoodie in Tokyo, in line for a breakfast restaurant with my wife, Wendy. When we reached the front of the line, the host, a Japanese man in his fifties, saw the logo and recognized it instantly. He didn't speak English and I can't speak any Japanese, but we were able to connect through memories that meant something to both of us.

The nWo really mattered to people back then. It still matters to people now. In this book, I'll attempt to do justice to the tale of how the nWo started, what made it so big, and how and why it has made a lasting impression on pro wrestling and beyond.

I hope you enjoy it.

PART I

CHAPTER 1

THE SPECTACLE
OF EXCESS

Hulk Hogan fidgeted in his seat. The world-famous professional wrestler was sitting on a gray sofa on the set of *The Arsenio Hall Show*. The host filled a chair adjacent to him. Hogan adjusted his oversized belt and pulled on his skintight jeans with his massive hands.

"I've got my shorts in a wad," he said with a forced smile.

Hogan knew exactly what Hall was going to ask him. The World Wrestling Federation (WWF), the company Hogan helped build into the biggest in the industry, was embroiled in a steroid scandal. Hogan was by far the WWF's biggest star, a six-foot-five blond muscleman who achieved mainstream fame in the 1980s. He had also been tied in reports to George Zahorian, a doctor facing federal charges for the distribution of illegal steroids to wrestlers.

Earlier in the day, in July 1991, WWF owner Vince McMahon held a press conference, admitting to prior steroid use himself and announcing that the company would start to implement anti-drug protocols.

Hogan going on Hall's show was another vehicle for the WWF's public relations. Hogan and Hall ran in the same Hollywood circles, and Hogan had been interviewed by him several times before. McMahon wanted Hogan to admit to his past steroid use or not sit down with Hall at all.

But Hogan had other plans.

For years, Hogan had been the most popular good guy—or babyface—in wrestling. His entire character was based around how he always did everything the right way. Hogan would tell kids to train, eat their vitamins, and say their prayers. He was terrified that if he admitted to using steroids, he would be labeled a hypocrite.

Hogan's audience was mostly children. And even the adults, while knowing the choreographed nature of professional wrestling, still believed in him. He was the blue-eyed hero facing down evildoers while never compromising his white, Christian principles.

So Hogan lied in an attempt to preserve his perceived values. He said he never abused steroids, nor was he a steroid user. Hogan said he used physician-prescribed steroids in the past to treat injuries, but that was it. For more than thirteen minutes, a stammering Hogan blamed the media, feigned ignorance about steroids, and intimated his size was due to genetics. Ironically, he was wearing a white "World's Gym" T-shirt with a jacked-up gorilla illustration in the middle of it.

McMahon was pissed off at Hogan's denials, and Hogan regretted lying before he even left the building. He has referred to the interview as his "biggest mistake." Hogan later admitted to steroid use while under oath, saying he started with the drugs in 1975.

"I see now that I should have taken all the bullets out of Arsenio's gun and said, 'Yes, I used steroids to bulk up,'" Hogan said. "I should have come clean. It probably would have hurt my career but not as badly or for as long a time. So I screwed myself."

Hogan traded in the feeling of being a charlatan for the feeling of being a liar. Fans saw through the platitudes in the Hall interview and, while it didn't necessarily hit Hogan in the pocketbook immediately, the relationship he had worked hard to build with the fan base had been damaged. He came off slimy and disingenuous, not befitting a role model to kids.

An even more important relationship had also been affected: the one between Hogan and McMahon, the two most significant figures in the history of the industry. The two of them—the promoter and the superstar—teamed up to grow the WWF into a pop-culture phenomenon in the eighties.

Once close friends and confidants, Hogan and McMahon started to drift apart after the Hall interview.

———

In the late 1970s, Terry Bollea debuted as a wrestler in his home state of Florida. He worked the territory circuit for two years in Memphis and Atlanta, but also in places like Jonesboro, Arkansas, and Booneville, Mississippi. Prior to McMahon consolidating the industry, there were thriving regional and local promotions throughout the country. That's where Bollea got his start, on the back roads of the southeastern United States.

Bollea wasn't a star at that time. But he stood out. He had long blond hair, a blond goatee, and was simply a large individual. A bodybuilder for years, Bollea was billed as six-foot-seven and weighed in the neighborhood of three hundred pounds. Steroids, which weren't made illegal in the United States until 1990, were pervasive in bodybuilding, some Olympic sports, and, of course, pro wrestling.

While already a large man by any standard, Bollea understood that injecting himself with steroids would allow him to increase his muscle mass. Strength is important in pro wrestling, but aesthetic is everything. It's show business. Bollea had an innate feel for that—what fans reacted to—from the beginning and the unique charisma to carry it out.

That included adapting things as part of his character from his own squared-circle heroes like "Superstar" Billy Graham and Dusty Rhodes and making them his own. From Graham, he borrowed poses and catchphrases, like referring to his bulging arms as "pythons." From Rhodes, he picked up in-ring mannerisms like finger wagging and pointing.

In 1979, Bollea was promoting one of his matches on a morning talk show in Mobile, Alabama, and the other guest was Lou Ferrigno. An actor and bodybuilder, Ferrigno had been portraying the live-action version of Marvel Comics' "The Incredible Hulk" on television for two years. The host of the show joked that Bollea was "bigger than the Hulk."

Bollea started working under the name Terry "The Hulk" Boulder from there, until he began with the WWF (which is now WWE), then promoted by Vincent James McMahon, the father of the McMahon who guided the WWF to national prominence.

The elder McMahon thought Bollea looked Irish, so he handed him a bottle of red hair dye and renamed his character to Hulk Hogan. Bollea's father was Italian, and his mother was French, Italian, and Panamanian. That didn't matter. Vincent James McMahon's characters in the WWF were defined by their nationalities, like Italian immigrant Bruno Sammartino, and Bollea was close enough. The New York–based WWF wanted to sell tickets to the area's substantial Irish community.

Bollea ditched the red-hair dye bottle. But the new name stuck. Bollea would be known as Hulk Hogan from then on.

With a new moniker, Hogan started carving out a path for himself in the WWF. But he was portraying a bad guy, or heel, which would likely only limit how big of a star he could become.

————

Professional wrestling features a fairly elementary framework for storytelling. There are heroes, called babyfaces, and villains, called heels. The babyfaces, in most cases, are the stars of the show, the ones who prevail in the end. The heels are the ones cheating and trying to do everything to overthrow the babyfaces' dreams of being champion or attaining whatever goal the storyline is outlining.

Heels have to win matches and establish credibility as legitimate threats to their enemies, the babyfaces. Heels can be champions and sometimes ascend to becoming a promotion's biggest star. But, especially in pro wrestling prior to the 1990s, the heel characters are mostly there in service to the babyface characters.

The babyface is the wrestler the fans are supposed to get behind, the one the audience is cheering for to emerge victorious. The heel is there for the fans to boo, to stack the deck against the babyface so that when the babyface finally wins, there is a feeling of catharsis. But that therapeutic reaction can only be achieved if the heel is effectively malevolent enough that fans want the babyface to dish out comeuppance.

Pro wrestling, at its core, is a morality play. It's Shakespeare in a ring.

————

Hogan got his big break in 1981—and it wasn't in the wrestling ring. While working for the WWF, Hogan received a Western Union letter backstage from Sylvester Stallone, one of the biggest action stars of the decade. Stallone said in the letter that he wanted Hogan to play a role in *Rocky III*.

Stallone was looking for a wrestler to be paired against the Rocky Balboa character in a charity exhibition match in the film. Hogan was a fan of the first two *Rocky* movies, both of which did well at the box office. Stallone was a megastar. He believed it was a no-brainer to take the part.

His promoter felt otherwise. Vincent James McMahon told Hogan that he was in the WWF's storyline plans and there just wasn't time for him to jet off to Hollywood to film a movie. The elder McMahon issued Hogan an ultimatum: If you do *Rocky III*, don't bother coming back to the WWF.

Believing that sharing time with Stallone on the silver screen would do wonders for his profile, Hogan walked out on the WWF and took the role.

Rocky III ended up doing very well at the box office, becoming one of the highest-grossing movies of 1982. The only two films that made more money were *E.T.* and *Raiders of the Lost Ark*.

Before *Rocky III* even had a chance to premiere, the American Wrestling Association (AWA) in Minnesota, promoted by highly respected former amateur and pro wrestler Verne Gagne, came calling for Hogan's services. So Hogan headed up to Minneapolis for another shot with a major wrestling company.

The problem was, the fans did not view the bronzed Hogan, billed from Venice Beach, California, as a bad guy, despite how his character was being scripted to act. He was booked to be a villain, but movie star and bodybuilder Arnold Schwarzenegger had made Venice—he trained at an outdoor gym there called Muscle Beach—a recognized and cool place in the 1970s, especially to parka-wearing Midwesterners. Hogan also had a personality that connected with the audience as something more than a one-dimensional, meathead heel.

Before the end of 1981, spurred by audiences, the AWA made Hogan a babyface. When *Rocky III* came out a few months later, Hogan started walking out to the ring with the Rocky theme song, "Eye of the Tiger," playing over the PA system. When he got to the ring, he ripped off his shirt, exposing his substantial pectoral muscles. Hogan also began a side hustle, printing T-shirts at the local mall and selling his own merchandise with catchphrases on it out of the back of his truck. Hogan's name was growing so much that Johnny Carson had him on *The Tonight Show* in 1982.

"That's where I started planting the seeds that would grow into Hulkamania," Hogan said.

A McMahon reached out to Hogan in 1983. But it wasn't Vincent James; it was his son, who had purchased the WWF from his father a year earlier. The younger McMahon wanted to take the WWF national, with Hogan as his lead character. He was signing some of the top stars from around the country, away from the regional, territory promotions. This was the opportunity Hogan had been waiting for, and it wasn't difficult for him to depart the AWA.

Hogan returned to the WWF in December 1983 and, in his fourth match back, on January 23, 1984, he won the WWF World Heavyweight title, beating hated villain The Iron Sheik, who played an anti-American character from Iran. The relationship between the United States and Iran fell out after the Islamic Revolution in 1979 and the two countries have not had diplomatic relations since then.

The Sheik, a real-life former national-team wrestler from Iran, represented America's biggest political foe at the time. Hogan would begin walking out to a new theme song called "Real American" in 1985.

Cyndi Lauper, one of the hottest pop stars of the time, was brought into the WWF fold that same year. Her then-boyfriend and manager Dave Wolff was a lifelong wrestling fan. Hogan, wearing a white tuxedo shirt (sleeveless, to show off his preternaturally large arms) and black bowtie, accompanied Lauper to the 1985 Grammy Awards as her bodyguard and came up onstage with her when she won in the best new artist category. The WWF and MTV soon joined together for a collaboration that was called the *Rock 'n' Wrestling Connection.*

The next step for McMahon's wrestling revolution and Hogan's burgeoning fame was a supershow at New York's Madison Square Garden that would be called *WrestleMania.*

The *WrestleMania I* headliner was built around a storyline involving Lauper. At a WWF event, Lauper awarded WWF manager Captain Lou Albano with a gold record. Albano played Lauper's father in the music video for her hit song "Girls Just Want to Have Fun." "Rowdy" Roddy Piper, the promotion's top heel, interrupted the ceremony, cracked the record over Albano's head, and then "kicked" Lauper. Hogan came out to save her and ran Piper off.

The angle, the pro-wrestling term for a non-match storyline development, was everything McMahon could have hoped for and more. *WrestleMania* just needed a little more star power to complete McMahon's vision to take wrestling mainstream.

McMahon looked down on what wrestling had been, events where storytelling took place in the ring through simulated fights. What he wanted to build was an entertainment company, so much so that he later banned the use of the words "professional wrestling" on WWF television, with "sports entertainment" as the substitute. Wrestlers could not be called wrestlers; they were "Superstars."

McMahon didn't think he could grow his promotion on the back of fake fights. He needed glitz and glamour. The first *Wrestle-*

Mania needed celebrities with the hope that their presence could elevate McMahon's "Superstars" to that same status.

Peter Young, Hogan's agent, also represented Mr. T, who was brought in to be Hogan's tag-team partner for the big main-event match. At the time, Mr. T was starring in the hit show *The A-Team*. That wasn't all. Muhammad Ali was hired as special referee. Billy Martin, the controversial then-manager of the New York Yankees, was a guest ring announcer. And Liberace, the flamboyant pianist, was guest timekeeper.

The injection of luminaries from the worlds of music, sports, and television worked wonders for McMahon's marketing of *WrestleMania*. And Hogan himself.

The week of *WrestleMania I* was a whirlwind of trying to drum up interest for the event. Hogan and Mr. T were all over TV, especially news programs after an incident that occurred on the Lifetime show *Hot Properties*, hosted by Richard Belzer. The man who went on to become most famous for playing a television detective was something of a victim that night.

Hogan reluctantly agreed to placate Belzer when the host asked him to demonstrate a wrestling move. Belzer had been talking trash jokingly with Hogan and Mr. T and actually asked Hogan why he was a "bad guy" and then became a "good guy," somewhat alluding to pro wrestling not being real, which was a no-no then. Belzer then asked Hogan to perform a submission on him.

Hogan, his hairline already betraying him before he became a household name, towered over Belzer as he explained that he would put the skinny comedian in a front headlock. Hogan gently grabbed Belzer's shoulders and pulled him downward, bent at the waist. Hogan then wrapped his giant right arm around Belzer's head and neck and connected his right hand with his left bicep.

Belzer looked like he was struggling as Hogan and Mr. T talked some smack. Then, Belzer's arms went limp. Hogan let him go and the comedian's body snapped to the floor, the back of his head cracking against the ground. The live audience gasped.

"You all right, brother?" Hogan asked as Belzer came to.

Hogan helped Belzer up and Belzer quickly seemed to regain his senses, throwing the telecast to commercial. Then Belzer turned around—and blood could be seen dripping from the back of his head down onto his blazer.

Belzer ended up going to the hospital. Hogan and McMahon were lucky. If Belzer had been severely injured or worse, the outrage might have gotten *WrestleMania* canceled. Instead, all that happened was the incident getting the WWF much more media attention.

Hogan and Mr. T hosted *Saturday Night Live* the night before *WrestleMania I*, which took place March 31, 1985. Pro wrestling was Hollywood suddenly, with Hogan playing the role of leading man.

The Associated Press reported the next morning that one million people watched *WrestleMania I* on closed-circuit television (the predecessor to pay-per-view). Several reports have put the attendance figure at 19,121. McMahon invested millions—his daughter, Stephanie, said years later that her mother and father "mortgaged everything they owned"—and the first *WrestleMania* was a massive success.

"It was funny, because nobody ever talked about wrestling except wrestling fans," said wrestling journalist and historian Dave Meltzer, who has been writing the *Wrestling Observer Newsletter* since 1983. "And then, that week everybody talked about wrestling. It was just *the thing* in pop culture."

Belzer ended up suing Hogan, a personal injury lawsuit that was settled out of court for $400,000. But the scene playing on news shows and hosting *Saturday Night Live* only helped the *WrestleMania* promotional tour's momentum—and Hogan's budding stardom.

Hogan's peers were noticing the changes in the business, too. Wrestlers did not have guaranteed contracts then, instead getting paid a percentage of whatever the ticket sales were for the shows they were on.

"We'd sometimes run two or three cities a night with different people [in the main events]," said Jimmy Hart, a legendary on-screen wrestling manager and Hogan's longtime confidant. "Well, all of us wanted to be on the show that Hulk was on, because we were going to make more money. . . . We knew if Hulk was on [the show], no matter where it was, it was going to sell out."

If Hogan was a master at manipulating a crowd and getting them to pay good money to see his matches, he was every bit as shrewd of a businessman behind the scenes, with his attorney Henry Holmes and Young backing him up.

Holmes said the first time he got into a verbal battle with McMahon was over merchandise and how much Hogan was getting for sold items with his name and likeness. There was one particularly combative meeting at the WWF offices in Stamford, Connecticut, that Holmes recalled vividly. McMahon was sitting at his desk and Holmes and Hogan were opposite him.

"Well, so you don't like this clause on merchandising?" McMahon said, according to Holmes. "I don't have to listen to any fucking lawyer about merchandising. This meeting is over."

But Hogan was too valuable to the WWF, and McMahon had to compromise. The two sides eventually came to an agreement that gave Hogan a larger percentage of his merchandise revenue and control of his name and likeness. Originally, the WWF owned the Hogan intellectual property (along with a percentage given to Marvel initially due to use of the Hulk name), but keeping Hogan happy and headlining events was paramount. Hogan was already the highest-paid wrestler in the world by several degrees. He had leverage, due to crowd demand, that no one else did. And Hogan never had any issue using that leverage.

"A lot of it was, initially the wrestling contracts were really, really one-sided," Holmes said. "And the control is owning the character and all that stuff."

Hogan headlined the second *WrestleMania* in 1986, beating King Kong Bundy in a cage match. It was a big event, but it paled in contrast to what came next.

In 1987, the WWF put together the biggest match in wrestling history up until that point, one many would argue remains the most significant ever.

If Hogan was the most famous wrestler in the world, Andre the Giant was a close second. Andre, whose real name was André Roussimoff, was billed as being seven-foot-four and five hundred pounds. In reality, he was probably closer to six-foot-ten. But his unprecedented combination of uncanny size and charisma made him the most unique athlete in the annals of professional wrestling. It also earned him attention outside the ring. Roussimoff had a role in the 1987 movie *The Princess Bride*.

For the preceding years, Hogan and Andre were both booked as babyface characters, and friends. They had tag-team matches alongside each other. But then, due to the manipulation of Hogan antagonist Bobby "The Brain" Heenan, Andre turned on his buddy. During one interview segment, he yanked Hogan's crucifix necklace right off his neck. In storyline, Andre had grown jealous of the attention Hogan was getting, when Andre was the one who allegedly had not been pinned or submitted for the last fifteen years (neither was true). Heenan said Hogan only maintained a friendship with Andre so he didn't have to defend the WWF title against him.

The WWF built the match as Hogan going up against an unstoppable foe, someone who had not even been body-slammed. In reality, Andre had been beaten outside the WWF and body-slammed several times all over the world, including on several occasions by Hogan himself. But, in pro wrestling, it's always the promotion and story that trumps reality. The truth hardly matters. The WWF had an audience that likely didn't know what was happening in wrestling outside its own storylines, and McMahon had no problem using that to his advantage.

The WWF claims 93,173 people packed the Pontiac Silverdome in Michigan on March 29, 1987, for *WrestleMania III*. The real number was closer to 78,000, but, in pro wrestling, exaggeration is the rule. The actual figure is impressive enough, in the same way the pain from a suplex or slam can be legitimate. But doesn't it stand out more when it gets embellished?

More than one million more tuned in on closed-circuit television to see if Hogan could topple his most fearsome foe yet.

Of course, he did. Hogan was the WWF's meal ticket, and people had paid to see the satisfying conclusion of the story: good over evil. Hogan slammed Andre, pinned him, and took Hulkamania to another level of stardom than wrestling had seen before.

The two men had a rematch eleven months later, on a card called *The Main Event*, which was on free-to-air NBC. The show drew 33 million viewers for a rating of 15.2, according to Nielsen. It still stands as the most-watched wrestling match ever in the United

States on television, and there's almost no chance that record will ever be broken with the deterioration of TV viewership due to other technologies.

"[My wife and I] would be out to dinner someplace and somebody at the next table would be talking about the WWF or Hulk Hogan or Andre or whoever," said Rob Wright, who was a producer and editor for the WWF in the 1980s. "It was so ingrained in pop culture, there really was no escape."

Hogan was pro wrestling's first real brand name in the modern era, someone who transcended the art. There is no formula to recognizing or building a star. Several things can help: someone's looks or sex appeal, their physical charisma, and how they can engage with fans in interviews. That doesn't just apply to wrestling; it applies to entertainment and sports, as well. As in Hollywood, the biggest stars are not always the best actors. Hogan was not a mat wrestler who produced classic matches. Tom Cruise has never won an Oscar, either.

McMahon went about building stars like he did most things: with blunt force. Hogan was on prime-time talk shows, Saturday morning cartoons, on the cover of cereal boxes, featured at toy stores with his action figures. Everywhere you looked.

Hogan wore the colors red and yellow. Psychologists have said that those colors are effective in marketing—think McDonald's—because of how they make consumers feel. And Hogan was indeed like the pro-wrestling version of the Big Mac. He wasn't a Michelin-starred meal—wrestlers like Ric Flair, Dusty Rhodes, Ricky Steamboat, and Terry Funk were the ones putting on the critically acclaimed matches of the day in the National Wrestling Alliance (NWA) and then World Championship Wrestling (WCW). Hogan's popularity was not because of how good he was in the ring, but because of how he resonated with the public. He didn't have a long list of attacks in the squared circle, sticking mainly to punching, kicking, a big boot, and a leg drop.

But Hogan had the magnetism and oversized personality to make it work. More important, he was so incredibly driven to be at the top that he put in all the necessary work, which included an exhausting amount of travel for media and promotional events while maintaining his impressive physique. And the latter, of course, involved taking steroids.

———

In his 1957 book *Mythologies*, the French philosopher Roland Barthes wrote an essay titled "The World of Wrestling," in which he described the art as "the spectacle of excess."

"The public is completely uninterested in knowing whether the contest is rigged or not, and rightly so; it abandons itself to the primary virtue of the spectacle, which is to abolish all motives and all consequences: what matters is not what it thinks but what it sees," Barthes wrote.

What wrestling really is, to those in the thick of it, is business. It started in U.S. carnivals in the late 1800s as real competition, a veritable toughman contest. People in the crowd of carnival-goers tested themselves on the mat against the touring roughneck. Pretty quickly, organizers started to realize the actual matches weren't nearly as exciting as the idea of them. By the 1920s, capitalism took over. The winners were predetermined based on what could make the most money, and the action was manufactured to be more pleasing to the eye.

The result was something infinitely more popular than the original idea of having an actual grappling contest. And professional wrestling has been a staple of American society ever since, one that has branched out and gained a big following in places like Canada, Mexico, Japan, Europe, and Australia.

Professional wrestling is more story than sport. There's a psychological and sociological aspect to it, too. What compels people to spend their hard-earned money to watch what are basically fake fights?

WWE today is a multibillion-dollar company that reaches every corner of the globe on Netflix. The success of professional wrestling cannot be argued. And the reasons for that success have been applied in just about every aspect of life. Conflict and controversy, manufactured or otherwise, can be powerful and lucrative.

Pro-wrestling promoters were the godfathers of that idea—"the spectacle of excess."

———

Hogan was the man on top when the WWF went mainstream. And he had done all the work to help pro wrestling—really, McMahon's sports entertainment—remain there into the next decade.

So when McMahon told Hogan that the Ultimate Warrior would be beating him to win the WWF title at *WrestleMania VI*, on April 1, 1990, you could imagine Hogan's reaction. Hogan didn't agree with the idea at first, but eventually gave in. Warrior pinned Hogan at Toronto's SkyDome to become champion. It was the first time Hogan had lost via pinfall without any shenanigans in six years, before *WrestleMania I*.

McMahon had forced the man who helped him fulfill his vision to pass the torch to someone Hogan deemed unworthy. That was the wrestling business. Promoters are always looking for the new, fresh thing. For McMahon, that was the Warrior, a preposterously ripped bodybuilder with off-the-wall (likely chemically enhanced) intensity and bizarre, snorting interviews.

Hogan had an idea for after the match, something that might continue his momentum despite the loss. He wanted to beat the Warrior up, turn "heel," and go on a run as a bad guy. McMahon shot it down.

"I wanted to attack the Warrior from behind after the finish at *WrestleMania VI* and drag him around by the hair and I'd be the worst guy ever," Hogan said.

Hogan would eventually be vindicated. Realizing that maybe Warrior was not the right guy to lead the WWF into the future, McMahon had Sgt. Slaughter win the title from him in January 1991.

Slaughter, dressed in camo with a drill sergeant's hat, had played a U.S. military veteran and proud patriot for years. He even had a character in the popular G.I. Joe comic and cartoon based on him with the same likeness. McMahon had the idea to have Slaughter break bad and reveal himself to be an Iraqi sympathizer—right in the middle of the United States' involvement in the Gulf War.

And who better to reclaim the title from a traitor to his country? America's hero, of course. Hogan. He beat Slaughter after a particularly jingoistic buildup to win the WWF title back at *WrestleMania VII* on March 24, 1991.

Hogan dropped the title to The Undertaker, an up-and-coming occult heel character, later in 1991 due to interference from Flair, who came in from WCW with the NWA title.

Flair proclaimed himself to be the real world champion. It seemed like a *WrestleMania VIII* main event between Hogan and Flair was in the offing. The two were the most popular wrestlers of the 1980s, but didn't cross paths due to being in different promotions. Even in 1992, that was a big-money match. But it didn't happen.

Why not? That depends on who you ask. The WWF mythology says Hogan and Flair wrestled on several untelevised events—called "house shows" in wrestling—and those shows did not sell well. In reality, it's more likely that McMahon and Hogan could not agree on a finish to that *WrestleMania* match, given what was going on behind the scenes.

McMahon had been roped into the federal steroid case against Zahorian. The U.S. government was accusing McMahon of distributing steroids to his wrestlers and encouraging them to use the drugs. The feds were going to call Hogan as a witness for the prosecution—against McMahon.

At *WrestleMania VIII*, Flair wrestled "Macho Man" Randy Savage for the WWF title and Hogan was in the main event, a nontitle match, against the six-foot-seven Sid Justice. Hogan beat Justice, then disappeared from WWF television for nearly a year.

Hogan returned to the WWF in February 1993 to set up a match for *WrestleMania IX* in what would be, in essence, his farewell run. It would end up being his final *WrestleMania* for nine years. Hogan's contract was expiring, and he and McMahon were ready to go their separate ways.

Hogan was to team with Brutus Beefcake, Hogan's longtime friend from Florida (real name: Ed Leslie), against Money Inc., the tag team of Ted DiBiase and Irwin R. Schyster. But the bout almost never happened, and Hogan nearly lost his life before he got the chance to close his chapter with the WWF.

Two days before *WrestleMania IX*, Hogan went out on Jet Skis with Leslie and their friend Ellis Edwards, who was the stunt coordinator on the popular TV show *Baywatch*. Leslie had a faster Jet Ski than Hogan's and offered Hogan a chance to try it out. Hogan made a mechanical error in driving the craft and hit a wave hard. The front end of the Jet Ski stayed down and launched the wrestling superstar headfirst over the top of it.

Hogan would have been fine. Except the Jet Ski then followed and hit him right in the head, near his left eye, at forty miles per hour. Hogan's orbital bone cracked on impact. Edwards was able to get Hogan onto his Jet Ski and to the beach. He and Leslie then rushed him to the hospital. Hogan was out cold and facedown in the water before Edwards got to him.

Hogan had a concussion, so Edwards stayed up the entire night with him, waking him up every hour. At *WrestleMania IX*, two days later, Hogan sported a nasty black eye and wore a bandage over the area. Hogan told the Nevada State Athletic Commission (NSAC) that it was just makeup, and the injuries were just part of the show. Given what wrestling is, that was surely plausible. But in this case, Hogan was actually hurt, and should not have been anywhere near a ring.

"That's really what it was," Edwards said of the injury. "Stitches are all in there. It's all purple and the eye is slammed, it's all swollen. He's got a mild crack up there. It's a big goddamn deal. And they did let him wrestle."

Not only wrestle, but Hogan came out after the main event between Yokozuna and Bret Hart and challenged the winner— Yokozuna, a 500-plus-pound Samoan wrestler playing a sumo character—to a title match right then and there. Hogan was booked to win. He pinned Yokozuna to claim the WWF championship for a fifth time.

That was essentially Hogan's WWF swan song. Hogan lost the

title to Yokozuna on June 13, 1993. The two had a series of house-show matches that summer and then Hogan was gone, letting his contract with the WWF run out.

The relationship between Hogan and McMahon by then was completely nonexistent. McMahon felt betrayed by Hogan after all they had been through together. Not only as business partners, but each considered the other a good friend before the steroid scandal. McMahon felt like his company, the one he invested all his money and time into, was at stake, as was his livelihood. He was facing jail time. And McMahon believed Hogan was helping the federal government dismantle all he had built.

The prosecution told Hogan that he would get immunity as long as he told the truth about McMahon. When Hogan agreed to testify, McMahon cut off all communication with him.

"He may have thought that I had turned on him," Hogan said of McMahon. "I would never have done that. But not being able to speak with him at that time put a tremendous strain on our relationship. And we didn't talk for a long time after that, even after the trial was over."

Hogan's testimony—he admitted to using steroids, but said McMahon never gave them to him nor told him to use them—wasn't damaging to McMahon in the least. It was more damaging to Hogan himself, who, under oath, finally came clean about what else he did to get his physique besides pumping iron. It wasn't just the vitamins he was telling kids to take.

Hogan's testimony also killed the government's case. They expected him to say McMahon bullied his wrestlers into taking steroids. McMahon ended up being acquitted due to lack of evidence.

It was evident to everyone that Hogan had indeed lied on the Hall show, that he didn't practice the principles that his character talked about on the air. Somewhat disgraced, even in a profession already treated by many as a disdainful fake sport, Hogan's career was at a crossroads.

Perhaps more television and film opportunities were in the future. One thing he had always promised to McMahon, though, was that he'd never compete against him in the wrestling business.

CHAPTER 2

BECAUSE THIS IS WHERE THE BIG BOYS PLAY

Eric Bischoff was just a few months into his new job in 1993, as executive producer of WCW, and trying to compete with the WWF was hardly his top priority. The WWF was far and away the biggest wrestling company in the world, and WCW was a distant second. Bischoff was simply trying to keep a promotion that was bleeding money afloat.

One of his first big ideas was to change the structure of WCW television tapings, which were mainly done in front of small crowds in the Atlanta area. WCW was owned by Ted Turner and with one flip of the remote control over to Turner Broadcasting System (TBS), where WCW aired, one could see where WCW stood in the pecking order. Audiences were sparse. Venues, almost entirely in the Southeast, were tiny. Production value was lacking.

In 1993, Bischoff visited Disney MGM Studios (now called Disney Hollywood Studios) in Bay Lake, Florida, near Orlando, and liked what he saw. There were soundstages there that, when filmed, looked bigger than they actually were. The production and lighting were superior to what WCW had on the road. Multiple TV shows could be shot in the same place in the same day, and that could add up to eight to ten shows in a single weekend. WCW could fly talent in to one place for a few days and film television cards for a month or more.

Plus, there was a captive audience. The theme park was full most days and WCW could give away free tickets. It isn't like they weren't doing that already. The Disney patrons may not have been wrestling fans, but they "had all their teeth," Bischoff said. So not only would it cut costs, it theoretically would look less small-time on TV.

In some ways, this was the opposite of what the WWF was doing with McMahon pushing for bigger arenas and larger-scale events. Wrestling shows had been held in every type of venue imaginable for decades, from football stadiums to VFW Halls. Television tapings were a mixed bag, depending on the size of the promotion.

But until the WWF started *Monday Night Raw* in 1993 on the USA Network, there were no weekly national-level, prime-time wrestling shows that ran (mostly) live on cable television. Even *Raw* was taped sometimes, which had been the norm previously. The WWF would tape shows in arenas and air them later. WCW would do the same, but in smaller, studio setups.

Bischoff's idea was to maintain the taped, studio-show model for WCW's shows, just with a Mickey Mouse–colored coat of fresh paint. It wasn't a popular idea internally. He got pushback from his higher-ups, as well as from Disney executives. Turner was based in Atlanta and officials weren't fond of moving production elsewhere. And Disney brass was afraid of kids there to see their characters running into Cro-Magnon wrestling fans.

And why would they have agreed with Bischoff anyway? He was in completely over his head.

Bischoff, a jet-black-haired, babyfaced Detroit native, had many jobs before wrestling, from meat delivery salesman to veterinary assistant to male model. At one point, Bischoff had been all in on a children's game called Ninja Star Wars with his business partner and longtime friend Sonny Onoo, whom he met when both were young karate competitors.

In 1991, Bischoff landed what he thought was the position of a lifetime—as a third-string play-by-play announcer for WCW. It was a $70,000-a-year gig and Bischoff thought he was rich. He had been working in marketing and advertising for Gagne's AWA before getting a shot in front of the camera when the promotion's main interviewer was arrested for drunk driving. Bischoff and his wife, Loree, left Minnesota for Atlanta, the home base of WCW, with some swiftness.

After two years of toiling on WCW's syndicated C-level shows, Bischoff was again the beneficiary of someone else's malfeasance.

Old-school wrestler and promoter Bill Watts had been running WCW as the promotion's vice president of wrestling operations for about a year when racist comments he made in an interview with the *PW Torch* wrestling newsletter surfaced. *Torch* reporter Mark Madden reached out to Hank Aaron, then Major League Baseball's home-run king and a Turner executive, for comment about Watts's remarks, which advocated for the ability of businesses to discriminate against Black Americans.

Shortly after, Watts was gone from WCW. Madden took credit for the departure, saying Aaron exerted power behind the scenes. Watts has denied that, saying he had already resigned before Aaron was made aware of his comments.

Bischoff, despite feeling like he had no chance, applied for Watts's old position, figuring he had nothing to lose. Bischoff pitched some ideas on how to modernize WCW. He felt like Watts was trying to bring wrestling back to the 1970s. Bischoff's proposals resonated. Turned off by Watts and the industry's old boys' club and wanting a fresh face, Turner executives Bill Shaw and Bob Dhue hired the then-thirty-eight-year-old as WCW's executive producer in 1993.

This did not go over too well internally. Legendary wrestling play-by-play announcer and executive Jim Ross, who had been Bischoff's boss, soon left WCW to join the WWF. Others who were far more qualified than Bischoff were passed up.

Bischoff himself knew he was out of his depth. But what was he going to do? Turn it down? Bischoff's son, Garett, was nine years old at the time and his daughter, Montanna, was eight. The job presented a significant raise. So with no further experience in TV other than being a backup broadcaster, Bischoff gave it a go.

What did he really have to lose? With or without him, WCW figured to never be in the same class as the WWF.

———

If there was one thing Bischoff was good at, it was persuading people. He was a smooth operator—he wouldn't have gotten the job as boss if not—and he was able to convince Turner execs and Disney people that WCW in Florida would work. Bischoff believed it would be a boon for advertisers and make WCW appear to be a national promotion, not just regional, southern wrestling.

It ended up doing much more than that.

The WCW TV tapings at Disney MGM started July 7, 1993. WCW filmed thirteen episodes of its syndicated show *Worldwide* over a four-day stretch and one episode of *WCW Saturday Night*, then the company's flagship show.

Coincidentally, or perhaps not-so-coincidentally depending

on who you ask, Hogan just so happened to be filming a television show—the syndicated *Thunder in Paradise*—during that same time period at Disney MGM Studios after the production moved from St. Pete Beach, Florida.

Hogan was free of his WWF contract—this was months after the Jet Ski *WrestleMania* mess and his title loss to Yokozuna—and still unsure about his future in wrestling. The one thing he was certain about was that he had more left to give in the ring, and he still loved the wrestling business. Hogan felt like McMahon had signaled to him that his run on top of the business was over. And Hogan vehemently disagreed.

"Everything in life is called a run," Hogan said. "You may have a run with your wife for two years, or it could be twenty-two years or thirty-two years. In the wrestling business, you can be a main-event guy and go make movies and have a four-year run and then become a big star. Or you can have a twenty-five-, thirty-year run."

One day in the summer of 1993, Hogan got a visitor on the *Thunder in Paradise* set: Ric Flair. Journalists Shaun Assael and Mike Mooneyham reported in their book *Sex, Lies, and Headlocks* that Hogan and Bischoff were already in communication before that. But Hogan, Flair, and Bischoff all maintain that Flair was the one who made the first contact between Hogan and WCW.

Flair had gone back to WCW from the WWF a year earlier and remained one of the most popular wrestlers in the world. Flair was also a heel, and the chance to do that major Hogan vs. Flair matchup that should have happened at *WrestleMania* was still out there. Flair, like Hogan, was also getting older. Hogan turned forty in 1993, and Flair was already in his mid-forties.

Flair surely would not have minded another big name to do business with, so he started pitching Hogan on the idea of coming to WCW. Then Bischoff started joining Flair on the *Thunder in Paradise* set and chatting with Hogan on the phone. Hogan began to see the potential of dollar signs in WCW. A storyline with Flair would make sense for his comeback.

But the words of Bischoff and Flair weren't good enough for Hogan. Bischoff was a neophyte wrestling executive, not someone like McMahon. Hogan just didn't trust or respect him on that level yet. So Hogan said he had to meet with Ted Turner directly.

Hogan showed up at CNN Center in Atlanta partially in his wrestling gear: yellow trunks, a pink shirt, and bandana. Hogan and Turner talked wrestling—Turner was a genuine fan of the art—and enjoyed each other's company. Turner told his top executive Shaw that he should "make this man a deal."

"Basically, I broke my word to Vince," Hogan said, "and went to WCW."

It was a remarkable coup for Bischoff. The wet-behind-the-ears exec managed to help lure wrestling's greatest drawing card to what was considered a second-rate promotion. There was more to it. Turner was a competitor and more than happy to jump in the ring, so to speak, with McMahon. And McMahon really did think Hogan's time as a marquee headliner was up.

Of course, it took an incredible amount of money and leverage for Hogan to commit. Bischoff said Hogan's first contract was worth around $2 million annually, which included $500,000 per pay-per-view event plus another figure for the TV shows to promote them. New England Sports Network reported at the time that Hogan alone would be making 40 percent of WCW's revenue. He would also get a major chunk of the promotion's merchandise and licensing money. Bischoff said that the report overestimated, but it was not far off.

It was by far the most lucrative contract a pro wrestler had ever signed at the time. On top of that, Turner picked up *Thunder in Paradise* to air on its Turner Network Television (TNT) channel.

"We kind of broke the bank and Eric will probably use certain cuss words," said Holmes, Hogan's attorney, who negotiated the deal. "But I thought it was a really good move for Hulk."

————

WCW didn't just give Hogan a mountain of money. It gave him what no wrestler ever had before him or after him: creative control. Hogan had complete say over what his character did or did not do on screen, and that extended to characters Hogan interacted with.

Plenty of wrestlers had leverage before, as Hogan did in the WWF. No executive wants to piss off their top stars, the people who make them the most money. There was always leeway given. But ultimately, the boss is still the boss, which is why Hogan abided by McMahon's wish in 1990 when he lost the WWF championship to the Ultimate Warrior. By giving him creative control, WCW essentially made Hogan a boss himself—part of the creative team that drew up the stories that made it on the air.

Creative control was valuable to Hogan, because he felt like McMahon no longer believed in him as a top draw and wanted him to pass the torch to younger talent when Hogan wasn't ready to do that. By getting this clause in his contract, Hogan never had to do anything with his character he didn't want to again. And if WCW tried to pull a fast one, Hogan could sue for breach of contract.

So not only did Hogan cement himself as the highest-paid wrestler of all time with his WCW contract at around $2 million per year, he ensured he'd remain on the top of the business for years to come because no writer or booker could move him off that perch. It said so right there in black and white.

———

Bringing in Hogan, the biggest financial draw in the history of the business, was a signal that WCW was ready to be a legitimate player. Bischoff said he was immediately able to engage in a conversation with satellite provider DirecTV and gain a better split of revenue simply by having Hogan on the roster.

"It's like, no wrestler was worth that," Meltzer said of Hogan's contract. "And, as it turned out, like so many deals that you hear about that sound ridiculous, they end up being worth it. Certainly, in the short term, it was more than worth it."

The promotion threw Hogan a ticker-tape parade at Disney MGM Studios on June 11, 1994, to christen the signing. WCW did everything in its power to make the acquisition a big deal in the mainstream. NBA superstar Shaquille O'Neal accompanied Hogan to the ring for his first match in WCW, which was in the *Bash at the Beach* pay-per-view main event against Flair on July 17, 1994, in Orlando.

Bash at the Beach followed the *WrestleMania I* formula. Hogan, with old friend Jimmy Hart in his corner, beat Flair to win the WCW World Heavyweight championship for the first time. He then celebrated in the ring with Mr. T and O'Neal, who presented him with the belt. It was a box-office success. About 14,000 people attended the show at Orlando Arena and WCW did what was then its best pay-per-view numbers ever: an estimated 225,000 buys.

Hogan viewed WCW as a "southern wrestling" company that prioritized in-ring work and having critically acclaimed matches— something Flair was known for—over entertainment and filling arenas with paying customers.

"This is a business about making money, not about who the best wrestler is," Hogan said. "When I came in, I said, 'Let's spike the vodka with a little more juice. Let's rock the house here.' I knew when I came in fresh with Hulkamania, with new people to work with, like Flair, a dream match—never saw us two together—I knew I had a heck of a run coming and it was up to me to adjust the dial."

The *Bash at the Beach* pay-per-view buys represented a 125 percent increase from the 1993 summer event *Beach Blast* and a 114 percent increase from the previous pay-per-view, *Slamboree* in May 1994.

Hogan and Flair had a television rematch at *Clash of the Champions XXVIII* in Cedar Rapids, Iowa, five weeks after Hogan won the title. That set records, too, airing on TBS. Hogan vs. Flair II had 4,126,000 households watching, making it then the most widely viewed pro-wrestling match ever on cable TV. It was also the largest audience for any match in WCW history, which extends back to its time as the standard bearer of the National Wrestling Alliance (NWA).

Flair won that match by countout, setting up a trilogy cage match with Hogan on pay-per-view at *Halloween Havoc* on October 23, 1994. That show produced the second-largest amount of pay-per-view buys for WCW at the time, an estimated 210,000.

While others saw a new level of success for WCW, Bischoff saw a downward trend. *Halloween Havoc* performed worse than Hogan's debut at *Bash at the Beach*. Bischoff felt like the sheen of Hulkamania, a decade after it started, was beginning to wear off in WCW already.

Hogan's presence helped earn WCW credibility. But it wasn't enough to truly compete with the WWF. WCW needed more stars. And there was one available.

———

Randy Savage, once McMahon's second-biggest drawing card after Hogan, left the WWF in late 1994. He was looking to jump ship because, like Hogan, he felt like McMahon's new direction didn't include him. Savage had been working primarily as a color commentator for the WWF before his departure.

In the wake of the steroid trial, the WWF started to move away from characters who looked larger than life due to the perception they might be on something (and probably were). McMahon started featuring smaller, more athletic wrestlers like Bret Hart and Shawn Michaels.

In addition to the public-relations hit of those allegations, the WWF was also struggling financially and "weakened" in multiple ways, according to longtime WWF and McMahon attorney Jerry McDevitt.

"It had a big impact," McDevitt said. "People were thinking it was going to be the end of the company. Usually when the feds charge you, they have a 95 percent rate of a conviction or plea. It's very unusual to beat the feds. I understand why people felt like they had to take care of their families and jump off a ship you think is sinking when it really was not."

Bischoff said Hogan "did a sales job" to get him to sign Savage. Hogan and Savage, once a tag team called the Mega Powers, alternated over the years in real life from being close friends to hated enemies. But Hogan knew Savage could help him make money like they had before, as a team and as rivals, and was always willing to do business.

It didn't take much of Hogan's persuading to sway Bischoff. Savage was still a big name. And he brought with him his partnership with the beef stick snack brand Slim Jim, which then started sponsoring WCW programming. Bischoff said the Slim Jim deal "offset the majority, if not all" of Savage's salary.

In the conclusion to *Starrcade 1994*, Savage came out to help Hogan fight off the bad guys in just Savage's second appearance with WCW. But he would not be the difference-maker that helped tip the scales toward WCW that Bischoff hoped.

Hogan spent the first part of 1995 in a storyline with Vader. Not Darth, but an agile, six-foot-three former All-American offensive lineman named Leon White who was billed at 450 pounds. White probably wasn't as heavy as the promotion said, but he was a large man still capable of pulling off impressive athletic feats, like a moonsault (backflip) off the top rope.

Vader was the kind of mammoth, menacing heel that fit a certain mold for Hogan, similar enough to some of the behemoths Hogan faced in the 1980s, like Andre the Giant or King Kong Bundy. And White was more mobile than either one of those guys and could put on a more entertaining match. But the interest level in the rivalry wasn't high, and Hogan's pay-per-view numbers started to plateau. His television ratings weren't necessarily moving the needle, either.

Hogan wrestled Vader in pay-per-view singles matches at *Super-Brawl*, *Uncensored*, and *Bash at the Beach* in 1995, plus a tag-team match with Hogan and Savage against Vader and Flair at *Slamboree*. Those events averaged an estimated 157,500 buys. Those were better numbers than the WCW pay-per-view shows without Hogan garnered in 1994 and the first half of 1995. But the WWF, in what was considered a down year, was beating those buy rates, even with off-brand pay-per-views like *In Your House*.

"In the beginning when Hulk first came in, it was, 'Oh yeah, it's Hulk!' Everybody is excited, 'yay!'" Bischoff said. "But after the new car smell went away, it was kind of like a 'seen that, done that, been there, what's next' kind of thing."

Bischoff even started noticing a "smattering of boos and smart-asses" when Hogan would come out. He wasn't the only one who heard them.

———

Turner and McMahon had something of a professional rivalry over the years, which would later turn personal. WCW had just brought in brand-name stars like Hogan and Savage, and Turner wanted to take things a step further. Turner told his executives that he wanted WCW to go head-to-head against the WWF's franchise *Monday Night Raw*. Every single week.

"When I walked out of Ted's office, I was excited, but I was overwhelmed, like, 'What the fuck am I going to do now?'" Bischoff said.

Bischoff got back to his office, sat down at his desk, and pulled out a yellow legal pad. For the next hour or two, he jotted down as many characteristics of the WWF as he could, from its production values to how it promoted events to its characters and to the demographics it was targeting. After he was done writing those down, he went to the top of the list and asked himself how WCW could be different at each thing.

The conclusion Bischoff came to right away was that the new show, which would be called *Monday Nitro*, had to be live. *Raw* was live only every few weeks, with most shows taped and aired later. The WWF, Bischoff said, appealed to a young demographic, mostly kids in their teens or younger. Bischoff decided *Nitro* would try to attract adults, ages eighteen to forty-nine, a significant group for cable television advertisers because those in that range are the nation's biggest consumers.

In order to hit that eighteen-to-forty-nine-year-old demographic, Bischoff realized WCW's storylines needed to be more based in reality.

Two other things stood out in Bischoff's mind. He had been visiting Japan regularly because of WCW's partnership with New Japan Pro-Wrestling. Bischoff noted that wrestling was treated more like a real sport in Japan, with a different kind of respect.

Men went to matches in suits and women in dresses. New Japan was packing the Tokyo Dome with 60,000-plus people while WCW could not even give tickets away to some TV tapings. Bischoff figured there was something there he could adapt, perhaps a storyline that involved wrestlers from a rival organization, UWFi, invading New Japan.

"When they sit down in front of their television, they all know this isn't real," Bischoff said. "But if you can create emotion, they'll forget that it's not real."

There was something Bischoff had in mind that would fulfill all those ideas and solve his budding Hogan problem, too.

What if Hulk Hogan was a bad guy?

Bischoff felt like the fans had spoken with their booing voices in arenas and Hogan's character needed to be revamped. He came up with his pitch—why the industry's greatest hero should turn heel—and rehearsed it over and over. Bischoff would tell Hogan how much it would reinvigorate his career and give him new stars to work with, like WCW's franchise wrestler Sting. He'd remind him how much of a success he was playing a heel in the AWA and in Japan.

"I was excited, I was fired up," Bischoff said. "I'm a pretty good salesman when I want to be. I thought, 'Yeah, this is going to work.'"

Bischoff flew down to Hogan's mansion in the Tampa area.

The two men grabbed a pair of beers and sat down on sofas in Hogan's living room. Bischoff recited his pitch, giving his best sell job. Hogan, politely, threw Bischoff out of his home.

"It was a very short and sweet conversation," Hogan said. "There wasn't much verbiage at all. I don't know if I was rolled up on the wrong side of the bed that day or what, but I don't think I was the nicest person I could have been that day."

Hogan dismissed Bischoff, but he was listening. To Bischoff and to the reactions he was getting.

"Everything was changing," Jimmy Hart said. "The merchandise sales were dropping off a little bit. All of a sudden, it wasn't cool being a good guy anymore. It wasn't cool to say your prayers and take your vitamins anymore.

"And Hulk and I both said, '[Turning heel] works, but you got to do it with the right person.' You gotta do it with somebody that's [popular]. You gotta do it with something that was going to really make sense."

———

Americans were in a much different headspace by 1995 than they were during Hogan's 1980s heyday. Hopes were high then. The Berlin Wall fell, communism was on the ropes. Technology was expanding into what we now know as the internet. Ronald Reagan survived an assassination attempt and the economy, for the most part, was in a good place.

Yuppie (young, urban professional) culture had taken hold, with the baby boomer generation coming into their own. With them came the rise of materialism. Blockbuster Video and MTV launched. People were consuming entertainment differently.

Indiana Jones, Star Wars, and *Back to the Future* all landed as epic franchises. *WrestleMania* could be thrown in there as part of that extravagant pop-culture craze.

By the early 1990s, though, things began to swing. The United States was at war in Iraq. The Los Angeles riots brought the issue of race and policing to everyone's collective doorsteps. Beloved former NFL star and comedy movie actor O. J. Simpson was accused of murdering his ex-wife and another man. The economy was in a recession. America was under siege, too. From outside and inside forces.

The World Trade Center was bombed in 1993 by al-Qaeda and a federal building in Oklahoma City was bombed two years later, killing 168 people, then the deadliest terror attack in U.S. history. The perpetrator in the latter was an American: Timothy McVeigh, a domestic terrorist.

The upbeat, poppy music of the eighties highlighted by Michael Jackson, Prince, and U2 gave way to Nirvana's grunge era and gangsta rap. America had lost its innocence. The enemy was within.

Two of the most popular movies of the early 1990s—*Goodfellas* and *Pulp Fiction*—were about mobsters. Another, *The Silence of the Lambs,* starred a cannibal. Television got more cynical, led by *Seinfeld.*

In that world, the preachy, nationalistic Hogan character just did not fit in.

———

After spurning Bischoff's plans to turn him heel, Hogan planned to stay the course and keep to the playbook.

Hogan met Paul Wight, a nearly seven-foot, 300-plus-pound former basketball player, through a mutual friend, actor Danny Bonaduce, in 1994. Seeing potential (and the clear possibility of making money with him in the future), Hogan brought Wight into WCW.

The impossibly large rookie, who had no prior wrestling experience, trained for just several months before debuting in May 1995. Wight's character was named The Giant and he was dubbed as the son of Andre the Giant, which, of course, he was not.

By the fall of 1995, Hogan was in a storyline with Wight and the dastardly group Wight joined up with: the Dungeon of Doom, a cheesy collection of pseudo-supernatural misfits led by Kevin Sullivan, who, in addition to being the head of creative, was an on-screen talent named The Taskmaster. Wight's second career wrestling match was against Hogan for the title at *Halloween Havoc* on October 29, 1995. The location was in Detroit, Michigan, but it was not the Silverdome, and it surely was not Hogan vs. Andre in 1987.

The pay-per-view did an estimated 120,000 buys, a 25 percent drop from the previous pay-per-view event Hogan headlined, which was *Bash at the Beach* against Vader in a steel cage. *Halloween Havoc* was the worst-selling pay-per-view with Hogan in a main-event singles match since Hogan arrived in WCW fifteen months earlier.

That made it clear that Hogan had indeed lost his mojo. It was the mid-1990s, and the formula that Hogan fell back on so many times was simply not working. Hogan knew it and so did Bischoff. The numbers were going in the wrong direction, and in a cruel twist, Hogan had lost the crowd that had been firmly behind him for more than a decade.

———

Monday Nitro premiered on September 4, 1995, going up against *Raw.*

Another thing Bischoff considered when drawing up ideas for

the new show was that, based on what focus groups had said, viewers liked surprises. So the debut episode of *Nitro* saw WWF star Lex Luger show up in WCW as a huge shock. Luger had been, at one time, the man McMahon hoped would succeed Hogan as his promotion's blond, gallant, well-muscled protagonist.

But someone in the WWF office made a brutal mistake and had not realized Luger's contract was coming up. And there he was at the Mall of America for *Nitro*'s premiere, a major salvo for Bischoff and the No. 2 promotion.

WCW had barely been a gnat for Vince McMahon to swat at. But *Nitro* had become a nuisance to the WWF right away. In the third week of the head-to-head battle, on September 25, 1995, *Nitro* beat *Raw* for the first time in the ratings, 2.7 to 1.9.

There were more moments like that to come.

"Different" was the word Bischoff had burned in his mind months earlier after the conversation with Turner. And his *Nitro* program was giving off different vibes from McMahon's *Raw*. There was a certain chaotic aspect to being live, a feeling like anything could happen. The WWF was still in a transition period post–steroid trial and Hogan's departure, still building up new stars like Hart and Michaels.

Nitro felt fresh, even if it featured older stars like Hogan, Savage, and Flair. Fueled by Bischoff, a cocky outsider, it had a certain brashness.

———

Debra Miceli was released by the WWF in late 1995. She had been the face of the WWF's thin women's division for about two years under the name Alundra Blayze. When she was let go, Miceli was still the WWF women's champion.

Bischoff and Miceli had known each other for years, going back to their time in the AWA, and Miceli worked in WCW before signing with the WWF in 1993. When he found out about her release, Bischoff told Miceli he had a spot for her on *Nitro*—and to bring the WWF championship belt along.

Miceli returned to WCW on December 18, 1995, under her former character name Madusa. Early in the show, she interrupted the commentators—Bischoff, Heenan, and former NFL star Steve "Mongo" McMichael—at the broadcast position and did an interview about leaving the WWF and joining WCW.

Wearing a black leather vest with gold stitching, Miceli pulled out the pink WWF women's title belt and grabbed a nearby trash bin. She lifted the bin over the commentary desk with her right hand and dropped the belt into it with her left.

"And that's what I think of the WWF women's championship belt," Miceli said on the show. "This is the WCW. I am now in the WCW. And they used to call me Alundra Blayze and not anymore. Because this is where the big boys play—and now this is where the big girls play."

Bischoff, one of *Nitro*'s play-by-play voices, feigned shock on television. But it was his idea all along.

———

Bischoff also started giving away the results of taped *Raw* shows on *Nitro*, making sure to mention that *Nitro* was always live. Luger's appearance caught the WWF with its pants down and Bischoff telling fans what would happen on *Raw* before it even aired really annoyed McMahon and company.

"That was really a pain in the ass for us," said Gerald Brisco, a former wrestler who became one of McMahon's top lieutenants. "I mean, a lot of people say, 'Well, it was just business as usual.' But it wasn't. We paid attention to what was going on and it was upsetting to all of us that our business was being exposed like that."

Miceli's stunt? That had WWF execs fuming. Miceli said years later that she regretted throwing away the title—and she wasn't welcomed back into the WWF again for two decades.

"It was a tawdry thing to do," longtime WWF producer Michael Hayes said. "It was a shot across the bow and pretty much a kick in the groin, I think, as it was meant to be. That was what got everybody's ire up. That is just something you don't do. You don't drop the flag on the ground, and you respect a title, a championship belt. It was the beginning of many traditions being broken."

But it was working for WCW. *Nitro* beat *Raw* in the ratings four out of the final five weeks of 1995.

————

McMahon was not going to take any of this lying down.

In an online chat the same day Miceli dropped the belt in the garbage, McMahon took aim at WCW, writing that Turner can only buy talent and WCW was unable to create its own stars. Bischoff, he wrote, was doing Turner's selfish bidding, and WCW showed no regard for wrestling fans by putting another show on Monday nights up against *Raw*.

At the end of the New Year's Day 1996 episode of *Raw*, a black screen popped up with white lettering that read: "Billionaire Ted's 'Wrasslin' Warroom.'" A video then played of a group of people sitting at a conference room table with a man who looked like Turner at the head of it.

"We need more action from our stars," the faux Turner stuttered. "We want them to pull out all the stops."

It was a parody of WCW. There was a frumpy, white-bearded man wearing yellow and red portraying Hogan called "The Huckster." A man portraying Savage was referred to as "The Nacho Man." WWF's former interviewer "Mean" Gene Okerlund, who had jumped ship to WCW, was satirized as "Scheme Gene."

An actor playing a WCW executive said they had some suggestions for "Billionaire Ted" and played clips of high-impact moves being performed by WWF wrestlers. The exec asked "The Huckster" if he could pull them off.

"Brother, at my age, my feet don't leave the ground," the Huckster, satirizing Hogan, said.

"Billionaire Ted" then asked "Huckster" and "Nacho Man" what they could actually do. And they stood up at the table and did the gestures that Hogan and Savage were known for—"Huckster" rotating his hand and putting it against his ear to hear the crowd and "Nacho Man" raising up his arm toward the sky and twisting his finger.

The one-minute segment ended with the tagline recited by a voiceover: "You can't teach old dogs new tricks. The new WWF generation—on top of the hill, not over it."

Brisco said in the WWF offices during production meetings that Turner was routinely referred to as "Billionaire Ted" prior to the skits and "Vince decided to take it and run with it."

None of the actors in the skit played a character based on Bischoff. McMahon continually tried to pit himself and the WWF against Turner, the absurdly rich media entrepreneur. Bischoff was really the man making the vast majority of the decisions for WCW, not Turner. But McMahon's underdog WWF going toe-to-toe with a billionaire had a lot more cachet as a narrative to fans and media than McMahon going up against Bischoff.

McMahon didn't just build manufactured storylines for his television show, he used such things in real life, as well. No one has ever understood pro-wrestling tactics and their application to audiences better than McMahon. Even the idea that Hogan and Savage were like dinosaurs was a stretch. Bret Hart was the WWF's champion at the time, and he was only four years younger than Hogan and five years younger than Savage.

The first "Billionaire Ted" skit was a cute jab and not particularly incendiary. But the sketches continued—for months. And kept escalating until USA Network bosses pulled the plug.

Bischoff said people at WCW found them humorous and Turner got a kick out of them. Dr. Harvey Schiller, the president of Turner Sports at the time and Bischoff's boss, said he doesn't recall ever having a conversation about the skits with Turner, who didn't really see McMahon as an equal.

Bischoff, meanwhile, was rolling up his sleeves in his office at CNN Center. The conflict between WCW and the WWF was intensifying. *Nitro* was starting to find its brazen groove. Bischoff, who at one point was playing with house money, had become intoxicated by his promotion's (and his own) growing success and obsessed with battling McMahon.

But the elephant with the twenty-four-inch pythons in the room was still Hogan and his waning popularity.

CHAPTER 3

SAY HELLO TO
THE BAD GUY

Scott Hall's contract with the WWF was coming up in a few months. Five months after the "Billionaire Ted" skits started in 1996, to be exact. Hall had always wanted to be a wrestler, but the travel schedule—and the money he was making in comparison to all those days on the road—wore on him.

Hall, then thirty-eight years old, had a young family with his wife, Dana Burgio. Their son, Cody, was four, and their daughter, Cassidy, was just ten months. In a perfect world, he would be able to spend more time with them.

Sean Waltman, Hall's close friend, knew all that when he took some time off from the WWF in January 1996 and flew to Los Angeles. Waltman, then twenty-three years old and one of WWF's top young wrestlers nicknamed The 1-2-3 Kid, was in LA for training and physical therapy. He was also looking to break into Hollywood.

Waltman crashed at the home of Rich Minzer, then the assistant director of Gold's Gym.

Minzer put Waltman in touch with entertainment agent Barry Bloom, who was already familiar with the world of wrestling and a lifelong fan of the art. He represented several wrestlers, including 1970s and '80s star Jesse Ventura, who later became a color commentator for the WWF and WCW. Bloom landed Ventura roles in several films, including *Predator* with Schwarzenegger and *Demolition Man* with Stallone.

Bloom and Waltman met in Bloom's LA office to discuss Waltman's potential as an actor. During the conversation, Bloom mentioned that Bischoff, with the support of Turner, over in WCW was "opening up the checkbook."

Waltman had not seriously considered making a move from the WWF, even though his contract was coming up later in 1996.

But he knew someone who was unhappy there.

———

Hall was at work the night of January 15, 1983, tending bar at the strip club Thee Dollhouse in Orlando, Florida. He was bracing himself. Hall knew an altercation—"of course it was over a girl"—was imminent.

It was early in his shift when Hall got word that the husband of the woman he had been seeing was outside in the parking lot. The man had busted all the windows out of Hall's car, and was fixing to get a piece of Hall next.

Hall, a well-built, six-foot-five bodybuilder, went outside to confront the man and knocked him down immediately with one punch. The man, named Rodney Perry Turner, reached for a firearm and a struggle ensued.

Hall took hold of the gun first—and shot Perry Turner in the head. He died instantly. Hall, then just twenty-four years old, was charged with second-degree murder. The case against him was later dismissed when sworn testimony was not enough to prosecute.

"I drilled him, and he went down, and his shirt went up and he was reaching for the gun, so I reached for it, too," Hall recalled.

A bar employee told the *Orlando Sentinel* at the time Perry

Turner had threatened to kill both Hall and Perry Turner's wife, Carol, when he found out Hall and Carol were dating.

Two months earlier, Perry Turner had fatally shot another man. Perry Turner claimed he was attacked after the man made a pass at Carol. Perry Turner was never charged, as the killing was ruled justifiable.

"I should have sought counseling right then, but I didn't know anything," Hall said. "I was a kid."

———

Hall was raised in a military family. He has referred to his father as a "big shot" in the U.S. Army. Hall's parents and grandparents had issues with alcohol, an addiction that definitely did not skip a generation.

"We come from a long line of hard-drinking rednecks," Hall said.

Hall went to high school in Germany where his dad was stationed and moved just about every year before his family settled in Florida when he was a teen. Hall's father was a pro-wrestling fan, and Hall himself wanted to be a wrestler ever since he was eight years old when his dad took him to a hair-versus-hair match. Hall took a piece of the losing wrestler's hair home with him.

"And I just was hooked since then," Hall said.

Hall had spent time working the regional circuit as a wrestler in the 1980s, including a stint in the AWA like Hogan. Hall had a run with Curt "Mr. Perfect" Hennig as the AWA tag-team champions, and Verne Gagne then wanted to position Hall as his No. 1 babyface. Hall absolutely looked the part. He was tall and handsome with light brown hair and a bushy mustache. With a wide chest, big arms, and bulging trapezius muscles, Hall looked kind of like a jacked-up Tom Selleck.

"When Verne started pushing him to be his top guy, I know other people were going like, 'Oh man, same size as Hogan, better body, better-looking,'" Meltzer said. "But when it didn't work, it was kind of like, 'Oh, he doesn't have charisma.'"

Things just didn't click for Hall as a generic good guy. The fans didn't get behind him. After taking a hiatus from wrestling, Hall found his way to WCW in 1991. He knew he had to change things up, because regular old Scott Hall, as impressive as he looked with his shirt off, wasn't working.

And Hall really committed to changing things up. His new character was called The Diamond Studd. He was a cocky ladies' man with slicked-back black hair, a toothpick between his teeth, and dark sunglasses. The bushy hair and mustache were long gone. The Diamond Studd wore a five o'clock shadow and didn't skip trips to the tanning bed. The leaner Studd looked nothing like "Big" Scott Hall from the AWA.

The Diamond Studd was managed on screen by Diamond Dallas Page, who previously had accompanied the very popular Fabulous Freebirds to the ring. Like Hall, Page had a background in the nightlife industry, managing several Florida clubs. Hall and Page got along well, in the ring and outside of it. And Hall started to have some success in WCW with Page by his side.

Hall had size, good looks, and could work an entertaining match in the ring. There might not be a blueprint for wrestling stardom, but he checked a lot of boxes. Still, Hall wasn't being positioned past the early matches on WCW cards. The main event wasn't even in sight.

That didn't matter to Hall so much. He was grateful just to have the job of his dreams. But Hall and his wife, Dana, had just had their first child, Cody. Making more money to support his growing family would have been nice. So Hall started having conversations with Pat Patterson, McMahon's right-hand man.

"Some guys were higher up [in WWF], but everybody was a star," Hall said. "So I said, 'I don't have to be a main eventer, I still want to wrestle.' Because even the lower-paid wrestlers are getting paid, and I had no education. So I thought, this is what I still want to do for a living. If I have to be a bottom guy, I'd rather do it for the best company."

"Bottom guys" in wrestling—or low carders and midcarders—are kind of like the fighters you see on the preliminaries of boxing or UFC events. They're talented enough and have a big enough following to earn a spot on the event, but don't have the skill level or star quality to make the main event. Their main role is to lose to wrestlers tabbed as stars as those would-be stars make their way to a headlining role.

Hall would never be a "bottom guy" again. He was pushed near the top of the card immediately in the WWF with a new character: Razor Ramon.

Hall, as Ramon, became an arrogant, well-dressed, and villainous Cuban American from Miami. It was basically a rip-off of Al Pacino's suave but brutally violent Tony Montana character in *Scarface*, which had gained a renewed cult following a decade after its release. McMahon had never seen the movie and when Hall came to him with the idea, he thought Hall was a genius.

For weeks on WWF television there were taped vignettes trumping up his arrival. Hall wore gold chains with an open, button-down shirt revealing his chest hair. He spoke with a fake Cuban accent, called people "chico," and borrowed phrases from *Scarface*, adding his own spin, like "say hello to the Bad Guy."

Hall was neither Cuban nor even Hispanic, just like Hogan

wasn't actually Irish. In wrestling, everything is about the performance. And Hall was more than believable enough as Razor Ramon.

———

In his first WWF storyline, Hall was placed with Flair, Flair's manager Heenan, and Hennig, Hall's old tag-team partner from the AWA. They all were in a major storyline opposite Savage.

Being attached to big names like Flair and Savage right away elevated Hall's character in the eyes of the fans—and his charisma and in-ring ability did the rest. By the beginning of 1993, Hall was in a storyline with Bret Hart for the WWF title, culminating in a match on pay-per-view. The former "bottom guy" was now featured on the event poster.

A decade after Hall killed another man in self-defense, things could not have been going any better for him. The then-thirty-five-year-old was a bona fide star in the business he fantasized about being in from childhood.

Hall and Waltman became friendly that same year, after Hall helped make Waltman's career to that point. The two created one of the most memorable pro-wrestling moments of the forgettable early 1990s.

Waltman was a lower-level wrestler in the WWF whose primary role was to get beaten and make the top stars look great. In wrestling terms, he was a jobber. A "job" in wrestling is the act of losing or getting pinned in a match. And "jobbers" are those wrestlers whose sole purpose is to lose.

That idea got completely turned on its head when Waltman, a lovable-loser babyface, shockingly pinned Hall during a match on *Raw* in May 1993. Waltman was an excellent in-ring worker and

McMahon had bigger plans for him, including an eventual heel turn. Hall was happy to help—he understood the more stars there were to work with, the better for everyone. Hall and Waltman continued to work matches against each other and eventually became tight outside the ring.

Waltman's underdog story was one of the most impactful of a down period of the WWF, because Hall, as Razor Ramon, was slotted as a main-event-level guy and people like him never lost to "jobbers" like The 1-2-3 Kid. Waltman had previously only been in "squash matches," where everyone knew he was going to lose—in dominating fashion—to his more popular opponent.

Those squash matches had been a fixture of WWF television in the 1980s and early 1990s and part of wrestling for a long time. Their utility was to get stars, or wrestlers the promotion wanted to become stars, to showcase their offense in front of crowds. By the 1990s, fans were kind of clued into what to expect in those matches.

So Waltman pinning Hall cleanly was a major surprise. It was one of those early moments in the decade where fans were fed a twist or swerve when they thought they knew what was going to happen, which became a staple of wrestling storylines later.

Hall and Shawn Michaels, who became one of the WWF's main headliners after Hogan and Savage left, had known each other from previous stops in Kansas City and the AWA. The two grew closer and started traveling together early in Hall's WWF tenure, because they wrestled each other so often.

The friendship was the origin of the most influential real-life group in pro-wrestling history.

Kevin Nash, a nearly seven-foot-tall former college basketball player whom Hall had once teamed with in WCW, signed with the WWF in June 1994. He was positioned on television as Michaels's bodyguard, with the ring name Diesel. Nash started riding with Hall and Michaels. The trio turned people off right away.

It was still an era when wrestlers protected the myth that wrestling was real. Nash and Michaels were heels and Hall was a babyface. They weren't supposed to be interacting with one another, even outside the ring. When the three of them pulled into gas stations on the road, they'd all put towels over their heads to obscure their faces.

Paul Levesque signed with the WWF in 1994 as the character Hunter Hearst Helmsley (later shortened to Triple H), a snobby blue blood from New England. Like Hall and Nash, Levesque had a lackluster run in WCW. He would join as the fifth member of this behind-the-scenes unit, which was dubbed "The Kliq" by either Luger or wrestler "The British Bulldog" Davey Boy Smith. Hall said the basis of the group was simply he and Michaels passing down what Hennig had taught both of them about the inner workings of wrestling.

"Then, when Kev came along, when Diesel came along, we taught him the way we thought business should be done," Hall said. "When Kid came along, Kid had to do business the way we thought it should be done because he was in our clique. And later, Triple H came in, we taught him, 'This is how we do business, this is the way we think it should be done.'"

The group even started to use its own signature hand gesture that they would flash to acknowledge the camaraderie. They would put their middle and ring fingers together with their thumb and point their pointer finger and pinkie upward. The gesture originated at North Carolina State University. The school's sports teams are nicknamed the Wolfpack, and fabled women's basketball coach the late Kay Yow has been credited with popularizing the sign going back to the 1970s.

Some of the Kliq members were babyfaces in the WWF script and others were heels, and the hand signal was their way to show unity in a world where they were not supposed to socialize behind the scenes. Some have called it the "too sweet," but The Kliq called it the Turkish wolf, due to its other origins as a Turkish nationalist symbol. It was first done by the group during a European tour and thought up by Waltman, who later would popularize another, more obscene gesture that went viral long before viral was a thing.

"When we did [the Turkish wolf sign] originally, we were sneaking it into places where we could get away with doing it," Levesque said. "A lot of it was breaking the rules, anyway. It really was more about sneakily breaking the rules and seeing if anybody catches on that we're doing it."

The Kliq loved to push boundaries and was gaining power as a unified force, inside and outside of the ring. Michaels even started to call his fan base "The Kliq" on screen as a nod to his backstage buddies.

At *WrestleMania X* on March 20, 1994, at Madison Square Garden, Hall beat Michaels (with Nash in his corner) to win the WWF Intercontinental title in a revolutionary ladder match. To win, a wrestler had to set up a ladder in the ring, climb it, and grab the title belt, which was hanging from the arena ceiling. The match drew major critical acclaim. Dave Meltzer wrote the following week in the *Wrestling Observer* that it was "probably the best match ever" on a WWF pay-per-view event.

With Hall, Michaels, and Nash all being pushed as stars and Waltman and Levesque getting increased television time, The Kliq had considerable clout backstage. And, according to those in the locker room, they used it to help one another and diminish non-Kliq members. They formed almost a self-contained union, even threatening on several occasions to go on strike—just the five of them—if they thought one member of the group was being wronged.

One of the chief victims of Kliq bullying was Chris Candido, who wrestled under the character Skip as a high-energy, colorful, and obnoxious heel fitness instructor. Hall admitted years later that The Kliq was too hard on Candido and it wasn't so much Candido himself, but the "stupid gimmick." Candido's manager was his real-life girlfriend Tammy Sytch, whose character's name was Sunny. Hall said it was a testosterone-fueled "shark-tank environment" that the two stepped into in the WWF, competitive and ruthless.

"We almost prided ourselves on how vicious our locker room was," Hall said. "It was a brutal, vicious, cutthroat kind of environment. I'm not saying it's the right thing, but [those] were the conditions. Some guys thrive on that; some guys don't."

To compound matters, Michaels and Sytch started dating during a lull in Sytch and Candido's on-again-off-again relationship. Michaels and Sytch would even sneak off during shows to quiet areas of the arena to have sex. Sytch, a pretty and charismatic blonde with a girl-next-door look, was gaining more popularity with fans than Candido, and she became one of the world's most downloaded celebrities in the early days of the internet.

Hall's favorite locker-room target was Shane Douglas, who wrestled under the name Dean Douglas, a college professor character who carried around a paddle. Hall had heard a lot about how good Douglas was during Douglas's run in Extreme Championship Wrestling (ECW), a small Philadelphia-based promotion that had a cult following. When Hall and Douglas first wrestled each other in 1995, Hall felt Douglas was "so overrated."

Hall and Douglas wrestled often that year, sometimes over the WWF Intercontinental title, a secondary championship. Douglas felt Hall played games with him, one night telling him that he could throw his punches and kicks a little harder and the next saying that Douglas was trying to "kill me out there," because the strikes were too hard. Douglas felt like he was a hot free-agent signing that the WWF had big plans for, and Hall and Michaels nipped all his momentum in the bud.

"It was sort of like the wolfpack mentality," Douglas said. "They would come around and they all had Vince's ear."

The Kliq was polarizing and controversial. But the five members of the group were some of the biggest stars in wrestling. They were well rounded, extremely talented, and creative, even coming up with ideas for characters and stories for others. They were also rebellious and cutting edge, representing a Gen X wave in the industry. The Kliq were as much known for partying and womanizing as their skills between the ropes. Hall, Michaels, and Waltman, especially, were into drinking and drug use. They did cocaine, popped painkillers, and abused muscle relaxers called somas. Nash partook in the activities, too. Levesque was completely sober and acted often as designated driver for the other four.

But despite their antics, The Kliq had the support of the most important person in the WWF: McMahon. The group was making him money and part of the nucleus that helped him move on from the days of Hogan. He told them as much in a meeting once.

"[Vince said,] 'What's the deal with this fucking Kliq?'" Nash said. "We just sat there like, 'Oh, fuck.' This is a different tone than he's ever taken. [Vince said,] 'Because, goddammit, I want in.'"

———

In late 1995, a few months after WCW aired its first *Nitro* episode, Hall pulled McMahon aside at a TV taping and asked him what exactly he had to do to start making more money. Hall at the time was one of the top babyfaces in the WWF, his merchandise sold well, and he felt like the Razor Ramon character could lose and still remain popular, or "over," as they say in wrestling.

"I said, 'Do I need to improve on my ring work or something that I can do better on my interviews so that I can make more money like the guys who preceded me?'" Hall recalled years later. "[McMahon said], 'No, no, no. I'm absolutely, certainly pleased with your performance and your interviews are fine.' I said, 'Well then, I just can't understand why my money isn't going up.'"

Hall had a meeting with McMahon and J. J. Dillon, who was WWF's head of talent relations, at the promotion's office in Stamford, Connecticut. According to Hall, McMahon had a check on the table and said it was Hall's to keep. McMahon then offered him a three-year contract. Hall told them he couldn't work the WWF's travel schedule for another three years. He now had two young children at home.

In 1995, Hall wrestled in 177 matches, which averages out to almost a match every other day for the entire year. In December 1995, Hall wrestled eight out of the first nine days of the month, all in different cities.

McMahon offered Hall a two-year deal and said he would consider a contract for just one year. Hall replied that he had to think about it.

"I said, 'I ain't no mathematician, but I get my merchandise statements,' and I said, 'If we move the decimal point a little bit over . . . would the McMahon family really notice it? Because the Hall family would notice it,'" Hall recalled.

McMahon told Hall he couldn't do that, because Hall was already making the same as what other top stars like Michaels, Nash, and The Undertaker (Mark Calaway) were getting. Hall then asked if he could go and wrestle in Japan for a few tours during the year; that way he'd be making more money, but it wouldn't be coming from the WWF's coffers. Hall even pitched the idea of raising the cost of his merchandise, so he'd take home a bit more cash. McMahon balked at both of those things.

In the WWF, wrestlers didn't have guaranteed salaries. As independent contractors, they got paid a percentage of whatever ticket sales and merchandise revenue were at the time, per event. The wrestlers at the top of the card made more. It was difficult for them to know what they'd be making month to month and, for the most part, if they didn't wrestle on a show, there was no paycheck.

"Vince had you so busy working that you didn't even think anybody else wanted you," Hall said. "You gotta go to Target and sign autographs for free and then drive two hundred miles to the town [for a show]."

Hall left Stamford without an agreement and with no clarity on what the future would hold for him.

———

Right after Waltman broke the news of Hall's unhappiness with the WWF to Bloom, the agent called Hall from his office phone and put him on speaker. Hall was interested in a potential move to WCW if the money and schedule were right. Bloom called Bischoff the very next morning.

Bischoff knew the call was coming. Hall and Page, formerly an ensemble on WCW television, had remained friends. After speaking with Bloom, Hall called Page to see what was going on. Was

WCW really shelling out money for free agents? Page said it was true. And then Page called Bischoff, his neighbor in Mableton, Georgia, to fill him in.

Bischoff was into the idea of bringing in Hall. It seemed like a no-brainer. *Nitro* was just four months old. What better way to help WCW and hurt McMahon than taking one of the WWF's biggest stars?

Hall at the time was motivated by two things: more guaranteed money and less time on the road. WCW was promising both.

The WWF wasn't going to let Hall go so easily, though.

Bloom sent a telegram to the promotion's offices, giving notice that Hall would be departing. That was a requirement in WWF deals. If wrestlers didn't inform the promotion they were leaving within ninety days of the expiration date, expiring WWF contracts at the time automatically renewed.

Soon after Bloom sent the notice, Hall was backstage at a WWF show in East Rutherford, New Jersey, on February 24, 1996. Hall was approached before his match by WWF producer Tony Garea, who told Hall he should call the company doctor.

Hall called and the doctor's wife answered. Mauro Di Pasquale, whom McMahon had hired after the steroid scandal to lead the WWF's antidoping testing, wasn't home. So Hall proceeded to start putting his wrestling gear on in the locker room. Garea came up to him again and asked what he was doing. Hall was confused. Garea told him that officials wanted him to leave the building. Hall realized what Garea was saying—that Hall had failed a drug test.

"As soon as he told me that, I said [to myself], 'I guess they got my notice,'" Hall said.

Hall was suspended for about six weeks and didn't wrestle again until April 7, 1996. He missed out on *WrestleMania XII* and the payday that would have come with it. When he returned, the Razor Ramon character was mostly used to "put over" other wrestlers. In other words, he did a lot of losing, to the likes of Vader, Jake "The Snake" Roberts, Goldust, and Jerry Lawler.

But no matter to Hall. He was about to embark on a new journey anyway.

CHAPTER 4

YOU GIVE THE PEOPLE WHAT THEY WANT

Eight days before Hall left the WWF for WCW, Hall and Nash ducked into a dark alleyway in Midtown Manhattan near Madison Square Garden and lit up a joint.

Other than getting high, there was one other thing the duo wanted to do to commemorate the moment. The WWF was on a tour of Europe a few weeks prior, and Hall, Nash, Michaels, and Levesque discussed in Germany the idea of doing some kind of farewell or thank you in front of the live crowd at the final WWF event for Hall and Nash, who would be joining Hall in WCW.

At the nontelevised event at MSG, Michaels would be defending his title in the main event against Nash, a steel cage match. In the semi-main event, Levesque was facing Hall. The idea was, after the main event, the four men would acknowledge their real-life friendships.

But there was a problem. This was pro wrestling. And while Nash and Michaels were close outside the ring, their characters were sworn enemies in the script. What The Kliq wanted to do that night was break kayfabe, something that was essentially unheard of in the industry.

Because of how controversial the thought was, Michaels and

Nash ran it by McMahon and Patterson. McMahon said that if it was that important to them to do it, then it was important to him, too.

―――

Kayfabe is the myth that wrestling, its matches, and its characters were 100 percent real, and, for almost a century, people in the business believed that myth must be preserved at all costs. Some still feel that way.

Their reasoning is that once you acknowledge that what's going on in and around the ring is all predetermined, it exposes the business as phony. It would be like a magician revealing that all his tricks were not actually the works of magic. The admittance would undermine what the very art was.

The fact is, though, that most people were aware that wrestling wasn't a real sport going back to the early 1900s, not long after it became choreographed in the first place. It's kind of like Santa Claus. Maybe some kids still believed, but everyone else was hip to the fact it was fictional entertainment.

In 1989, McMahon himself confessed wrestling was not a legitimate athletic contest to the New Jersey legislature. He did so to avoid the costs that came with individual states regulating and sanctioning wrestling as they did with boxing. McMahon's vision was "sports entertainment," after all, and he didn't shy away from it.

But that was behind closed doors in front of a group of politicians. Wrestlers still were not supposed to break kayfabe in public in the mid-1990s.

―――

Michaels pinned Nash in the MSG main event, as scripted. Then Hall came back into the ring—he had lost to Levesque earlier— and greeted Michaels with a hug and The Kliq's signature wolfpack hand gesture. Michaels then "woke up" a prone Nash, who was still acting as if he was really hurt from the match, an act in wrestling called selling. Michaels turned Nash over, straddled him, and gave him a kiss on the forehead.

Hall and Michaels called out Levesque. They all greeted each other with the wolfpack gesture and engaged in a four-way hug. They held each other's hands up in a show of triumph and then each got into one of the four corners of the ring, climbed onto the turnbuckles and posed. The crowd in New York, many of whom were privy to the knowledge that all of these guys were friends and Hall and likely Nash were leaving the WWF, ate the moment up, cheering vociferously.

"It just became organic," Nash said. "I mean, when you looked out there, there were people crying. There were people cheering. There wasn't a person that was sitting on their ass. And that's what you learn in this business as a performer. You listen to the people, you give the people what they want."

———

Nash grew up in southwest Detroit, raised mostly by his mother, Wanda, who worked at the local Ford Motor Company factory. His father, Robert, died of a heart attack when Nash was just eight years old.

Nash's size—he was six-foot-ten—and athleticism were conducive to sports from early on. He starred as a basketball player at Aquinas High School in Southgate, Michigan, and attended the same hoops camp after his junior year as Magic Johnson. A year later, they were on the same team in an exhibition game.

"Early in the game, Magic came down the lane, I had my hands by my chin and all of a sudden, I had the ball in my hands," Nash said. "If Magic Johnson was my point guard, I probably could have had a couple of scrub years in the NBA."

Nash earned a scholarship to play at the University of Tennessee, where he majored in psychology and educational philosophy.

But Nash was maybe too smart for his own good. He got into fights often in Knoxville off the court and clashed with his coach, Don DeVoe. In 1980, Nash was disqualified from a game in his junior year against Kentucky for throwing a punch and, after Tennessee lost the contest, he got into a physical altercation with DeVoe.

"He grabbed my jersey and tried to spin me around," Nash said. "He kept running his mouth so I bitch-smacked him."

Nash was dismissed from the team. At first, Nash was going to transfer to Bowling Green, but he ended up enrolling in the U.S. Army. He spent two years in the military and then played basketball professionally in Europe for one season before needing knee surgery. Nash returned to Detroit for the procedure with the expectation of eventually getting a job as a laborer in the automotive industry, as most, including his parents, did in that city. That wasn't a sure thing, either. Detroit had been struggling since the oil crisis of the early 1970s.

When he was home, Nash caught a WWF event at Joe Louis Arena and became intrigued. It was the first time he had watched wrestling since he was a kid. Nash still wanted to be an athlete; he was considering a basketball comeback. But he knew his oversized body wasn't going to stay healthy running up and down a court.

Evading the assembly line, Nash moved down to Georgia, got a job managing a strip club, and began training in wrestling under Jody "The Assassin" Hamilton. WCW was based in Atlanta, and if you wanted to meet a wrestler, the two best places were the gym or a gentlemen's establishment.

Nash worked hard enough as a wrestler, and his size could not go unnoticed. Hamilton thought he was destined for greatness. It was only a matter of time before WCW signed him. Nash debuted in 1990 as one half of the Master Blasters tag team.

In 1991, Nash was given the character Oz, based on *The Wizard of Oz*. For gear, Nash was draped in a lime green robe with white stars all over it. The idea came from Dusty Rhodes, a top star from the 1970s and 1980s who was running WCW's creative at the time. It was a silly gimmick for someone who had the potential for much more.

"I wrote then, 'This guy is gonna make a lot of money and it's probably not gonna be with this company,'" Meltzer said. "I just felt like they had no idea what to do with him. And Vince would."

———

No matter how talented in the ring and on the microphone a wrestler is, his or her character—or gimmick, as it's called in wrestling—can make or break a career. Sometimes, it takes several attempts through trial and error to bring out the best possible character for a wrestler, like how Hogan went through several different iterations before finally becoming the persona that fans connected with.

Some wrestling veterans have said that a character should be the wrestler's real-life personality turned up to eleven. In other cases, wrestlers have made off-the-wall gimmicks that are nothing like them work because they were talented enough actors. Even if it wasn't authentic, if it felt authentic, that was good enough. Kind of like wrestling itself.

Hall's "Big" Scott Hall character in the AWA was generic and had a ceiling for how popular it could get. With the Diamond Studd gimmick, Hall got closer to his potential. And then that evolved into Razor Ramon, which made Hall one of the biggest stars in the industry. It was the same man playing all three roles, but the character—and Hall's performance of said character—took him to a new level.

———

In early 1992, given a bit more creative freedom, Nash became Vinnie Vegas, a tongue-in-cheek mobster gimmick inspired by Steve Martin's role in the movie *My Blue Heaven*. The character played more to Nash's strengths. He was witty, sharp, and charismatic.

The Vinnie Vegas character still didn't ascend past the midcard, like Diamond Studd. But there was one influential person who was enjoying Nash's work from afar: Michaels, who convinced McMahon to hire Nash away from WCW.

"I saw a guy that was incredibly talented and thought he should be on a much bigger stage," Michaels said.

Bischoff, who was about to become WCW's executive producer, asked Nash to stay. Nash agreed, mainly just to shut Bischoff up. Nash asked for his release the next day. Nash didn't actually think Bischoff would rise to become WCW's top decision-maker.

Nash, sporting jet-black hair, black sunglasses, and dressed all in black leather, joined the WWF in June 1993. He became Diesel, Michaels's on-screen bodyguard and a play on his Motor City upbringing. Nash would eventually turn on Michaels, who played an arrogant, self-absorbed heel character, and become a babyface.

McMahon saw big money in Nash where WCW had not. In fact, he saw him as a potential successor to Hogan as the company's No. 1 good guy.

Within a year of his arrival, Nash won the WWF World Heavyweight title from aging legend Bob Backlund on November 26, 1994, and held on to it for nearly a full year—358 days—before losing it to Bret Hart.

Despite the monster push he was getting from management, Nash knew portraying Diesel as the cookie-cutter hero didn't necessarily play to the charming-yet-flippant Nash's strengths.

At one point, Nash tried to plead his case to McMahon about his generic character, using the movie *Heat* as an example. In it, Al Pacino plays a Los Angeles cop tracking a relatable criminal played by Robert De Niro, whose crew is planning a major heist.

"At the end, did you want De Niro to [win] or did you want Pacino?" Nash asked McMahon.

"Well, De Niro," McMahon replied.

De Niro, Nash explained to his boss, was the heel.

When Hall told Nash the news that he was going to WCW, they were at a WWF television taping early in 1996. Hall knew Nash's contract was expiring thirteen days after his in May 1996. He wanted Nash to join him—not only because the two were close friends, but because of a stipulation in Hall's contract: a "favored nations" clause.

That meant that if specific main-event wrestlers signed with WCW from the WWF in the future, Hall's salary would get elevated as a result. Bloom submitted to Bischoff a list of names that included Nash. Hall told Nash what he was going to be making in WCW and told him to sign there and "get more," so Hall would end up getting more, too.

Nash was happy for his buddy. But he wasn't that interested in leaving the WWF.

———

Like his friend Hall, Nash had his fair share of run-ins backstage. Bigelow and Candido were buddies, and heavily tattooed heavyweight wrestler Bam Bam Bigelow took exception to how The Kliq—especially Michaels and Nash—were treating Candido.

"Now, all of a sudden, [other wrestlers] were scared of these guys, and I was the only one that stepped up to the plate and said, 'Fuck all you guys, man,'" Bigelow said. "It's not right, it's wrong. And they went to Vince and just said, 'Look, this guy, he's got a bad attitude, it's bad for morale. Let's abuse him.' And I didn't let them abuse me as much as they wanted to, and I just left."

Bigelow wrestled NFL all-time great Lawrence Taylor at *WrestleMania XI* on April 2, 1995, in a match that went on last as the headliner. It was far better than it had any right to be with a neophyte wrestler, as good of an athlete as Taylor was. Bigelow was a strong in-ring worker, especially for his size—he was billed at six-foot-four and 390 pounds—and was obviously trusted enough to work with a big name from the sports world. But Bigelow felt like The Kliq was burying him backstage and he left the WWF seven months later.

"Some of the midcard or low-card guys hated Shawn at the time and to an extent Nash," Meltzer said. "But they were also afraid of Nash. It was like, 'Oh, I want to beat up Shawn. But then Nash is always around' type of thing. Shawn really had a lot of heat with a lot of people at the time. But Bigelow was the first one who talked to me and just said, 'They're fucking with me and I'm going to end up being out of there.' And I thought, 'You just fricking did the *WrestleMania* main event and carried a guy who never wrestled to a good match.'"

Bruce Prichard, a longtime producer for the WWF, said Bigelow "convinced himself" that things would go bad for him because The Kliq didn't like him and "that wasn't the case."

Carl Ouellet, who wrestled in the WWF as a tag team with Jacques Rougeau as The Quebecers and as Jean-Pierre LaFitte, said he also had his troubles with The Kliq. Ouellet said he is "good friends" with Nash now, but at the time he felt like the guys in the group were "cocky and arrogant" and that Michaels especially was intentionally holding other wrestlers back from making it big. In 1995, Ouellet and Nash got into a legitimate physical altercation after a match. In pro-wrestling terms, when a cooperative situation turns into an actual fight, it's called a "shoot."

Ouellet had a match scheduled against Nash on September 15 of that year in Montreal, not far from where Ouellet grew up and a place where he had a significant fan following. Ouellet said he didn't want to put Nash over, a wrestling term for letting him win.

Nash wasn't pleased by Ouellet's stance and one day, while the two were at a television taping, Ouellet said Nash approached him and said their match would solely consist of Nash landing a big boot and his jackknife powerbomb finishing move. Ouellet said he stood his ground and said that's not what he would do. What was agreed upon was a double disqualification.

In the actual match, Ouellet said the blows he and Nash traded got "harder and harder" as it went on. The next night, the two were booked for a match in Quebec City, which Nash was supposed to win cleanly. Things went off without incident until Ouellet went to the top rope for one of his signature moves, a leg drop. Ouellet said he misread the distance and landed with his leg on Nash's nose.

"And then he got up and started swinging at me," Ouellet said.

Ouellet said he called for the finish of the match, because he didn't want to escalate things. Nash hit him with his powerbomb, and Ouellet said he was "really upset" when they got backstage because he wasn't aware he hurt Nash's nose. The two men were supposed to wrestle the next night in Toronto, Ouellet said, but the match was called off because WWF officials were "afraid that something big would happen."

Battle lines had been drawn in the WWF locker room, between The Kliq and everyone else. The Kliq had considerable power with McMahon, but Bret Hart was also a favorite of the boss and a key part of the promotion's foundation in a post-Hogan era. Bret Hart and Michaels couldn't stand each other, and The Kliq was nothing if not loyal. They tolerated Bret, but things were tense.

Nash was scheduled to wrestle Bret, then the WWF champ, in a cage match in the main event of the *In Your House* pay-per-view February 18, 1996. The bout was supposed to advance two other storylines heading into *WrestleMania XII* six weeks later. At *WrestleMania*, Bret would face Michaels and Nash would have a match against The Undertaker.

At the *Royal Rumble* a month prior to *In Your House*, the storyline had Diesel screwing The Undertaker out of the WWF title by interfering in Undertaker's match with Bret Hart. At *In Your House*, the plan was for the same thing to happen, but the other way. The Undertaker was going to cost Diesel the belt, by reaching up through the bottom of the ring, grabbing Diesel, and pulling him underneath.

That was agreed upon by all parties, however Nash and Bret Hart didn't see eye to eye on the exact finish. Nash wanted to powerbomb Bret and be on the way to a clear victory before Undertaker snatched him, thereby protecting the Diesel character and adding more fuel to the fire for the Undertaker match at *WrestleMania*.

"I would've cost [Undertaker] the championship," Nash said. "He would've cost me the championship. . . . And Bret was already going to be in the [*WrestleMania*] main event."

Nash, Bret, and The Undertaker were in a room backstage discussing the finish before *In Your House* and Bret was questioning what was in it for him. Bret wanted his character to maintain an air of strength and not look like he was in danger of losing the title before the Michaels match.

"And fucking Taker, who never really goes off, he goes, 'Motherfucker, this isn't about you, it's about me and Kev—it makes our match better,'" Nash recalled. "[Bret said], 'I don't want to do it.' And we just went back and forth."

That infuriated Nash. So much so that, in a fit of anger and frustration, he decided to make a career-altering decision.

Nash walked down to the ring area, where Hall was going over his match with Waltman before the show.

"Tell Bischoff," Nash told Hall, "I'm coming, too."

———

There was just the little detail of convincing Bischoff that signing Nash would be in the best interest of WCW. Bischoff didn't trust him. Nash had lied to his face less than three years earlier, saying he wouldn't leave for the WWF. But Page went to bat for Nash hard.

Page connected Nash and Bischoff on the phone, and they met in person twice. Bischoff also flew out to Phoenix where Nash lived and the two went to a strip club called Bourbon Street Circus. Unlike Hall, Nash didn't hire Bloom until later.

It was there, inside the gentlemen's club, where Bischoff told Nash the nascent idea of how he planned on re-debuting Hall and Nash in WCW. But Nash wasn't completely sold on Bischoff nor WCW. Nash went back to McMahon and gave him a chance to match WCW's offer. McMahon did not.

Beating McMahon was consuming Bischoff, and he knew Nash could be a game changer. More than the ability to add Hall and Nash to the WCW roster, Bischoff would be taking them away from the WWF, where they were featured acts.

With the signings of Hall and Nash, WCW had signaled that it wasn't just going to be a southern wrestling company anymore, but one that would compete with the WWF on every level, including for high-level free-agent talent.

McMahon told Meltzer that WCW was "buying my guys," to which Meltzer replied that McMahon did the same thing to other promotions in the 1980s when he was looking to take the WWF national.

"No, I didn't," McMahon told Meltzer. "I had to use my own money. They're using Ted's money."

For the remaining months of 1996, Hall's WCW salary was $379,295 and Nash's was $336,261. The average WCW salary for all of 1996 was $110,319. The only WCW wrestlers who made more than Hall and Nash that year were Hogan, Savage, Flair, and Luger— and they were with WCW for all twelve months. In 1997, only Savage and Sting made more than Nash, and Hall was fifth behind Luger.

McMahon took Nash's departure, in particular, personally. McMahon reiterated that in an interview with WWF-owned *Raw* magazine, taking a shot at Nash in the process.

"Each individual is different, we all have different values," McMahon said. "Kevin Nash is looking for security. He's 37 years old, he is busted up physically and he doesn't have a love for the business and respect for the business as many individuals do who have grown up in it."

Meanwhile, Bischoff was developing plans for Hall and Nash in WCW. Perhaps they would end up being great adversaries for Hogan and Hulkamania would rise again. Bischoff already had a big idea, one that he was keeping under wraps.

CHAPTER 5

WHO'S THE THIRD MAN?

Hogan kicked back in his trailer, which sat in the tree-lined hills of Calabasas, California, northwest of Los Angeles, and pulled out a cigar. It was around 11 p.m. on a weekday night in June 1996, less than a month after Hall and Nash arrived in WCW.

"So," Hogan said, "who's the third man?"

———

Two weeks before Hogan's question, Bischoff climbed into his wife Loree's red Jaguar. He considered taking his Porsche, but the man he was about pick up—Hall—was too tall for the small car.

The plan was for Bischoff to leave his Georgia home, pick up Hall where he was staying at the Atlanta airport Marriott, and then Bischoff would drive them both the ninety minutes or so down to Macon, where Hall would make his surprise WCW debut. This was the first time Bischoff had seen Hall since Hall left WCW for the WWF in 1992.

Hall was known as a big partier and had developed something of an infamy in the WWF for having an attitude. After the beginning of *Nitro*, Bischoff felt the morale in WCW had reached new heights. A promotion that had been primarily a doormat for the WWF had become legitimate competition.

With things copacetic behind the scenes, Bischoff didn't want to upset the apple cart, which is why he wanted to be the first one to see Hall and get a read on where his head was at. He also wanted to get a feel for whether or not Hall was under the influence of anything.

"I was so concerned about upsetting this [newfound morale]," Bischoff said. "Finally, WCW had a really fun roster, locker room. People were enjoying themselves. And I thought, I'm going to bring these two guys in, and it's going to be right back to the way it was."

Bischoff was struck by how down-to-earth Hall was, which was a far cry from his reputation as a bully, avid drinker, and drug user. Once he got to the arena, Hall greeted officials and other wrestlers. Hall felt some tension backstage among his new WCW peers. No one wanted to cede their spot on the card, because that could equal a lower profile on television and a drop in income.

On the date of Hall's debut, Bischoff celebrated his forty-first birthday. As far as their discussion about how Hall would be introduced that night, Bischoff believed Hall understood the basic idea of what Bischoff wanted the storyline to be—an invasion—but there was a disconnect with regards to the speech Hall was going to deliver.

Partly because he hadn't fully hashed the whole thing out yet, Bischoff kept the debut storyline for Hall and Nash under wraps. There's an old saying in the industry: "Telephone, telegram, tell-a-wrestler." In other words, if you wanted to communicate something widely, tell a wrestler and everyone would end up knowing. Bischoff clued in just Nash and brought in Kevin Sullivan, his head of creative, about halfway through the process to help him work through it.

One of Bischoff's biggest fears was this storyline idea leaking to the "dirt sheets," a pejorative term in wrestling for the industry's media. Mainstream newspapers and television didn't really cover wrestling other than one-off stories here and there. Filling the void for that lack of coverage were newsletters, like the *Wrestling Observer* and *Torch*, that published insider information on the business weekly, mailing it out to subscribers.

In an effort to make things clearer for Hall, Bischoff went to the production office set aside for him backstage at Macon Coliseum and wrote out some loose guidelines as to what he wanted Hall to say on TV.

Hall was to portray himself as someone who was not supposed to be in the building. Everyone else on the broadcast would treat it like a total shock he was there. No name was to be given for him, especially not Razor Ramon.

The Razor Ramon character, though played by Hall, was trademarked and owned by the WWF. It was the company's intellectual property, much in the same way Captain America belongs to Marvel and Batman belongs to DC.

There was a meeting called before showtime with Hall, Bischoff, producers, and the broadcast team about exactly how Hall was going to enter the ring. Would he have entrance music like every other wrestler?

Hall was supposed to interrupt a match between "The Mauler" Mike Enos and Steve Doll. Larry Zbyszko, a former wrestler and one of *Nitro*'s color commentators, suggested Hall should walk through the crowd before doing so, to make it feel more organic. It was also decided in the meeting that Hall should not attack them, because that would be too much like other wrestling storylines.

When WCW came back from a commercial break during the

first hour of *Nitro*, Hall could be seen in the crowd walking down the Macon Coliseum steps on the top left part of the screen. As he got closer to the ringside area, fans were unsure exactly what was happening.

Wearing a denim vest and jeans with no shirt, the well-stubbled Hall, his hair slicked back with a single curl on his forehead, climbed over one barricade with fans trying to reach out and touch him.

"Wait a minute," WCW play-by-play announcer Tony Schiavone said on the call, acknowledging the intruder. "What the hell is going on here?"

Hall walked behind the ringside broadcast and asked for a mic. Hall grabbed one from ring announcer David Penzer at the table at ringside, climbed up the ring steps, and entered the ring.

Enos and Doll were still in the middle of their match. Hall put the microphone to his mouth and Enos just looked at him and left the ring with a confused expression. Enos, Doll, and referee Nick Patrick were aware of what Hall was going to do. They were informed of the plan before the show. But they sold it as if this was something not in the script.

Pro-wrestling storylines exist in their own universe with their own particular rules and specific ways of how characters interact with one another. When a wrestler enters the ring during a match, it almost always means he's going to attack one of the competitors, like when The Undertaker's interference cost Nash's character the match against Bret Hart. That's a standard method of beginning and advancing wrestling storylines.

When Hall did what he did on *Nitro*, it was so outside the fabric of wrestling's usual presentation that it felt like a rift in the space-time continuum.

"You people, you know who I am," Hall said on the microphone, clenching a toothpick between his molars, with a staccato delivery. "But you don't know why I'm here."

———

In wrestling, promos are as important as the matches, arguably more so. A promo, which is short for promotion, is a talking segment (or interview) that builds to a match or the next beat in the story. Promos explain the storyline, the stakes at play, and what a character's motivations are. They are the essential connective tissue of professional wrestling.

If you're a good promo artist and you can get people to believe in your persona, it almost doesn't matter as much if you can't perform entertaining matches in the ring.

A classic promo can define a wrestler's career. Flair's 1985 monologue about being a limousine-ridin', jet-flyin', Rolex-wearing son of a gun exemplified exactly what his character was supposed to be. Same for the blue-collar Dusty Rhodes's promo about the working class and falling on "hard times" from the same year. In 1987, Savage's "cream of the crop" interview, complete with tiny plastic half-and-half containers, is remembered as much as any of his matches.

A promo can come in many forms. The WWF has long preferred a script written by a writer with input from the wrestler. In other promotions, the wrestlers write promos themselves or go on screen with a few bullet points memorized and fill in the rest themselves. The most talented wrestlers on the microphone can go out there in front of a crowd with just an idea in their head and construct their words on the fly, listening for the crowd to send them in the right direction.

Cutting a promo is an art unto itself—an art within an art.

Hall's promo on May 27, 1996, has gone down as one of the best of all time, as much for its unprecedented content as for Hall's delivery.

"Where is Billionaire Ted?" Hall went on, referencing the WWF's skits. "Where is the Nacho Man? That punk can't even get in the building. Me? I go wherever I want, whenever I want. And where oh where is Scheme Gene? 'Cause I got a scoop for you. When that Ken Doll lookalike [Bischoff], when that weatherman wannabe comes out here later tonight, I got a challenge for him, for Billionaire Ted, for the Nacho Man. And for anybody else in [*here Hall puts on an exaggerated southern accent*] 'Dubya Cee Dubya.' Hey, you want to go to war? You want a war? You're gonna get one."

According to Bischoff, the story was supposed to be about Hall returning as a star after being mistreated in the past by WCW. Perhaps Bischoff is sticking to that story for legal reasons (which we'll get to later), but if that was truly the case, he was the only one who felt that way, and everyone else in the wrestling world and beyond missed the point completely.

It was clear to viewers that Hall was acting as an invader working for the WWF who had come to declare war on WCW.

The 4,309 fans in attendance didn't even cheer. They were completely stunned. Hall started walking toward the entrance ramp and *Nitro* went to commercial with him flicking his toothpick at the camera, a trademark of the Ramon character.

Bischoff felt there were some other issues in the details, too. Hall was slick-talking and charismatic. But his delivery of the speech was somewhat mechanical. That was because he basically just recited what Bischoff had written down "word for word," Bischoff said.

Hall didn't quite have a feel for the promo, as Bischoff suspected, so he played it safe and recited the script. The carefulness of Hall's words probably only contributed to the feeling of authenticity. It almost felt out of character.

The second hour of that *Nitro* opened with Bischoff and Heenan at the broadcast position. Bischoff, wearing a denim button-down shirt and a black leather vest, addressed Hall's appearance.

"We aren't even going to dignify the interruption that occurred here earlier," Bischoff said on commentary. "He wants to come out and say something to me—'Ken Doll lookalike'—I'm right ready, willing, and able."

At the end of the show, *Nitro* panned back to Bischoff and Heenan at the broadcast table, recapping what transpired on the episode. Hall then popped up to their right with a microphone in his hand.

"Lookie here, Ken Doll—you have such a big mouth," Hall said. "And *we* are sick of it."

"Who's we?" Bischoff responded.

"You know who," Hall said. "You want a war? You got one."

Hall flicked his toothpick at Bischoff, who told him, "You're out of here." Hall left the broadcast set as Bischoff and Heenan both shrugged.

"I don't know what to say," Bischoff said to cap the show. "We'll see you next week."

———

Bischoff wanted to lean into the idea of episodic television with storylines developing week to week. He was adapting wrestling programming to the fast-moving, rapidly expanding world of cable TV. WCW vice president Sharon Sidello, Bischoff said, used to refer to wrestling as a soap opera for men. The storylines were sensational, like something out of *One Life to Live*, but contained inside the confines of a pseudo-sport. Bischoff leaned into that idea, creating a live-action, episodic melodrama with cliffhangers, swerves, and stories that advanced from week to week.

A week after his shocking appearance, Hall was back at the end of *Nitro* to confront Bischoff on the broadcast set. Hall shoved Bischoff back into his chair and Sting, long WCW's unwavering good guy, came out to save the executive/announcer. Sting slapped Hall as security intervened.

That episode of *Nitro*, on June 3, 1996, beat *Raw* in the ratings, 3.0 to 2.3. The beginning of the "invasion" storyline was the talk of the wrestling world, with fans wanting to see what happened next.

But the debut of Hall in that manner did come with consequences, for him and for WCW. The WWF sent a legal letter to Hall after his appearance, threatening to withhold merchandise and pay-per-view pay he was still owed due to alleged trademark infringement. The WWF felt like its "Razor Ramon" intellectual property was being stolen.

McMahon also read a lawyer's letter on the June 3, 1996, episode of *Raw*, stating that Hall and Nash were not part of the WWF. A WWF lawsuit, claiming copyright violations, followed.

None of that deterred Bischoff. Nash made his debut on the June 10, 1996, episode of *Nitro* in Wheeling, West Virginia. Hall came out to the broadcast position again at the end of the show. Bischoff stood up and Nash appeared, towering behind the exec.

"This is where the big boys play, huh?" Nash said. "We ain't here to play."

Hall and Nash made it clear they were there for a fight—in the ring. They wanted a three-on-three match: WCW's best trio against the two of them and the mystery man they were bringing with them.

Nash was also not given a name when he appeared, like Hall. Marcus Bagwell, who was then in a tag team called the American Males with Scotty Riggs, said none of the wrestlers could even say "Razor Ramon" or "Diesel" in the building during shows or WCW would have fined them $10,000.

————

Hall and Nash were getting dressed in other parts of the building during shows, rather than with the rest of the wrestlers in the locker room. Bischoff said he wasn't trying to fool the other talent into thinking it was real, but he didn't want people who worked in the buildings to see Hall and Nash congregating with WCW wrestlers and officials to preserve the integrity of the tale they were trying to tell.

Resentment started to build right away against Hall and Nash, with many wrestlers seeing their potential spots being taken by carpetbaggers from the WWF.

Brian Knobbs (Brian Yandrisovitz) of the Nasty Boys tag team was friendly with Hall and Nash. But he felt they had come in with "that attitude" from the WWF that they were superior to WCW and its talent.

"They were talking to us like Ric Flair and Lex and Sting and those guys and kind of putting down WCW a bit, because they came from the WWF," Knobbs said.

Not everyone was unhappy that Hall and Nash were there. Konnan, a Cuban American wrestler who came to WCW after being one of the biggest stars in Mexico, hit it off right away with Hall and Nash, as did Konnan's protégé Rey Mysterio Jr.

"[Hall and Nash] look cool, they talk cool, they were good-looking, they were tall, they were in good shape, they had funny lines," Konnan said. "The casting was perfect."

———

Sting came to visit Bischoff in the spring of 1996 at Bischoff's home in Cody, Wyoming. The WCW star was planning on buying property down the road.

Bischoff described Sting as "very smart," but "very cautious," a guy who would listen when being pitched on ideas as if "he was in a lecture." Sting had been the cornerstone babyface for WCW going back to the 1980s. WCW fans had never seen him as a villain.

But that's exactly what Bischoff was proposing: for Sting to turn heel—to turn against WCW—and join Hall and Nash as the third man.

At thirty-nine years old, Sting wasn't dying his hair blond and spiking it up like he had in his younger days when he portrayed a surfer-like character. Bischoff felt that Sting's self-motivated alterations might have been a sign he was ready for an even bigger change. And Bischoff was right. Sting agreed in principle to make a major shift in his career and be part of the new storyline alongside Hall and Nash.

And then, Bischoff got a call from Hogan.

Hogan had been taking some time off from WCW to work on projects in Hollywood. He was filming the movie *Santa with Muscles*, starring alongside Ed Begley Jr. and a young Mila Kunis, which would be released later that year. Hogan was keeping track of what was happening on WCW television and pay-per-view. Every Tuesday morning, Jimmy Hart would overnight Hogan a VHS tape of *Nitro* via FedEx.

Hogan took particular interest in how WCW introduced Hall and Nash. He called Bischoff out of the blue and asked him to fly out for a conversation about "where we're going."

Bischoff was surprised. Hogan returning to the ring was not even on Bischoff's radar. He had that thought on the back burner, planned for sometime later in the year.

Bischoff flew out from Atlanta to Los Angeles. He arrived late and Hogan was waiting for him. After some small talk, Hogan got down to the reason why he wanted to meet with Bischoff: he wanted to know who the third man was going to be.

"Who do you think it should be?" Bischoff shot back.

Hogan's answer floored him.

"You're looking at him, brother," Hogan said.

Bischoff was elated and knew Hogan would make the biggest splash. On the flight back home to Atlanta, though, Bischoff couldn't help but think about WCW's stalwart who had already agreed to the role.

"In the back of my mind," Bischoff said, "I'm thinking, 'How the fuck am I going to tell Sting?'"

———

The Great American Bash pay-per-view took place at the Baltimore Arena on June 16, 1996. Before the main event, which featured The Giant defending his WCW championship against Luger, Bischoff came out onto the stage in front of the entranceway and called out Hall and Nash, still without using their names. Bischoff said before he answered their challenge, he had some questions.

"Do you work for the WWF?" Bischoff asked, clearly trying to lower the temperature from a legal perspective.

Hall and Nash both said no. They then asked Bischoff who

the three men were whom Hall, Nash, and their "surprise" would be facing at the *Bash at the Beach* pay-per-view the following month.

Bischoff said he couldn't tell them yet, but would be able to the next night on *Nitro*. Hall, miffed that he didn't get a straight answer, punched Bischoff in the gut. Nash grabbed Bischoff, put the executive's head between his legs, picked him up by his torso end-over-end, and threw Bischoff back first through a table off the stage. Bischoff was not a wrestler and him being attacked with that level of violence was startling to viewers.

Bischoff didn't rehearse the stunt at all. He knew there was a "pretty good chance" he'd get hurt, as far as pain. But he felt like it wouldn't be anything serious where he'd need a hospital stay. Meltzer wrote in the *Observer* that the angle got big cheers among some fans, "but left others pretty much stunned."

"I wanted it to be shocking," Bischoff said. "This goes back to making things believable. When you see things you've never seen before, your brain automatically shifts into, 'Oh my God, I've never seen this before—it must be real.'

"Rather than just kneeing me in the gut, folding me up, I said, 'What if you powerbombed me off the stage?' Kevin was like, 'Are you crazy?'"

Meanwhile, back in Los Angeles on a movie set, Hogan was watching things unfold with a keen eye.

"Eric was thinking about putting Sting in there and, in my opinion, Sting wasn't WWE to the core," Hogan said. "Nobody was more WWE than me. And so, once I saw Scott show [up and] Big Kev powerbomb Eric off the stage, I went, 'Oh boy, when I turn heel, this is going to either destroy my career or this is going to be the greatest thing that ever happened in wrestling.'"

The night after *The Great American Bash* on *Nitro*, the three WCW representatives who would face Hall, Nash, and the third man were announced: Sting, Luger, and Savage. Gene Okerlund, during the announcement, referred to Hall and Nash as "The Outsiders" for the first time, and that would go on to be their tag-team name.

Sting was going to be in the match on the babyface side with Hogan now in play as the partner of Hall and Nash. But that didn't mean Sting was off the hook. Bischoff told Sting that WCW was going to move forward with Hogan as the third man. But Bischoff needed Sting to be the backup teammate of The Outsiders in case Hogan changed his mind.

Despite what Hogan was saying, Bischoff didn't think he'd actually go through with it. He remembered the conversation the two had a year earlier about a heel turn when Hogan threw him out of his house.

———

Bash at the Beach was scheduled for July 7, 1996, at the Ocean Center in Daytona Beach, Florida. Hogan flew in the day before with his agent, Peter Young. WCW's head of creative, Kevin Sullivan, was put in charge of keeping things on course. Sullivan owned a condo about a mile away from the arena, and Hogan and Young stayed over with him that night.

Sullivan's job was to keep Hogan's appearance at the show a secret—and, most important, to make sure Hogan followed through with the storyline plans.

Bischoff said he knew Hogan could change his mind on things after talking to people in his inner circle, which included Young, who was "second only to Hulk's wife," Linda, in not wanting him to turn. Jimmy Hart was also in favor of Hogan staying a babyface, Bischoff said.

"Hulk trusted Peter," Bischoff said. "Peter had been with Hulk from Day One. Peter was with Hulk through a lot of shit in WWE. . . . But Peter was like, 'Oh my God, you're Hulk Hogan! Merchandise! Oh my God! Movie deals, oh my God!' Peter was looking at what he was going to lose, as opposed to what it was going to do for the business."

Young said he remembered being at Sullivan's home, but denied having any input into what Hogan would do the following evening on the pay-per-view show.

"I really didn't have any say in Hulk's wrestling," Young said. "That's like WWE lore that I had anything to do with it. I wish I had the power to do that."

Bischoff said he wasn't convinced Hogan would actually pull the trigger on the turn until they both got to the Ocean Center before *Bash at the Beach*. But Bischoff didn't tell anyone Hogan was sold on it. Not Hall. Not Nash. Not the commentary team. The plan was for the six-man tag-team match—Sting, Luger, and Savage against Hall, Nash, and Hogan—to begin without a third man for The Outsiders' team.

Legendary boxing ring announcer Michael Buffer did the intros for the match, as he did often for WCW in the 1990s. This one had a little more gravity, though. Buffer, in his baritone voice, boomed that the "very existence of WCW" was on the line in the headlining bout. The match was entitled "The Hostile Takeover."

———

Early in the match, Luger was "injured" and taken out on a stretcher. The idea was to remove him from the equation to even up the teams, two on two. Hall and Nash were the heels, and in wrestling, for story purposes, you want the good guys with their backs against the wall, battling back against the odds. It didn't make sense for the babyfaces to outnumber the heels, especially with what was coming next.

With Luger out, Hall and Nash took over the match. Hogan then appeared, coming down the entranceway in his yellow and red gear to a big reaction from the crowd. That's the moment when Hall and Nash were sure that Hogan would join them.

As Hogan made his way to the ring, Heenan on commentary exclaimed: "Yeah, but whose side is he on?!" It could have been an all-time gaffe if things didn't end up so overwhelmingly successful.

When Hogan got to the ring, Hall and Nash cleared out. Hogan played to the crowd like he always did—and then dropped his signature leg drop on a prone Savage.

The crowd didn't understand what was going on.

"Hulk Hogan has betrayed WCW," Heenan said on commentary. "He is the third man."

Hogan then tossed referee Randy Anderson out of the ring and laid on Savage for the pin.

Hogan stood in the middle of the ring with Hall and Nash on either side, all of them holding each other's hands up in a pose of victory. The fans in Daytona, realizing what had just happened, started to throw trash into the ring, a cascade of paper soda cups and junk food wrappers.

One fan even tried to enter the ring. It was not part of the script. The fan jumped over the barricade from the front row and slid under the ropes. Nash was there waiting for him and decked him with a left forearm shiver. The fan went down, and Nash and Hall stomped on his head—hard—until arena security came to take him away.

Okerlund came into the ring with a microphone. Hogan didn't really know what he was going to say, but, as he always did, he was going to follow the reaction of the crowd, which was incendiary.

"I didn't back off," Hogan said. "I could have pulled back a little bit on the verbiage, but I'm like, 'Nah.' I just shoved the gas pedal down."

What came out almost seemed therapeutic.

Hogan told the fans to shut up, compared them to the garbage in the ring, and told them to "stick it." Hogan said he was fed up with the fans' reactions after all he had done for them and for charity. He intimated he only did it to line his own pockets. As far as WCW went, Hogan said he was bored, and that Hall and Nash represented "the new blood."

"If it wasn't for Hulk Hogan, you people wouldn't be here," Hogan said. "If it wasn't for Hulk Hogan, Eric Bischoff would be still selling meat from a truck in Minneapolis. And if it wasn't for Hulk Hogan, all these Johnny-come-latelies that you see out here wrestling wouldn't be here."

Hogan named the trio for the first time—the New World Order—and then botched it the second time around, calling them the "new world organization." Bischoff said the name was his idea and he told Hogan to say it backstage before *Bash at the Beach*. In reality, Zbyszko was actually the first to use New World Order in reference to the group, six days earlier on *Nitro*.

Was it the smoothest execution from all parties? Hardly. But maybe that made it seem even more genuine. There was nothing fake about the palpable fury of the fans at Ocean Center that night. They knew what was happening was all part of the script, but they couldn't help but empty out their emotions.

The man who was the hero of pro wrestling for more than a decade had put a dagger in the collective backs of those who cheered him. And it made for an incredibly compelling and chaotic scene.

Those were just getting started.

PART II

CHAPTER 6

ARE PEOPLE IN DANGER?

Mike Weber was WCW's director of marketing for most of the 1990s. The first time he heard the words "new world order" in a wrestling context was when they came out of Hogan's mouth at *Bash at the Beach* 1996. There were no monthslong plans for a marketing campaign, no systematic rollout of new branding for this group. Weber and his team had to jump on it when they realized how big of a deal it was shaping up to be following the reaction Hogan's heel turn got from fans.

Weber had been the WWF's head of media relations in the 1980s at the height of Hulkamania. But this was something completely different. Hulkamania was something built up and carefully manicured. The New World Order was a spontaneous convergence that became bigger than anyone had counted on.

"The whole thing was about the most organic, reactionary type of a thing I've ever seen," Weber said. "And everything we did was reacting to it and then trying to like expand upon it. From merchandising, how it's marketed, how it was promoted, how it was licensed and all that stuff."

The nWo needed a logo.

———

Floodlights beamed through a twenty-foot panoramic window behind Jenni Sloan from the left, the same way they would every thirty minutes as a Disney MGM Studios people mover escorted visitors on a tour of the Orlando theme park.

Sloan, then a twenty-six-year-old blonde whose maiden name was Hines, worked for Disney i.d.e.a.s., a postproduction studio on the park's grounds. Her main job was designing special effects for Disney MGM attractions, stages, and rides. But one day in July 1996, there would be a departure from her typical work.

Three producers from WCW, Craig Leathers, Annette Yother, and Rob Wright, came into her office and said they needed a logo for their big, new pro-wrestling storyline: the New World Order. The group had a name, and it was exploding as the topic at the forefront of every wrestling conversation. But in order for WCW to capitalize on that, the nWo needed merchandise.

Leathers, Yother, and Wright told Sloan's boss that they needed a logo—that day. And they only had the budget for one hour of Sloan's time. No one involved remembered the exact dollar figure, just that the execution of such a thing would have normally been done by WCW in-house at its offices in Atlanta. But the Summer Olympics were being held that year in WCW's home city and there were simply no production trucks available to roll for WCW television, so the promotion was using the in-house operations and production at its second home in Orlando.

Leathers had come prepared with some ideas in his head. He spent hours perusing the magazine stands at places like Walgreen's, buying biker and skater magazines and ripping out pages afterward in search of the right aesthetic.

"I knew I wanted it kind of grungy," Leathers said. "Something easily readable."

Leathers, Yother, and Wright stood behind Sloan in the corner of a long editing suite, their backs to the huge window. Sloan sat in a red chair with a gray Macintosh computer in front of her and got to work. With a short amount of time, Sloan didn't even have time to sketch anything out on paper. She said Leathers told her maybe just start laying out some ideas with the letters "NWO" on the computer, suggesting something that looked a little "rough" and like "graffiti."

"Of all the work I've ever done that was like the fastest, quickest, did-not-think-it-would-last-any-time-at-all [thing]," Sloan said. "I mean, they couldn't even afford color. I was like, 'All right, well, I guess a black T-shirt with a white logo.'"

Bischoff estimates the T-shirts alone have sold somewhere in the tens of millions of dollars. He briefly came back to WWE in a leadership role in 2019 and he said nWo T-shirts were still in the current-day top-ten things most sold in WWE's merchandise catalogue.

Sloan didn't see a penny of the revenue from the logo she helped design, either. She said at the time she was making somewhere just north of $50,000, which for 1996 was a decent salary (more than $100,000 now, accounting for inflation), especially given she was one of the only women in the country doing that type of postproduction work.

Sloan said she rarely saw or thought about the nWo logo for about two decades, until several years ago, before the COVID-19 pandemic, when she was waiting in line at the Waldorf Astoria Golf Club in Orlando. There was a man there standing in front of Sloan and her family wearing an nWo shirt. She said she asked him where he got it. It turns out, that man was Hulk Hogan's son, Nick, who was six years old when his father turned heel.

———

The September 2, 1996, *Nitro* was the first time Hogan, Hall, and Nash wore the classic nWo T-shirt—black shirt, white graffiti-like lettering—on television. The following week, more than two months after *Bash at the Beach,* was the first commercial aired during *Nitro* promoting the shirts and explaining how to buy them.

That was one of the biggest early challenges of marketing the new group, Weber said. WCW could not officially sell the shirts, because the nWo was supposed to be a completely separate, rival organization. Weber said when the nWo first formed, the people who worked for the third-party vendor that sold WCW merchandise in arenas used to go outside, about a block away from the building, and sell the nWo shirts from a cardboard box separately from WCW ones, as if they were bootleggers.

The T-shirt "was the storyline," Weber said. As the group grew, the shirt became synonymous with membership. Hogan, Hall, and Nash would give prospective members the shirt and if they put it on, they were in.

The shirts had taken on a gravity and meaning all their own. If you had one on, you weren't just wearing something. You were a part of something.

Before the turn, Hogan was expected back in the fall of 1996, returning to his role as the good-guy face of the company. In advance of that, WCW's then-director of merchandising Kelley Merwin (née Komminsk) had ordered more than five thousand yellow and red tearaway Hogan shirts. They never saw the light of day.

Once the logo was in hand, Merwin ordered nWo T-shirts at five thousand per clip from printers in Las Vegas and Atlanta. Most merchandise items, if she was unsure how they would sell, would be ordered starting with five hundred and Merwin would see how things went. The nWo shirt was a hot seller right from the beginning.

Right before the dawn of the nWo, WCW had hired 4Kids Entertainment, a children's entertainment and merchandise licensing company run by Alfred Kahn. 4Kids became the largest merchandise trading entity in the United States in the 1990s on the back of their work with *Pokémon, Yu-Gi-Oh!,* and *Teenage Mutant Ninja Turtles.*

With the help of 4Kids, WCW was able to get nWo products sold at Spencer's Gifts, a favorite mall store at the time for kids, teens, and young adults that sold offbeat items, as well as pop-culture merchandise. WCW and 4Kids licensed whatever they could with the nWo brand—"we went full tilt on everything," Weber said—from sneakers to bandanas to baseball caps to women's apparel to pennants to replica belts to action figures to credit cards to even a bowling league.

WCW also teamed up with NASCAR to develop an nWo-sponsored Chevrolet. It was driven, fittingly, by Kyle Petty, who was considered one of motor sports' biggest villains.

"I got noticed more for wrestling than for Coca-Cola and Mattel," Petty said, referring to his other sponsors.

The nWo logo was everywhere you looked.

Meltzer wrote in the week ending July 7, 1996, the day of *Bash at the Beach,* that all WCW programming on television was viewed in 6.88 million homes on 175 stations, compared with 4.2 million homes on 153 stations for the WWF. There were more eyes on WCW in the wake of the nWo storyline than on the No. 1 promotion in the world.

"The term *viral* was not there, but that's what it went—it went viral," Weber said. "And people went crazy over it."

Funnily enough, once the WCW and nWo merchandise started

selling incredibly well at shows in 1997 and beyond, WCW actually had to hire someone to come to events and bust counterfeiters selling fake nWo shirts outside the building, Merwin said. Life had imitated art.

There was no online shop for people to buy things on the internet then. WCW's website was primitive by today's standard, at best. The only way to buy nWo merchandise was over the phone, at events, or through a catalogue. Merwin's team sent out four catalogues to fans in the mail annually—two for WCW and two for the nWo. The two brands were kept completely separate.

"We had different phone numbers for both [merchandise shops], too," Merwin said.

Then there were the video games. Weber said a deal with developer THQ was signed late in 1995 and when the nWo started in July 1996 they had to hit the metaphorical pause button and overhaul the original plan to include the group. What WCW and THQ ended up agreeing on was a game cobranded as both WCW and the nWo. THQ was completely fine with that, Weber said, because they saw how "the nWo took over the business in days."

The group's name, the New World Order, did not end up being controversial. Nash and Bischoff discussed its relationship with conspiracy theories and the idea that there was a higher power somewhere pulling the strings on everything, like "the World Bank and the Illuminati and the different Rothschilds." They wanted a sinister theme for the group that had the curiosity factor that Bischoff pined for. The nWo fit the bill.

———

Hogan, Hall, and Nash were inside a soundstage at Disney MGM Studios in Orlando one day in July 1996. The idea was to get the three of them together while Hogan was in town—not in Los Angeles filming a movie—and tape several segments for the fledgling New World Order group that would air on *Nitro*. The promos were supposed to set the tone for what the nWo would be, how it would look.

And, frankly, things didn't go well.

"When we first started out, none of us liked each other," Hogan said.

One of the things that initially made him hesitate to become a heel was that he wasn't entirely sure about being packaged with Hall and Nash as a unit. It wasn't that he didn't think those guys were good. He just didn't know if he could trust them yet. Hogan was also well aware of the stories about The Kliq in the WWF.

"If I was a bad guy on my own, I knew how to handle that," Hogan said.

He had been the alpha dog in the industry for so long and he was being asked to run in a pack with a pair of guys who had unsavory reputations from their days in New York. Hogan was put in somewhat of a position of vulnerability.

Sullivan believed Hogan figured it would also be a mistake to enter into a storyline opposite Hall and Nash. Hall and Nash were physically bigger than Hogan, and Sullivan's theory was that Hogan felt like Hall and Nash would not make him look strong in matches.

After about an hour of shooting the first nWo interviews, Hall and Nash called for a break. They went outside the soundstage near a picnic table and pulled aside Neal Pruitt, one of WCW's features producers who was assigned this project.

Hall and Nash felt like Hogan was approaching it all wrong, saying the same old, tired lines from the 1980s that made him big as a babyface. Hogan was yelling into the camera like it was 1990 and he was trying to build up a *WrestleMania* match against the Ultimate Warrior. He was going on long monologues and dominating the camera time while Hall and Nash could only slip in sound bites and catchphrases here and there.

Hogan was just five years older than Hall and six years older than Nash. But there was a generation gap in terms of when they all came up in wrestling. Hall and Nash listened to contemporary music, especially hip-hop, in a period when gangsta rap was taking off. "California Love" by 2Pac and "Gangsta's Paradise" by Coolio were near the top of the charts. Hogan was a major superstar a decade prior to Hall's and Nash's emergence in the business and his musical taste was stuck in the eighties.

Hall and Nash still didn't know how it would all work out with Hogan and the future of whatever it was Bischoff was putting together with the nWo. But they did know having Hogan next to them in photos only elevated their profile.

There's a term in wrestling called getting the "rub." It basically means someone taking their star power and having it "rub" off on someone else. Hogan was the beneficiary of it, sharing screentime with Stallone, Mr. T, and Shaq previously. His relationship to those men grew Hogan's profile. Now he was the one sharing his fame with Hall and Nash, who were too cunning to blow things up this early in the process.

"This is how smart Hall and Nash are," Sullivan said. "They put Hulk up in front and laid back and let him run with all his stuff until he felt comfortable and blended in with them."

Pruitt was the unsung hero in all of it. He cut up all the video from that first day of promos into small parts, made it black and white and grainy looking for a grittier feel. Pruitt brought his personal handheld camera with him, and Hall used it to shoot Hogan and Nash, giving the vibe that this was something the nWo was doing on its own and not part of WCW's production.

Perhaps most important, Pruitt spliced everything together to make it seem like Hogan, Hall, and Nash were all on the same page, speaking in a similar cadence, with everyone getting turns to give their lines.

Later on, when the three of them felt comfortable enough with one another, Hall and Nash had the conversation with Hogan about the style they wanted to push with the nWo, something more modern. Hogan was receptive to it.

———

With Hogan absent, the July 8, 1996, *Nitro*, the day after the nWo was formed, was filled mostly with interviews with WCW talent reacting to Hogan's heel turn. It wasn't just main-event-level wrestlers like Sting and Savage talking about it; even midcard wrestlers like Mysterio got an opportunity. The nWo story was all-encompassing, unlike much of what was going on at that time in wrestling.

For the most part, wrestling stories prior were told in segments, almost in a vacuum, without an overarching theme. There have been some exceptions throughout wrestling history. But with multiple voices up and down the card talking about the nWo, it really hammered home the idea that this was a bigger deal than everything else. Savage, in his promo, referred to the nWo's head baddie as "Hollywood Hogan," which ended up sticking as the moniker of Hogan's new heel character.

Hall and Nash showed up in a black limo toward the end of the episode and were interviewed by Okerlund. Nash quipped that the reaction to the newly formed nWo at *Bash at the Beach* made him feel like "Mark Fuhrman at the Apollo [Theater]," a reference to the O. J. Simpson trial.

The fallout of the Hogan turn led *Nitro* to a 3.5 to 2.5 win over *Raw* in the ratings. The number was tied for the second-highest rating yet for *Nitro*.

———

Hogan walked to the ring wearing all black clothing and a pronounced sneer on the July 15, 1996, *Nitro*, signifying his character's new direction.

In his first words since *Bash at the Beach*, Hogan said the nWo was taking over professional wrestling. Hogan took aim at Savage specifically. He said Savage blamed him for Savage's divorce.

Savage's on-screen split from ex-wife Miss Elizabeth (Elizabeth Hulette)—they had already been divorced for years in real life—was the most popular storyline on WCW television before Hall and Nash showed up. Elizabeth had joined up with Flair, with the implication that they were sleeping together, as well as jointly spending Savage's alimony money to further their lavish lifestyles.

Savage and Elizabeth had been an on-screen pair in the WWF on and off from 1985 to 1992.

Hogan continued with the promo, teasing new members of the nWo and saying he would be facing the current WCW World Heavyweight champion, The Giant, at the next pay-per-view, *Hog Wild*. Hogan then challenged "the whole WCW" to come out. WCW wrestlers Rick and Scott Steiner, Meng, The Barbarian, and Arn Anderson all emerged from backstage to confront him as the show went off the air, establishing the onset of the war between WCW and the nWo.

Pro wrestling, as a medium, has a tendency to rehash stories and segments from a decade or more earlier with a new sheen. The nWo was not going to be a nostalgia act.

More of that originality was on display during the July 22, 1996, *Nitro.*

Hall and Nash broke into the control room at Disney MGM Studios, where top WCW producers and directors like Leathers and Keith Mitchell were positioned. During a tag match, WCW cut to a camera in the room with Hall and Nash attempting to hijack the show.

Nash put on a headset and Hall instructed producers to pan the crowd, because they were "looking for someone," teasing that maybe a fourth nWo member would appear.

For the first time on *Nitro*, Hall flashed the Turkish wolf with his hand, a signal to The Kliq. It became the nWo's signature sign.

The *Nitro* episode a week later set a new standard for professional wrestling on television. It combined the suspension of disbelief sought after by Bischoff and a completely different feel from anything else that came before it, which was desired by Hall and Nash.

Four underrated people in how the nWo was built and how it came across on TV sat down before the show inside one of the trailers WCW was using outside the makeshift Disney MGM Studios venue.

There was Sullivan, the blond-haired, mustached, old-school wrestler and creative lead. There were Leathers and Mitchell, who had experience producing and directing wrestling television going back to the early 1980s. And there was Pruitt, whose broadcasting experience before WCW was solely in traditional sports, like college football and the Goodwill Games.

The idea was to do a beatdown by the nWo of several WCW wrestlers in the outdoor trailer area.

Pruitt, who would be the field producer on the ground for the segment, had the idea of shooting it with one camera. He was inspired by the police procedural series *Hill Street Blues*, whose showrunners preferred the use of handheld cameras over studio ones. Pruitt didn't want any camera cuts; it would be done in one shot.

They then got together all the wrestlers and production people and told them the plan. The behind-the-scenes workers had to be on camera to give off the feeling of realism.

"Everybody knows wrestling, to a certain degree, is a work," Pruitt said, using the industry term for "predetermined." "But what [the fans are] going to do is, they're not going to look at the wrestlers' faces to see if it's real. They're going to look at us production people and see what this is all about. I said, 'We've got to convince them that this is the most real thing you've ever seen, and you are freaking out yourself and panicked. We all have to have that look. Not one of us can make the mistake of not doing that.'"

Pruitt and the crew then walked through the segment step by step, four or five times. They "rehearsed it like crazy," he said. Different people—wrestlers and backstage employees—were stationed in different areas that the single camera would pan to, waiting for their cues.

The second match of the show was a six-man tag pitting Flair, Chris Benoit, and Steve McMichael against Sting, Luger, and Savage. Flair, Benoit, McMichael, and Arn Anderson made up the Four Horsemen, a legendary pro-wrestling heel group led by Flair that began in 1985 and had several iterations since.

During the match, Jimmy Hart, who had been working in WCW as a heel manager, came out and asked the six men for help. The Outsiders were in the back, he said. The scene established the significance of what was going on right away, because it was a villainous manager asking two teams—one of babyfaces and one of heels—to work together to help against a greater evil.

One cameraman started walking from the ring area to the back near the outdoor trailers and the segment that Pruitt led began. The first shot was Arn Anderson down on the concrete floor, holding his arm, with someone coming over to tend to him. The camera shifted left, and Hall and Nash were there, holding aluminum baseball bats, standing over a prone Marcus Bagwell.

A limo could be seen in the background. Hall and Nash dropped their bats and the aluminum clanged off the cement. The implied violence was more powerful than if they had actually shown it.

"We both were huge [Alfred] Hitchcock fans, in that your mind is way more powerful than any visual," Nash said of himself and Hall.

Scotty Riggs, Bagwell's tag-team partner, then came over from behind Hall and Nash and saw Bagwell on the floor. Riggs went over to tend to him as Hall bent down and grabbed a piece of lighting equipment. Riggs confronted Hall, who clocked him with the light.

Mysterio, a cruiserweight wrestler who stood about five-foot-five, then leapt from the railing of the elevated entrance area of one of the trailers. Nash caught him out of the air and threw him headfirst into the side of the trailer. The dangerous spot was Mysterio's idea.

"Just throw me," Mysterio said. "I'll fucking land."

After the brutal attack, Hall and Nash jumped into the waiting limo. Savage arrived to the area just as the limo was pulling away and jumped up onto the top of the vehicle while it was in motion, grabbing on to the sun roof and trying to get in. He remained there, hanging on to the vehicle as it drove out of the sight of the camera. It looked like a scene from *Mission: Impossible*, which premiered in theaters two months earlier.

Multiple wrestlers were down, with others standing over them, trying to help. Production people and security, wearing orange shirts, were tending to the fallen. It almost resembled a war movie. A woman offscreen screamed, "Somebody call an ambulance, please!"

The scene seemed so legitimate that, due to the noises being produced, park attendees, neighbors, and some WCW viewers started calling Disney MGM Studios to ask what the hell was happening.

"Disney was so pissed off at us after it was over with," Pruitt said. "Their switchboard got jammed up. 'Is there a riot going on over there? Are people in danger?'"

There is a symbiosis that pro wrestling has with its fans that doesn't exist in other entertainment mediums. When wrestling is at its best, the decision-makers and wrestlers respond to real-time, in-arena fan feedback. They try to match the fans' energy and go in the direction they believe the fans want.

When Hogan turned, the intensity inside the arena ratcheted up to a degree where people were throwing garbage into the ring. This scene at Disney MGM Studios was, in some ways, WCW's response. The chaos and violence—and most important, the authenticity—were turned up another notch.

The show continued with matches in the ring, but the producers kept cutting to the back near the trailers throughout the episode to see wrestlers being taken via stretcher into ambulances and getting driven away.

The fans who were there live started chanting "boring," because they couldn't see what was happening back there, just the action in the ring. During the nWo era, there were just as many storyline developments shot backstage for just the television audience as there were in the ring, if not more. That eventually prompted promotions, by the late 1990s, to invest in large video screens for the arena that would show what was happening in the back to those in attendance.

Regardless, the nWo's Disney MGM Studios trailer attack established that WCW was going to continue to deliver things to wrestling fans that were outside the established norm.

"I can just feel my heart beating right now, thinking about that scene, because it worked so well," Pruitt said.

Nitro walloped *Raw*, 3.1 to 2.1, on July 29, 1996. It was *Nitro's* seventh straight time winning the battle and earning a rating of 3.0 or higher.

———

The following week, a black screen appeared when *Nitro* was about to go to commercial. In white, grainy text were the words: "The following announcement has been paid for by the New World Order." At the bottom of the screen was the newly minted nWo logo created by Sloan.

A deep voice—Pruitt's, actually—read the text while a familiar-sounding music played in the background.

After the Disney MGM soundstage promo taping, Pruitt got together with editors Kemper Rogers and Tim Scott and started poring through the Turner music library. Much like there wasn't a huge budget or time for the logo, there were limitations on audio, too. Many WCW wrestler entrance themes at the time came from generic music out of the Turner catalogue. The nWo's music was no exception.

Pruitt, Rogers, and Scott picked out three different tracks. Bischoff and Leathers came to the studio to listen to them. The one they chose, Pruitt said, was catalogued as "FCD115 Track 14." It was later discovered that it was an instrumental song called "Rockhouse" by musician Frank Shelley, but WCW wasn't aware of that at the time. All they knew of it was as a generic music bed owned by Turner that sounded like it would have fit in the background of a porn.

"FCD115 Track 14" did carry a tune that seemed recognizable. It was basically a mashup of several different Jimi Hendrix beats, including from the songs "The Stars That Play with Laughing Sam's Dice," "Hey Joe," and "Voodoo Chile."

After the advertising message, Hogan appeared in front of a screen with the nWo logo on it. Nash was on his left and Hall on his right. They were all wearing black with dark sunglasses. It was a snippet from the trio's first promo, produced by Pruitt.

The camera cuts were quick, and the angles were unique. Pruitt said they were inspired by the Paul Mitchell male hair product commercials that were airing at that time on television.

———

Hog Wild was scheduled for Sturgis, South Dakota, on August 1, 1996, as part of the annual motorcycle rally in the city, which attracts around 500,000 people every year. Bischoff and many others in WCW were into motorcycles, especially Harley-Davidsons.

The "arena" area was a unique setup. The ring and set were built outdoors. There were no traditional seats or bleachers—just rows and rows of bikers sitting on their motorcycles or the grass. The situation was an odd one for the nWo's pay-per-view debut, because the fans in attendance were there for the motorcycle rally and not necessarily wrestling. It was pretty clear by how quiet they were and how they cheered Hogan, rather than booed him, that they were not exactly up to speed on current storylines.

Hall and Nash defeated Sting and Luger in a tag match that had a controversial finish. Nick Patrick, the referee for the match and WCW's senior official, stumbled onto Luger's leg, which led to Hall getting the pin. That was a storyline seed planted for later. Also on the undercard, Flair cut a promo saying the nWo had gone too far in beating up Arn Anderson, his best friend.

In the main event, Hogan beat The Giant to win the WCW World Heavyweight title. Hall and Nash came out to help. Giant was able to fend them both off, giving them each his chokeslam finishing move. But Hogan clobbered Giant with the belt and got the three count.

There was a time when WCW prided itself on compelling and athletic in-ring action, especially in the most important matches. Pro wrestling is a simulated sport and, during most time periods, part of the equation consists of entertaining contests. But during this era, things were going in the opposite direction. Story twists and turns became the only thing that mattered, rendering the action in matches an afterthought.

After Hogan won the title, Ed Leslie, Hogan's longtime friend and then a WCW character named The Booty Man, came out with an nWo shirt and a cake. Hogan's birthday was the next day. Leslie congratulated Hogan on becoming "the nWo heavyweight champion," and the appearance seemed to indicate he would be the fourth member of the group. He was not.

It was all a scene to set up Hogan's next match, against Flair.

Hogan said on the microphone that Flair was going to get the beating of his life and that Flair had a "soft spot" for Arn Anderson. Hogan then instructed Hall and Nash to beat up Leslie, which they did. Hogan whacked him with the belt.

"That is business, brother—and that was my best friend," Hogan said, with the words aimed at Flair. "If I do that to my best friend, what am I gonna do to you?"

Hogan capped the segment by grabbing the iconic WCW title—dubbed the "big gold belt" in wrestling circles with a history that went back a decade—and defacing it. He took a can of black spray paint and graffitied the championship with the letters "NWO."

The takeover was on.

CHAPTER 7

THAT DIRTY LITTLE FUCKER

Hogan's first title defense as "nWo champion" was scheduled to be against Flair at *Clash of the Champions XXXIII* just three days later, airing on TBS. While the two legends had a major series of matches in 1994 that were a massive financial success, this was the first time they'd be meeting with Hogan as a heel.

Savage had to be Hogan's title defense opponent at the *Halloween Havoc* pay-per-view in October. The event's main sponsor was Slim Jim, and Savage was the product's chief spokesperson. And the money was too good for WCW to ignore that kind of advertisement cohesion.

Hogan was sporting a much more pronounced, dark five o'clock shadow to go along with his blond Fu Manchu on the *Nitro* two days after he graffitied "nWo" on the belt. That was a look that Hall was already rocking going back to his days as The Diamond Studd. There would be several little things like this over the months and years of the nWo, with Hogan almost co-opting some of the things that defined Hall and Nash.

But Hall and Nash didn't take this particular thing personally. They thought it was all part of how Hogan was trying to evolve his character from white-meat hero babyface to sinister, yet contemporary villain. A bond between Hall and Nash and Hogan was starting to develop.

"Once we trusted each other and I said, 'OK, these two guys aren't a-holes and they're really cool' and they trusted me and figured out how to mold me to fit in, [we were good]," Hogan said.

Clash of the Champions XXXIII took place in Denver, Colorado, on August 15, 1996. There was a three-way match for the WCW tag-team titles on the undercard, pitting champions Harlem Heat against Sting and Luger and the Steiner Brothers. Patrick was the referee. Hall and Nash showed up on the outside of the ring and Patrick called for a disqualification right as Scott Steiner had Booker T of the Harlem Heat pinned.

After the finish, Okerlund pulled Patrick aside to ask him about what had been going on with him the last few days. Patrick, the son of legendary wrestler, trainer, and Nash mentor Jody "The Assassin" Hamilton, feigned ignorance and played his role as the self-righteous, yet slippery official to a tee, while clearly having something to hide.

The creative team was toying with the idea that anyone could be the next member of the nWo—even WCW's respected senior referee. Could Patrick be on the take?

Flair beat Hogan by disqualification in the *Clash* main event after a ton of outside interference. Championships do not change hands on disqualifications or countouts in American wrestling, so Hogan remained the WCW champion.

It was supposed to be a big week from a financial perspective—Hogan's first two singles matches since forming the nWo. Tickets were not sold to *Hog Wild*, because it was in the middle of the motorcycle rally, and the pay-per-view buys were an estimated 220,000. That buy rate was up from *Great American Bash* and *Slamboree*, but down from *Bash at the Beach* (250,000) and even *Uncensored 1996* (250,000), which featured Hogan's last match before going heel.

Clash of the Champions XXXIII did a solid 3.5 television rating on TBS, but for a Hogan vs. Flair match it was disappointing.

Meltzer also highlighted an issue the promotion was facing in the *Observer*: "NWO has become the cool thing because of how lame WCW has portrayed its side as being."

One of Sullivan's greatest skills as the head of creative (or booker, in wrestling speak) was getting his heels "heat." In other words, having the heels look dominant and fearsome, but also loathsome, so the fans will be invested in them getting their comeuppance. So far, that was working almost too well.

To further solidify how the nWo's invasion was bigger than WCW characters' past differences, Sting and Luger made peace with their longtime rivals The Four Horsemen. It was decided that Flair, Arn Anderson, Sting, and Luger would face the nWo in a War Games double-cage match at the upcoming *Fall Brawl* pay-per-view.

The role of televised wrestling shows at that point was to garner ratings, but also to advance the storylines toward big matches on pay-per-view. Those events represented wrestling promotions' biggest profit margin. Pay-per-views were promoted relentlessly on WCW and WWF TV shows and were where most of the biggest matches took place.

———

Hogan, Hall, and Nash showed up outside the arena in Palmetto, Florida, on the August 26, 1996, *Nitro* with black spray paint cans. Hogan tagged the WCW production truck with "NWO" and Hall crossed out the CNN logo. Hall and Nash graffitied "4 LIFE" on the side of the truck.

Inside the building, the cameras picked up Ted DiBiase in the stands, walking down toward ringside seats. DiBiase, a veteran wrestler and manager who was known in the WWF as "The Million Dollar Man," sat down in a front-row seat and put four fingers up. He mouthed the words "next week, five." The nWo was now apparently a quartet, soon to be a quintet.

Hogan, Hall, and Nash came out during the main event, which was Sting and Luger taking on Benoit and McMichael of the Horsemen. The nWo took out those four men, then Arn Anderson and Flair when they ran in to attempt to make the save. Hogan spray-painted "NWO" on McMichael's back and then graffitied Flair's trademark platinum blonde hair, turning it black.

———

Gangsta rap crossed over into the mainstream during the mid-1990s. The group N.W.A.'s *Straight Outta Compton* was the first record from the genre to go platinum. Doctor Dré departed N.W.A. and released *The Chronic* in 1992. It went triple platinum. *Yo! MTV Raps* became a popular show on the music network in the early 1990s.

The battle between West Coast rap, led by Death Row Records and Tupac Shakur, and East Coast rap, led by Bad Boy Records and Notorious B.I.G., intensified toward the middle part of the decade. Shakur was shot dead after a Mike Tyson fight in Las Vegas less than a month after Hogan christened the WCW title with "NWO" graffiti.

Hall and Nash were inspired by gangsta rap and the culture surrounding it. They started wearing bandanas tied onto their heads with the knot in front like Shakur did. The "4 life" came directly from West Coast rapper Mack 10, who debuted the single "Foe Life" in 1995.

WCW had little to no urban appeal previously. It was still, at its heart, a wrestling company in the Deep South with a good old boys' club in place.

Hogan wasn't necessarily a part of that, but he wasn't bumping to Westside Connection on his car tape deck, either.

Hall and Nash felt like the real-life Terry Bollea was actually a pretty cool guy. He had played bass in local rock 'n' roll bands as a kid in Florida. But he was not exactly up to speed on hip-hop culture. Nash put him on to the likes of Doctor Dré and Run DMC.

"He just basically sat down and goes, 'Where are you guys getting this from?'" Nash said of Hogan. "And then we just thumbnailed some stuff for him to listen to and he was on board."

By 1997, the middle-aged Hogan was wearing wide-leg JNCO jeans, a staple of late-nineties streetwear.

———

Nitro on September 2, 1996, in Chattanooga, Tennessee, was a big one. Patrick did another interview denying he was involved with the nWo and then he was embroiled in some more controversy, calling for another inexplicable disqualification in a tag-team match between the Steiners and Sting and Luger.

A limo had pulled up backstage, as was the norm as a sign of the nWo looming. Sting and Luger chased Patrick outside the arena and saw DiBiase getting into the limo. Sting threw a brick through one of the limo's windows as it pulled away and then he and Luger commandeered a police car to chase the vehicle.

This was all during an eight-man tag team match between the Horsemen and the Dungeon of Doom (Sullivan, Big Bubba, Meng, and The Barbarian). The limo was a decoy. With Sting and Luger out of the building, Hogan, Hall, and Nash attacked the eight men in the ring. The Giant came out to make the save for WCW.

Except, he wasn't there for WCW. The man whom Hogan had just defeated to win the WCW title—the biggest athlete in pro wrestling—had turned and joined the nWo.

Factions had long existed in pro wrestling as a plot device. It was an easy way to show viewers who was aligned with whom. Groups, or stables, were typically a vehicle for heels, who could outnumber the babyfaces before the good guys eventually overcame the bad. Typically, there was a defined hierarchy in these factions, with one clear-cut leader and supporting players behind him. The nWo was different already. Hogan, Hall, Nash, and The Giant were all main-event-level players. It was an elite assemblage.

Hogan, Hall, and Nash were wearing the classic nWo shirts—black with white graffiti-like lettering—for the first time during this segment. Savage then came out with a chair and started hitting nWo members, but Hogan landed a shot below the belt and hit Savage with a chair. The Giant chokeslammed Savage. Hogan then took a can of yellow spray paint and tagged a streak down Savage's back.

Hogan, Hall, Nash, and The Giant made their way over to the commentary position. Hogan and Giant grabbed headsets and explained that Giant had joined the nWo because of the opportunities and money it could earn him. Giant said he visited Hogan at his 25,000-square-foot home, where he kept twenty Harleys and five Mercedes.

"Is there any question now what's the most powerful organization in professional wrestling?" Hogan said into the headset.

Hogan and Giant tossed over the WCW broadcast table and spit on the WCW logo. They were actually not supposed to damage what was a very expensive *Nitro* set. The bill ended up being around $40,000, Meltzer reported. WCW ate the cost.

———

The nWo era was the first time pro-wrestling promotions began using the entire arena—from the ring area to backstage to the parking lot—as the setting for its television shows. Previously, for the most part, stories would transpire in the ring and in a set interview position.

By the mid-1990s, WCW was using its arenas as a living, breathing, three-dimensional environment. Attacks would happen in locker rooms and on loading docks. Conversations would take place in hallways. The breaking down of those past norms created a much more dynamic ecosystem to tell stories.

It made sense. How believable could any of this be if these characters only interacted in the specific setting of a wrestling ring? Just because everyone knew wrestling was "fake" didn't mean audiences wanted their intelligence to be insulted.

With the help of Ellis Edwards, who was brought in as stunt coordinator, WCW became very active in using all kinds of props and devices, including vehicles, to make things feel more realistic.

———

An nWo street team showed up outside the arena in Columbus, Georgia, with fliers and picket signs during the September 9, 1996, *Nitro*. Young men in their teens or twenties could be seen in the crowd passing out nWo propaganda. Zbyszko, on commentary, grabbed one of the pieces of paper and it read: "You haven't seen bad . . . but it's coming."

Later in the show, there was a shot of Hogan, Hall, Nash, and Giant putting nWo fliers on car windshields in the parking lot. It was oddly political, as if the nWo wanted fans to vote for their preferred candidate.

There were also several nWo commercials on the episode promoting the new T-shirts, plus another with Hogan, Hall, Nash, and DiBiase pumping up War Games in another grainy, black-and-white ad, this time inside a chain-link fence. Hogan explained DiBiase's significance in the group, saying he made Turner "look like a pauper" and pumping up the idea that DiBiase was the nWo's money man. DiBiase demanded that if Team nWo wins the War Games match, WCW must give the nWo its own TV segment and a tag-team tournament which The Outsiders would be in.

A few segments later, Patrick came out to ringside during a match between Luger and Rick Steiner. Patrick alerted Luger to a situation outside the building and pleaded with him to go to the parking area. Luger obliged—and walked right into an ambush.

The nWo and a man who looked an awful lot like Sting jumped Luger and left him lying in the rain. It appeared that Sting, whom Bischoff first tabbed to be the third man, had now joined the nWo in earnest.

In an interview with Okerlund toward the end of the episode, Luger and the Horsemen went off on Sting. Arn Anderson said he was "sick to my stomach," because the one thing WCW thought it could count on was Sting. Luger said his best friend stabbed him in the back and he knew where Sting lived and worked out. He was going to get some answers.

Fall Brawl took place six days later, in Winston-Salem, North Carolina, long a hotbed for Flair and the Horsemen. After another sketchy moment from Patrick in a match between The Giant and Savage, the Horsemen and Luger had an interview segment with Okerlund. Sting interrupted and told them it wasn't him who attacked Luger on *Nitro*. He pleaded with Luger, but Luger said he knew it was Sting and he couldn't believe him.

The main event was the War Games match, a four-on-four battle inside two rings, both enclosed by a single, roofed cage. Hogan, Hall, and Nash were named as participants for the nWo, but a fourth man was not revealed. The WCW team was made up of Flair, Anderson, and Luger, with the status of Sting as their partner still up in the air.

The last Team nWo member to enter the cage was Sting. Or at least someone who was dressed and made up like him. The commentary team sold it as if it were the real Sting.

But then the actual Sting came into the match next for the WCW team. He beat up all four members of the nWo team—and then left.

"Is that good enough for you? Is that proof?" Sting said, furious that his loyalty to WCW had been called into question.

With Sting walking out on Team WCW, Team nWo had the four-on-three advantage and the nWo Sting forced Luger to surrender with the Scorpion Death Lock, the legitimate Sting's submission finishing move.

Savage came out and attacked Hogan after the match, but succumbed to an nWo beatdown. Elizabeth, who had been with Flair and against Savage in storylines, ran into the ring to save her ex-husband. With Elizabeth lying on Savage to protect him, Hogan spraypainted "NWO" on the back of her dress.

"This is the lowest point of WCW," Schiavone said on commentary, "and [Hogan] is the lowest wrestler ever."

———

Jeff Farmer was approached in the summer of 1996 by Page, who was a talented wrestler himself and something of a liaison between management and "the boys" (the wrestling term for the wrestlers or talent). Farmer had been a lower-tier wrestler for WCW off and on beginning in 1993.

The creative team, Page told Farmer, had an idea for a new character. Sort of. And Farmer had the right physical attributes to play it.

Soon after, Farmer was sitting in a chair in Marietta, Georgia, getting a mold taken of his face. WCW had contracted André Freitas of AFX Studios to do several costumes and special effects for them during that time period.

For this particular job, Freitas's task wasn't to come up with something new and creative. He was supposed to make Farmer look exactly like someone else: Sting.

In addition to molds of Farmer's face, molds were taken of Sting, as well. Farmer was then fitted for facial prosthetics and contact lenses—he had light eyes and Sting had brown—to complete the look.

Before his debut as the fraudulent nWo Sting on the September 9, 1996, episode of *Nitro*, it took Farmer more than an hour to have the prosthetics glued to his eyebrows and forehead, along with the application of the Sting face paint. Sting let Farmer have a pair of his tights and one of his jackets. Farmer also studied how Sting moved in the ring and how to apply the Scorpion Death Lock submission move.

Farmer was sworn to secrecy about being Sting's nWo doppelgänger. Bischoff told him that if word of the fake Sting swerve got out publicly, WCW would drop the whole idea.

The prosthetics worked well, though Farmer eventually ditched them when it became obvious he wasn't the real Sting and he was simply attempting to be a satire of the character. The contact lenses lasted an even shorter time. One got stuck awkwardly in his eye during his big reveal, when he was beating down Luger in the rain in Columbus, Georgia.

"I couldn't even really see Lex, hardly," Farmer said. "I'm hitting him in the back, going, 'I hope I'm hitting him.'"

Farmer said he "felt a lot of pressure" during the War Games match and then a sense of relief when the match was over. It was by far the biggest moment of his career.

"You look at a Picasso painting and you're like, 'Oh my God, I could never paint something like that' or 'I could never do something close to that,'" Farmer said. "But in some instances, you're in there painting, too. And you're not gonna be a Picasso. But guess what? You're both sitting there with a canvas."

———

The nWo grew even stronger in numbers—and star power—the *Nitro* one night after *Fall Brawl*. It took a little longer than he had hoped, but Sean Waltman debuted in WCW.

On *Nitro*, Waltman, sporting a new goatee and wearing a Jim Morrison T-shirt, showed up in the crowd and was interviewed by WCW broadcaster Mike Tenay. Waltman didn't give away that he was joining the nWo.

During a tag match pitting Flair and Arn Anderson against Chris Jericho and Bagwell, Waltman was shown with some kind of remote control. He hit a button and nWo leaflets fell from the top of the arena in Asheville, North Carolina. The messages on the papers said things like "nWo, we beat you, now you're paying all the bills" and "nWo, we'll do TV our way." The nWo street team, which had been seen in previous weeks, started walking through the crowd again with signs. Arn Anderson and Flair grabbed some of the papers and crumpled and ripped up them up. Some fans did, too.

On commentary, Bischoff said DiBiase had increased the nWo's demands. They no longer wanted a segment—they wanted an entire nWo television show. And WCW had to give it to them, because Team nWo won the War Games match.

At the time, Bischoff actually did have a plan of giving the nWo an entire show on another day of the week. That's how hot the storyline was. People couldn't get enough.

Bischoff also said on commentary that Waltman should be called "Six," because that was now the amount of members the nWo had. That was later stylized to "Syxx" or "Syxx-Pac."

On the same episode, Sting—the real one—came out and took the microphone for a speech. He said he saw people, including his best friends, doubt him and not believe him when he said he had not joined the nWo. Sting said he had been a "babysitter" for Luger and given him the benefit of the doubt "a thousand times." He "carried the WCW banner" and gave his "blood, sweat, and tears" for the promotion. He now considered himself a free agent.

———

Coming off the War Games match and Waltman's debut, the nWo was increasingly becoming an even bigger focal point for WCW. A week later, the group essentially took over the second and final hour of *Nitro*.

The nWo also added a new member: Mike Jones, who was known for about a decade in the WWF as Virgil, the bodyguard for DiBiase's "Million Dollar Man" character. Jones was given the name Virgil in the mid-1980s, because it was the real first name of Dusty Rhodes, then one of the top stars (and the booker) of the competing Jim Crockett Promotions, the forebearer to WCW. This was a joke (or a rib, a common wrestling term) on Rhodes, because Jones was essentially a jobber.

Jones debuted in WCW as the nWo's head of security under a

new name. Hogan introduced him as Vincent, a clear shot at Mc-Mahon.

That *Nitro* was built around the story that WCW's top stars were away on a tour with New Japan Pro-Wrestling. Except for Savage. There was even an ad in that day's *USA Today* supposedly taken out by the nWo that read, "While WCW is away, the nWo will play."

The nWo jumped Savage during his match with Greg Valentine, leading to an extended beatdown. As advertised, no one came out to help him, even though there were obviously other WCW wrestlers backstage. Bischoff, on commentary, said WCW was being "held hostage."

Hall and Nash took over the broadcast desk and provided some hilarious commentary for the second hour. It was difficult for fans to boo the duo, because they were so entertaining. Not so much for Hogan, who spraypainted Savage's bald spot with graffiti and later was in the locker room area tagging walls with "NWO."

Meltzer reported around this time that a woman called the WCW offices, furious that her five-year-old had spraypainted "NWO" on her one-year-old.

Boundaries were being pushed on television, too. On an episode of *WCW Saturday Night*, one of WCW's taped weekend shows, the nWo destroyed a Cadillac that allegedly belonged to Luger. Giant ended up having to buy the vehicle, because the amount of damage exceeded the rental agreement, Meltzer reported.

———

Reality television existed for decades prior, but the show credited with making it into its own genre was MTV's *The Real World*, which premiered in 1992 and featured a group of twentysomethings in a new city all living together under one roof. They were allegedly filmed 24/7 and edited episodes of their goings-on aired later on MTV.

Television showrunners were already hip to the idea that American audiences didn't necessarily want real life. That was far too mundane. What they really wanted was a version of reality, taking bits and pieces of truth infused with storylines created by producers. Did the things on camera really happen? Sure. Were they set up to happen in a certain manner? Absolutely.

It was like what pro-wrestling promoters realized around the 1920s. Fans at carnivals didn't want a real athletic contest as much as a dramatic spectacle that could at least pass for legitimate competition. That way you could suspend your disbelief, just like the millions of cable viewers did when they watched *The Real World*.

There was something voyeuristic about watching people go about their "real lives." Audiences were more than willing to consume reality television as if everything happening was on the up and up and not at all influenced by the cameras or those wearing headsets.

What professional wrestling was able to do in the mid-1990s was use people's willingness to believe to pull its own genre closer to "reality."

Survivor and *Big Brother* took reality television to new heights in the late 1990s and early 2000s. But there is an argument to be made that mid-to-late-1990s pro wrestling bridged that gap as a proof of concept. Bischoff and company were more than willing to leverage American consumers' desire for scripted reality.

———

The nWo spent the September 30, 1996, *Nitro* in a Marriott hotel suite in Cleveland. Petty, the NASCAR driver, joined them. WCW attempted to gift Sting his own stock car on that episode, as an olive branch. Sting did not show up to accept it. He wasn't around, because in real life he was filming a scene (later cut) for the movie *Liar Liar* with Jim Carrey.

Nitro ended with Elizabeth in the nWo's hotel room and the group trying to sell her on joining them. Savage showed up to confront the nWo, only to see his ex-wife leaving their suite. A furious Savage shouted, "Son of a bitch!" as the scene came to a close.

Patrick, donning a neck brace, did an interview with broadcaster Mike Tenay on the following *Nitro*, demanding Savage be suspended and fined $1 million for attacking him several weeks earlier out of frustration. Patrick was still doing his shtick as a corrupt ref potentially working for the nWo.

The episode ended with another beatdown of Savage from the nWo. On this occasion, The Giant held Elizabeth's face, making her watch the attack. Hogan spraypainted an outline around Savage's body like it was a murder scene. Hogan then told nWo members to destroy the broadcast area (again). Waltman came out driving an nWo monster truck, knocking over the set. That time, it was planned.

Everything seemed fine on screen, but the nWo's honeymoon period was beginning to wear off after barely three months.

Meltzer was reporting that Hall and Nash were getting sick of playing second fiddle to Hogan and didn't love that Hogan was getting paid so much more than they were. There was also anger from those in WCW who were not involved in the nWo storyline at all and were no longer featured as often on television. Bischoff's entire focus was on the nWo, and other wrestlers felt neglected.

Hogan, according to Meltzer's reporting, was beginning to extend his creative control to all aspects of the nWo, not just his matches and segments. Meltzer wrote that *Nitro* episodes would be written out and Hogan would show up and make a ton of changes, rendering some story beats filled with narrative holds. Bischoff and the creative team began writing *Nitro* episodes the previous week, not long after an episode ended. But it wouldn't be finalized until hours—or sometimes minutes—before the show went live. Especially if Hogan was making tweaks.

Bischoff has denied that Hogan meddled to that degree, and several wrestlers and backstage personnel said it was clear that the buck stopped at Bischoff with regards to creative decision-making. Sullivan was still leading the creative team and reporting to Bischoff. Many on the undercard, with Bischoff concentrating on the nWo, had a lot of freedom to pitch their own ideas.

Some in WCW, though, felt like they didn't know who exactly was pulling the strings. Scott Steiner, who has long had issues with Hogan, said WCW's biggest star had more than his fair share of input.

"Everybody knew one guy was in charge," Steiner said. "Besides Bischoff, it was Hogan. Hogan put his thumb on a lot of shit. He actually ran the whole shit. He had to give the thumbs up on every fucking match."

It was rarely personal between Hall, Nash, and Hogan. Hall and Nash might not have liked that Hogan was the clear nWo frontman, but they respected who he was, what he did in the business, and that he earned the right to position himself in key spots.

Hall and Nash did get a resolution to one of their issues in the fall of 1996.

Bret Hart was a free agent and WCW made a play for him. Bret ended up re-signing with the WWF, a historic twenty-year contract that Meltzer reported would pay him more over four years than anyone ever in wrestling outside of potentially Hogan. Bret, Meltzer wrote, would be guaranteed $2.8 million for the first three years.

While WCW didn't sign him then, the possibility opened the door for Hall and Nash to get a raise. Hall had that favored nations clause in his contract. If WCW signed Bret Hart, Bischoff would have had to pay Hall a similar amount to him. To avoid having to do that, there was a compromise. Hall and Nash both got new contracts for more money, their agent Bloom said.

This also coincided with the WWF bringing in two wrestlers to play the characters Razor Ramon and Diesel in the absence of Hall and Nash. It was a legal flex for the WWF with the idea that it was the promotion and its marketing that made stars out of the characters, not the wrestlers themselves.

Of course, fans rejected it immediately and the storyline was dropped quickly, though the man who played the fake Diesel, Glenn Jacobs, went on to have a WWE Hall of Fame career as the character Kane.

———

Bischoff sat in a locker room inside the Civic Center in Mankato, Minnesota. It was around 4 p.m. on October 21, 1996. *Nitro* was going to air live from the arena in a few hours. Sting, who had returned from Hollywood, was there, beginning the process of putting on his face paint for an appearance where he'd once again declare himself a lone wolf.

Hall, who was there with Nash, asked Sting if he had ever seen the movie *The Crow*. Sting had not. The film came out in theaters in 1994 and starred Brandon Lee as a white-faced specter who came back from the dead to avenge the murder of himself and his fiancée. Hall told Sting that he should pattern his face paint—and his character—after The Crow. Hall said Sting should "rip off" WWF's The Undertaker, as far as the vibe of a darker role.

Sting's former character, which featured bright-colored face paint and gear, simply did not fit on a program with the violent actions of the nWo. How could that cartoony version of Sting be seen as a legitimate threat to the nWo's gang warfare? Just about everyone knew Sting needed a change, and Hall "gave it to him on a silver platter," Bischoff said.

"This is the thing that people never recognized about Scott to the degree they should," Bischoff said. "He was one of the most generous people I've ever worked with creatively. . . . When he was committed to you and believed in you, he gave you everything he could to get you over."

Sting (real name: Steve Borden) came out that night in Minnesota in the white face paint with some black streaks, wearing a black trench coat and black pants. He beat up the nWo Sting before the rest of the nWo entered. DiBiase offered him an invite to join the group. Sting said he might be out of their price range and "the only thing sure about Sting is . . . nothing is for sure."

Sting would go on to keep that Crow look for the next three decades.

"Steve is usually really, super analytical," Bischoff said of Sting. "He'll just give you a dead face. You don't know if he loves it, hates it. He's just poker [face]. I looked over at Steve [that night] and his eyes were like *this* fucking big, man. You could have landed a small helicopter on his eyeballs. He was so fucking excited."

———

The rest of the build toward the next pay-per-view, *Halloween Havoc,* consisted of more Hogan and the nWo beating up Savage and humiliating Elizabeth.

On paper, Hogan vs. Savage was a big main event. Savage was one of Hogan's biggest rivals of the 1980s, but Savage was the heel then against a babyface Hogan. Now, Savage was the hero trying to help WCW stop the seemingly invulnerable nWo.

Halloween Havoc took place October 27, 1996, in Las Vegas. On the undercard, The Giant beat Jarrett and Syxx defeated Chris Jericho with a little help from Patrick. Hall and Nash cheated to beat Harlem Heat to win the WCW tag-team championship for the first time.

Cheating is a significant part of how heels are presented in professional wrestling. And the necessity of cheating is really twofold. For one, it frustrates the crowd, who is dying for the heel to get his or her just due from the babyface in the form of an ass whupping. Second, it gives the good guys an excuse when they lose—the bad guy had to do something underhanded to gain an advantage. The babyface could argue that, in a fair fight, he or she would have won.

There's another insider wrestling phrase for this: keeping someone strong. Even if a good guy must lose to a villain in order to advance the storyline, you can keep him or her strong by having the heel cheat to win.

Cheating and using outside interference to win matches behind the referee's back was long a heel trope in professional wrestling. And the nWo used it—excessively.

———

Hogan came out for the main event with DiBiase and the Giant. He wore what appeared to be a wig on his head. Hogan was doing a sequel to the 3 *Ninjas* movie, and apparently the role required him to have hair on the top of his head. Hogan had been balding since the eighties, but he still bravely kept his long hair down the sides and the back for decades.

During the match, referee Randy Anderson was injured, and Patrick came out to take his place. Savage landed his signature top-rope elbow drop, but Patrick grabbed at his own neck like he was injured before making the three count. The rest was a complete mess. Savage hit Hogan with a foreign object. The Giant came out and chokeslammed Savage. And Patrick counted to three when Giant draped Hogan over Savage.

To everyone in the building, including those who worked for WCW, the event was finished. But Bischoff had another surprise up his sleeve, one he kept from everyone except those directly involved.

Bagpipe music hit the PA system and out walked Roddy Piper, Hogan's old rival from the first *WrestleMania*. Hogan, with a look of astonishment on his face, sold it like he had just heard an anthem from beyond the grave.

Piper had been known for his work as a bad guy, but at this point he was forty-two years old, banged up with a hip replacement, among other injuries, and way too beloved to be booed. He would be the third straight opponent for Hogan, after Flair and Savage, that was a retread of past storylines. But Piper was still a star. And the adult fans who were watching in 1996 remembered very well being kids during the eighties at the height of the Hogan vs. Piper feud.

Piper came to the ring and said he wasn't there to represent WCW or the nWo. He came to give Hogan a "reality check" that "I'm just as big an icon as you are." Piper said he was a Hollywood star and a millionaire, too. Hogan said they used to run together and fought together, and he didn't have a problem with him.

Piper asked Hogan if he remembered *WrestleMania* and then asked a question that he almost certainly felt in his heart. It applied in the story WCW was going to tell, but it was also how Piper felt.

"If they didn't hate me so much, you think they would have been cheering you?" asked Piper, who had a complicated relationship with Hogan behind the scenes and felt he wasn't given as much credit as he deserved for being the heel that helped Hogan take his stardom to the next level.

The segment was incredibly effective. Piper, who could sometimes be rambling and borderline incoherent during interviews, kept things on track and told a credible story about Hogan and their shared history. Hogan did his part to make Piper seem like a legitimate threat to him and the nWo when those were few and far between.

Halloween Havoc 1996 was the first major business success of the nWo era. WCW set its all-time records (at the time) for live ticket sales and souvenir sales, Meltzer reported. The event earned $224,660 from 8,390 tickets sold (about 10,000 total were in the building) and about $69,000 in merchandise, about half of which were nWo items. Meltzer wrote that merchandise revenue at non-televised house shows had "skyrocketed" due to WCW giving the nWo its own merch areas.

The storyline was no longer just creating buzz among wrestling fans and helping WCW beat the WWF in the ratings. It was making a real difference in the promotion's finances. And the addition of Piper and the ongoing storyline with Sting was about to take WCW—and the industry at large—to another stratosphere.

———

One night after *Halloween Havoc* was the first time Sting, with his new look, appeared on *Nitro* standing high up in the arena on the catwalk, looking down on the matches and segments in the ring. Hogan ended the episode cutting a promo on Piper, saying he couldn't lace Hogan's boots.

Bischoff, on commentary, hammered home the story beat that Piper was not signed with WCW and just wanted to confront Hogan at *Halloween Havoc*. The seed for another storyline was planted, as well, with Hall and Nash cheering on Diamond Dallas Page, teasing that he could be the next WCW wrestler to join the nWo.

A brooding Sting was back in the rafters the following week. Luger did an interview saying he hoped the nWo's propositions to Sting fell on deaf ears and all he wanted was a chance to talk to him.

Bischoff, who was allegedly away trying to come to a deal with Piper for a Hogan match, called in to the commentary desk and said things weren't going as well as he wanted on that front.

It wasn't directly stated on WCW television for years that Bischoff was the man running the company. On screen, he was just a play-by-play announcer. This was one of the first times where he was implicitly treated like an executive on television, since he was the one trying to sign Piper to a contract.

Sting attacked wrestler Jeff Jarrett, who had become part of The Four Horsemen, in the ring on the November 11, 1996, *Nitro*. He attacked Jarrett from behind, giving him a reverse DDT move—an act that features grabbing an opponent in a headlock and falling as if to drive his or head into the mat—that would later be dubbed the Scorpion Death Drop. Sting randomly attacking Jarrett was a nod toward the possibility that Sting was indeed joining the nWo. Luger did another promo later in the show, calling Sting the "Phantom of the Opera," apologizing and asking him to come back to WCW.

Sting came through the crowd and confronted Luger in the ring during an interview segment the following week. He had a baseball bat with him and pushed Luger in the chest with it. Then, Sting handed Luger the bat and turned his back on him, leaving the ring.

Bischoff's rhetoric about Piper from the previous week would all come to make sense on that episode. In the final segment of the show, he came out and said WCW was going to do everything in its power to make Piper sign to face Hogan.

Piper's bagpipe music then hit to a huge reaction from the Florence, South Carolina, crowd. Piper came out and accused Bischoff of being dishonest about trying to sign him, quipping, "I have never heard so many lies in my entire life, other than from me."

The Giant then attacked Piper from behind. He was followed by Hall, Nash, Syxx, and Vincent. Hogan came into the ring behind them and gave Bischoff a big hug. He said Bischoff was "the foundation of WCW" and "now he works for the nWo."

Piper spit at Hogan as the nWo and then security and police tried to hold him back. Piper said he'd have a contract at the upcoming *World War 3* pay-per-view for a future match against Hogan.

The nWo was already flexing its muscles with big names, and now the actual behind-the-scenes leader of WCW had joined them. It was logical to an extent. Hall and Nash did rough Bischoff up at the beginning of the storyline six months earlier. But nWo members were able to get away with so many things, coming and going on WCW television whenever they wanted and having matches on TV, house shows, and pay-per-view. There had to be some kind of storyline explanation as to why the group was able to seemingly do whatever it wanted.

Of course, the nWo had an inside man. It was Bischoff.

"We gotta make sense out of this shit," Bischoff said. "Otherwise, it's just fallen from the sky and nobody knows why. It kind of makes sense all along if I was the guy that allowed all of this crazy shit to happen. It's kind of like one of those, 'Oh, now I see.' Even [six months] after the story began, it's like, 'Oh, he's that dirty little fucker that let that happen.'"

CHAPTER 8

WE'RE STILL
THE SHIT

One week after Bischoff's shocking turn, Hall and Nash were in the ring holding chairs when *Nitro* began.

It was explained on commentary that there had been an incident prior to the show going on the air. The Nasty Boys tag team, Brian Knobbs and Jerry Sags, had run into the ring during a match that took place only for the live crowd and beat up the competitors.

The Nasty Boys, a brawling duo who were real-life close friends of Hogan's, were involved in a storyline where they were rejected nWo membership and angry about it. Hall and Nash came out after the Nasty Boys and attacked them with chairs. A replay of this was shown on *Nitro*, but the clip was stopped because, according to the commentators, it was too graphic.

There was some reality to that. Hall hit Sags in the head with one of the chairs and it connected hard. Too hard. Sags rolled out of the ring and turned his back to Hall, who almost hit Sags again. But Sags was no longer in the act of performance. He was really hurting.

Later backstage, Hall was talking to Nash and the two were having a laugh about the situation, specifically that it was good that Hall didn't hit Sags again. The force of the first blow was accidental. Sags, according to Hall's recollection, came around the corner with a huge bruise on his head and saw Hall and Nash chuckling.

Hall and Nash had been friendly with Knobbs and Sags for years, but The Outsiders also felt like the Nasty Boys were among the wrestlers who were annoyed that Hall and Nash were in WCW.

"[Sags is] thinking, 'They're taking my money, they're taking liberties with me, that guy [hit] me on purpose and he thinks it's funny,'" Hall said.

Two months later, Hall and Nash were wrestling in a three-way tag match at a house show in Shreveport, Louisiana. House shows are events held only for the live audience in the arena and not taped for television. They were (and still are, to a degree) a significant part of pro-wrestling economics, because they allowed promotions to get to smaller cities that might not have warranted larger-scale events. The WWF and WCW held multiple shows across the country (and sometimes abroad) every week, but not all of them were for TV.

On this particular house show, the opponents of Hall and Nash were the Nasty Boys and the Faces of Fear, Meng and Barbarian. During the match, Hall hit Sags in the head—the back of it, Sags said—and Sags flew off the handle for real. He started smashing Hall with legit punches. Vicious ones.

Sags went into the match with head and neck injuries. He was furious, because he thought Hall was again trying to hurt him purposely. Sags's attack resulted in one of Hall's teeth getting knocked out. The tooth cut Hall's cheek, causing an infection.

After the match, Hall asked Nash if his face was all messed up. Nash said it was and Hall told him how it happened. Nash was furious. He grabbed one of the baseball bats Sting was using as part of his new character and brought it into the Nasty Boys' locker room. Nash cracked the bat against the wall and said, "We'll see who has the stroke."

Knobbs said he didn't know what Nash was talking about, but

Luger, who was in the room, explained it to him. Nash was saying he and Hall had the power in WCW and the Nasty Boys were going to face consequences for what Sags did, despite their friendship with Hogan.

Sags was in the shower. When he came out, all covered in soap, he asked what was going on. Knobbs told him, and Sags left the locker room naked to look for Nash.

Hall spoke with Bischoff later that night and Bischoff was ready to fire Sags. Hall told Bischoff that he'd known Sags and Knobbs for more than a decade and Sags had a family. Hall didn't want to work with him anymore, but he didn't want to see the guy fired.

Sags didn't stop getting paid initially after the incident, but he was effectively done with WCW. He never wrestled another match for the promotion.

After seeing the tape of what happened in Shreveport, Sags learned that it was actually a blow from Nash with one of the tag title belts that hurt him during the match, not a strike from Hall. He ended up suing Hall, Nash, and WCW for negligence. According to the *Orlando Business Journal*, Sags claimed he was left with a concussion and permanent spinal disc injuries as a result of the incidents.

The publication only even picked up the story because the lawsuit went into how professional wrestling was scripted or choreographed and the athletes were not actually trying to hurt each other. That was the hook of the article. Even in the mid-to-late 1990s, this idea that wrestling wasn't real was still considered novel by mainstream media, though it had been common knowledge for quite some time.

"Scott was different when he came down to WCW," said Sags, who had been friendly with The Kliq. "I don't know if it was chemically altered. Everyone changes when they come out of that pressure cooker in WWF. It's stressful. Some of the guys turn into backstabbers; some guys deal with the pressure in different ways."

Bischoff said there was a clear change in Hall developing, compared to that drive they took to the arena in May 1996 on Hall's first day in WCW. He was falling back into some habits that included drug and alcohol abuse.

"Once he got familiar, once he felt like he was comfortable in the situation in WCW . . . once the nWo angle happened, once they had a certain amount of stroke just because of who they were and where they were [in] the hierarchy at that time, the Scott Hall with the baggage, that Scott Hall started showing up much more frequently," Bischoff said.

Hall and Nash also butted heads with Sting. There was a house show in Tupelo, Mississippi, and The Outsiders were in the main event against Harlem Heat. They wanted to walk out to the ring to the song "Ready or Not" by the Fugees, which they could get away with on a nontelevised card without WCW having to purchase the license.

Back then, WCW's production for house shows was bare bones. The wrestlers were required to bring cassette tapes with them for their entrances, and David Penzer, the ring announcer, was partly in charge of coordinating the music. On that night in Tupelo, there was an error. Penzer said there was an "eighty-year-old guy" cueing up the music in the building and he put the tape in on the wrong side, playing the incorrect song.

Hall and Nash would not come out. They expected the right music, and it was difficult trying to communicate with the music guy about what the right song even was at that point. Penzer said Sting and Luger were backstage and told Hall and Nash to just walk out, that no one would even know it wasn't the right song. Sting then told them, according to Penzer, that "it's only Tupelo."

Hall and Nash weren't happy with that kind of philosophy. The rest of the show went off without incident. But at the next TV card, Bischoff held a meeting with the wrestlers, and he said that Hall and Nash had come from the WWF, which had more modern production. WCW, Bischoff said, should strive to be just as good, if not better, and if anyone said something like what Sting did again, they'd be fired.

"The point that Kevin and Scott were trying to make was if we're gonna make this thing work, we've gotta start doing things the right way," Penzer said. "And there can't be 'it's only Tupelo.' It has to be the right way every time."

————

The main development coming out of the *World War 3* pay-per-view on November 24, 1996, in Norfolk, Virginia, was the contract signing involving Piper and Hogan. Piper came out with said contract and Bischoff, DiBiase, and Vincent walked to the ring next. Bischoff said Hogan was busy reading movie scripts, but he had given Bischoff his power of attorney. Piper said he would face Hogan at *Starrcade*, WCW's signature event of the year, usually held in November or December.

Hogan and the rest of the nWo, including Elizabeth, who in story had begrudgingly started to associate with the group, then came out. Hogan told Piper he couldn't get it done a decade ago when they were equals and now he was broken. Hogan lifted Piper's kilt—Piper's character was a Scotsman—to reveal a scar from his hip down his thigh from hip replacement surgery Piper had in 1994. Hogan called Piper a "cripple" and a "gimp."

Piper slapped Hogan, but the nWo grabbed him and held him, commencing a beatdown. Hogan hit Piper's bad hip with a chair. Hall and Giant held Piper while Hogan spraypainted Piper's right thigh with "NWO." The nWo left the ring. Piper got up, turned over the table that was set up for the contract signing, and told them if that was the best Hogan could do, "you're in trouble."

The *World War 3* main event was a sixty-man battle royal across three rings, a super-sized yet far more mundane answer to the WWF's annual *Royal Rumble*. Wrestlers got eliminated by being tossed over the top rope to the floor until there was one survivor still in the ring. The Giant won the match, pushing Nash and Luger over the ropes when they were the final three left.

The next night on *Nitro*, Bischoff did an interview explaining why he joined up with the nWo. He said after Nash powerbombed him at *Great American Bash*, he asked himself, "Do I want to be consumed by the power or do I want to be part of it?" He said now he was the highest-ranking executive in both the nWo and WCW. Bischoff said that everyone in the WCW locker room had thirty days to convert their contracts to nWo.

The American Males tag team, Bagwell and Riggs, then came out to the ring. Bagwell shook hands with the nWo members there: Bischoff, Giant, Syxx, Hall, Nash, and Vincent. Riggs did not do the same and Bagwell turned on him, hitting him with a neckbreaker. Bagwell became the tenth member of the nWo.

There was no formula to who joined the nWo, Bagwell said. The one thing everyone knew was that Nash had either the final say, or at the very least veto power. At the time, Bischoff and company were looking to expand the group, because the plan was to give the nWo its own show on another night of the week. Hall and

Nash couldn't work every match and Hogan had a limited amount of dates on his contract. The nWo needed bodies.

Bagwell was the first part of this phase of the group. He said Nash sat down next to him in the locker room before the show in Salisbury, Maryland, and asked him if he wanted to join. Bagwell said yes right away. The nWo was the hot thing and the wrestlers going up against them were ice cold. Attaching yourself to the nWo was attaching yourself to relevance.

"It's definitely what made Marcus Bagwell go to the next level," Bagwell said. "And the [wrestlers] who weren't picked were upset."

On the December 9, 1996, *Nitro*, DiBiase came out during a match between wrestlers Michael Wallstreet and Mike Enos. DiBiase handed Wallstreet, his former WWF tag partner formerly known as Irwin R. Schyster, a piece of paper that seemed to be an nWo contract. Wallstreet smiled and DiBiase left. That apparently added Wallstreet to the growing nWo roster.

A week later, Masahiro Chono, one of the top stars from New Japan Pro-Wrestling, did an interview segment with Onoo, Bischoff's longtime friend who had become a WCW on-screen manager. Chono opened his shirt to reveal an nWo tee. The nWo was about to go worldwide. Chono brought it back to Japan, recruited Japanese wrestlers to join, and it became a massive hit there.

On the same episode, Big Bubba (Ray Traylor) and Scott Norton both turned on WCW and joined up with the nWo. Bubba had previously been a popular act in the WWF under the name Big Boss Man.

Wallstreet, Bubba, and Norton were all solid wrestlers, but certainly not the A-list names that had previously joined the red-hot group. The strategy Bischoff, Hall, Nash, Hogan, and the creative team had for the nWo by late December was much different from what the lore of the group became.

At the time, they felt like the nWo name alone was selling tickets and fans demanded an nWo presence be on every show, whether that was in Chicago or some small city on a WCW tour stop. The focus wasn't on how to keep the nWo an exclusive group as much as it was how to milk as much money out of those three letters as possible in the short term.

While in hindsight, it's easy to say the nWo should have remained an elite assemblage of big-name talent, that was just not how it was being looked at in late 1996. Bischoff saw it almost as an offshoot wrestling promotion, and the roster of a wrestling promotion can't be all main-event stars.

The biggest criticism of the nWo years later became that there were too many members. It's a valid critique. Bischoff and company just didn't know exactly what WCW had yet in the nWo and what its legacy would end up being. So the expansion continued.

––––––––

Starrcade took place December 29, 1996, in Nashville, Tennessee. It was announced during the show that the nWo would be holding its own pay-per-view card the following month. On the *Starrcade* undercard, The Outsiders retained the WCW tag titles by beating Meng and Barbarian, and Luger defeated The Giant with a little incidental help from Sting.

Patrick was the referee for the Luger vs. Giant match, and Sting came through the crowd and shoved Patrick with his bat. Sting then said something to both Luger and Giant before dropping his bat in the ring and leaving. Luger got to the bat first and hit Giant with it, leading to the victory. After the match, Giant stared at the entranceway, seemingly wondering why no one from the nWo had come out to help him, which was the group's usual modus operandi.

Hogan vs. Piper was the *Starrcade* main event, and it was a non-title match, which was only sparingly mentioned on television. That might have given away how it was going to go down.

Late in the match, Giant came down to help Hogan. A fan came into the ring and grabbed Hogan's leg, which was not part of the script. Hogan and referee Randy Anderson fought him off. After the confusion, Piper was able to evade Giant, kick Hogan, and then put Hogan in his sleeperhold finishing submission move.

Randy Anderson lifted Hogan's lifeless arm three times and the arm dropped each one, signaling Hogan was unconscious. Piper was ruled the winner, though he wasn't the champ because it was a nontitle match.

Afterward, Hogan and The Outsiders argued with Giant, who told them he watched Hogan's back, but no one watched his during his match earlier. Hogan told him he "dropped the ball."

Starrcade, as a show, did not drop the ball. Quite the opposite.

The pay-per-view earned an estimated 345,000 buys, making it the best-selling pay-per-view in WCW history to that point. Meltzer reported in the *Observer* that it was believed to be, at the time, the best-selling non-WWF wrestling pay-per-view event ever.

Hogan and Piper, both in their forties and well past their athletic primes, were limited in what they were able to do physically. But it didn't matter. The in-ring athleticism had become secondary to everything else around it.

The storyline with Piper was by far Hogan's best work as a heel to that point. Hall and Nash had swagger and used humor. They were cheered. But Hogan? He was a true asshole. Even fans wearing nWo shirts at *Starrcade* were cheering their heads off for Piper.

Despite the defeat, Hogan was still WCW champ and the biggest drawing card in wrestling. The nWo had turned WCW's ratings momentum into tangible business success. And, courtesy of the Hogan vs. Piper finish, all signs pointed toward a blockbuster rematch.

Hall and Nash were waiting for Hogan in a limo outside the Nashville Municipal Auditorium after *Starrcade*. They were the ones who convinced Hogan to put over (lose to, in wrestling parlance) Piper. Hogan was extremely protective over his character and did not believe it made sense for him to lose often.

But Hall and Nash told him that it wouldn't matter, that the nWo was so popular he wouldn't be sapped of any cachet with a defeat. Piper winning would give him even more fuel for a return bout. Remember, Hogan got paid a percentage of WCW's pay-per-view buys, so that was an incentive for him to help those shows sell as well as they did.

Hogan was still green to the whole heel thing. In fact, he really didn't enjoy it on a personal level. His then-wife Linda described it as a "mental trip" for him. People would approach him in public or, worse yet, kids would come up to his children, Nick and Brooke, in school and ask why their father had changed. But on that night in Nashville, Hogan was thrilled everything turned out the way it did.

"He was so excited," Hall said. "It made me feel great to see Hulk that happy. Because he [lost], and he was happy. We were like, 'See? It doesn't even matter, man. We're still the shit.'"

Hall and Nash then coached Hogan on what to do next. Hall told him to go out to the ring the next night on *Nitro* and tell the crowd he beat Piper's ass and was waiting for who was next.

Heels lie. The idea was it would make the crowd angrier—because they saw Piper put Hogan to sleep at *Starrcade* with their own eyes. The fans would want to see Hogan get his comeuppance all over again.

The next night on *Nitro*, Hogan said Piper was a coward and the fans would never see him again. He also added a line that he would run for president of the United States with all the support he had, but that he would have to take a pay cut to do so.

Piper came out at the end of the show and set the record straight that he was the winner at *Starrcade*. Hogan and Bischoff came to the ring and Piper challenged Hogan to another match. Hall, Nash, and Waltman then attacked Piper from behind. Fans started to pelt the ring yet again with beer and soda cups, some of them filled. Hogan hit Piper in his surgically repaired right hip with a chair. Patrick also came out during this beatdown, wearing an nWo shirt for the first time.

Hogan told Giant to chokeslam Piper, but Giant would not do it. Hogan told Giant he dropped the ball again and slapped the big man. Earlier in the episode, Giant had asked Hogan for the title shot he earned by winning the *World War 3* battle royal. Hogan said he shouldn't worry about it, because all that mattered was the championship was already with the nWo.

The enormous Giant grabbed Hogan by the neck and told him, "I want the gold! Do I have a title shot?" Hogan whined out an apology and shook Giant's hand, saying he loved him. Hogan agreed to give Giant the opportunity and "may the better man win."

Hogan then instructed the rest of the nWo to attack The Giant. They ripped off his nWo shirt and Hogan slapped him while he was down, saying, "This is my belt, this is my sport." Giant was the first wrestler on the growing nWo roster to be ousted from the faction.

The Giant joining the nWo was Hogan's decision. Hogan was a mentor to the young wrestler, who was only twenty-four years old and had only been in the business for two years. Bischoff felt there was "nothing cool" about The Giant and he just didn't fit into the group. It didn't help The Giant and he didn't help the nWo, Bischoff said, especially Nash, who already had the role as the team's towering muscle.

The fallout from a big *Starrcade* show led to *Nitro* beating *Raw* by two whole ratings points, 3.6 to 1.6. It was the biggest margin of victory of the Monday Night War to that point.

The nWo beat up the Giant again on the following week's *Nitro*, the first of the new year. Even Bischoff got in a kick to the head, showing off his karate background. The nWo then took over the broadcast area while Sting came out to the ring. He pulled the prone Giant up by his hair and said something to him. Sting pointed his baseball bat at the nWo and then left.

A week later, the WCW executive committee—a storyline sanctioning body—ruled that Hogan had to face The Giant that night in New Orleans, Louisiana. But it did not have to be a title match.

Hogan vs. Giant ended up being the main event and it extended past the end of *Nitro,* into TNT's airing of the movie *Robin Hood.* During *Robin Hood* commercial breaks, TNT would cut back to the match. It was a ratings ploy to get people to watch the movie. The match ended anticlimactically with the nWo running in and beating up The Giant, resulting in a disqualification.

Savage returned for the first time since *Halloween Havoc* on a big January 20, 1997, *Nitro* from Chicago. He had been a free agent, but re-signed with WCW on a seven-figure deal annually. Savage would make $1.9 million in 1997, according to data from a future racial discrimination lawsuit compiled by journalists Chris Harrington and David Bixenspan. That's the most any wrestler in WCW earned in salary that year by a wide margin, even more than Hogan, whose contract seemed to be frontloaded. WCW couldn't risk losing Savage back to the WWF in the middle of the heated battle between the two promotions, and his salary was largely subsidized by the Slim Jim sponsor deal.

Savage opened the show in the ring and seemingly joined up with Sting, who had rappelled down from the rafters on a cable to confront him.

The end of that *Nitro* featured another segment between the nWo and The Giant, where both sides were held back from a brawl. It was announced that Hogan vs. Giant for the WCW title would headline the nWo's first pay-per-view, called *Souled Out*.

—————

WCW's creative team wanted to double down on Sting as this avenging, Crow-like dark angel, and his just coming to the ring through the regular entranceway—or even through the crowd— didn't really have the effect Bischoff and the creative team wanted. So the idea was for him to swoop in from above, specifically from his perch high above the arena. Edwards, the stunt coordinator, was tasked with executing that process, and he brought in specialist Barry Brazell to rig the equipment.

Edwards and Brazell used caving equipment—a harness, carabiner hooks, cables, a rig descender, and a C-drome—and tested it multiple times with a weighted bag around 400 pounds. Sting was a big guy, about six-foot-two, 250 pounds, so they figured that would be a good trial weight.

The first time they tried it, they woke Sting and Bischoff up and called them to the arena at 2:30 a.m. the morning of an event. Edwards and Brazell rigged the bag to come down on the cable and stop right before hitting the ground. It did not end up going as planned.

"The first time we do it, the cable jumps, the bag comes all the way down—slams," Edwards said. "The shit goes everywhere. I just looked at him and was like, 'Go back to bed. I need to perfect it a little more.'"

Sting turned to Bischoff and said, "I ain't doing this."

Edwards and Brazell tweaked things a bit more and everything went smoothly for *Nitro* in Chicago on January 20, 1997. Sting rappelling down from the rafters became a staple of WCW television that year, and it made him one of the hottest acts in pro wrestling, a mysterious vigilante who would appear when you'd least expect him.

Some more changes did have to be made to Sting's entrance process. Edwards had previously researched all the equipment, including going to the BlueWater Ropes factory in Georgia where the cables were manufactured and witnessing how they were essentially unbreakable. But with the original way they were doing it, Sting would come down fast—so fast that the television cameras would miss his descent. Edwards would get messages on a walkie-talkie while at the top of the arena saying Bischoff is "going nuts," because the fans watching at home couldn't see Sting come down.

So to remedy that issue, Brazell came up with the idea to have Sting come down on what's called a rack. They started using two different cables: a static line that got Sting down straight with no give, and a rappelling line with give, so "in case you fell off the cliff, it doesn't break things on you [with] that hard jolt."

Edwards would "belay" the rope, exerting tension on it to counterbalance the descending wrestler. With the new method, the rope would change color when it hit a certain point, indicating when Edwards and Brazell had to stop or slow Sting down.

"But you don't know how many times, 200, 280 feet coming

down from the ceiling, I get him eight feet down and we stop him—we went to commercial break," Edwards said. "I'm like, 'Goddamn.' Eric knows, too. You can't go to commercial break with my talents. This is no bullshit. You can't stop that stuff right there when we do this. But we saved it. Nobody saw him."

Edwards and Sting flew out to Los Angeles for some practice runs. Edwards took Sting to Calabasas to do rock climbing on cliffs there. Then they went to Malibu Canyon for rappelling. They also went to indoor rock-climbing places and rappelled together there. Sting learned everything, including how to tie a figure-eight knot for climbing.

Sting would get up to the top of the arena before every show three hours prior and he'd have to be there until the end, so more than five hours each Monday. Because they had to be up there so long, Edwards would bring up drinks and a bucket so they could go to the bathroom. They'd also need lighting equipment so they could see what they were doing.

"You have some good, deep talks about your life up there, because it's just you and him all the time," Edwards said. "Incredible guy."

Looking back, it seemed crazy that WCW was able to do such a dangerous stunt every week and that Sting was all too willing to go along with it even after his initial hesitance. Sting ended up being a bit of an adrenaline junkie and he knew it would make his character stand out in what was an evolving, ruthless pro-wrestling ecosystem. Edwards, Brazell, Sting, and everyone else were able to pull it off dozens of times without anything horrible happening.

Tragically, Owen Hart, brother of Bret, died in the WWF doing a similar stunt, rappelling down from the rafters in 1999. The WWF had taken the idea from Sting and WCW, and Owen's Blue Blazer character was doing it as somewhat of a spoof.

———

Garbage trucks and snowplows came rumbling down a Cedar Rapids, Iowa, street with nWo flags on them and nWo members riding on their backs. It was the middle of a blizzard, the night before *Souled Out*, the first pay-per-view fully branded as nWo. And WCW taped an nWo parade that would air on the show. The frigid weather was just the first of several bad omens.

It was not exactly the greatest presentation of the nWo. No offense to Cedar Rapids, but Iowa in the middle of the winter did not scream "the new, cool thing in pop culture." The odd portrayal would only continue as the show started.

After the pre-taped snowy mess, the January 25, 1997, show cut to a Bischoff promo that had been taped in Chicago at *Nitro*. It was him speaking at a lectern like a politician with microphones all around. The speech was produced by Pruitt, who said it was inspired by *Citizen Kane*. At the end of the monologue, Bischoff addresses the wrestlers who chose to go against the nWo at *Souled Out*. Bischoff asks menacingly, "What the hell were you thinking?" The line was written by one of the prop guys a night earlier while everyone was drinking at a bar.

Another Bischoff line from that promo, "we are in control," was later repurposed as an audio clip during the nWo entrance music by Joe Sparacino from WCW's sound department. Sparacino also recorded the "for life" in his own voice for use in the entrance music. The "nWo" audio clip in the theme song was a slowed-down version of Bischoff's voice. And Pruitt voiced one of the clips in Hogan's first nWo entrance theme: "The biggest icon in wrestling."

Souled Out, though, didn't get all of WCW's production resources. It was a piecemeal operation. And it showed.

The lowlight of the show was the Miss nWo contest, hosted by then-eighteen-year-old Jeff Katz, whom Bischoff and WCW live-event promoter Zane Bresloff discovered as a teen prodigy radio host in Michigan. One would imagine that for such a competition, WCW would find conventionally attractive women from the area or fly them in. Models, perhaps.

Not so. Bischoff wanted to go completely in the other direction.

Bischoff said the idea came from a friend of his, who told him a story about how in college he and his friends would have a contest "to see who could bring home the most hideous beast for the weekend."

"I specifically [told WCW employees], 'Do not bring back any hot-looking women—I want trucker women,'" Bischoff said.

Bischoff picked the winner of the contest, a woman called "Miss Becky" who appeared to be in her fifties. And her reward for winning was a brief make-out session with Bischoff.

Yes, that's right. Bischoff kissed her. With tongue.

Bischoff's wife, Loree, was "gagging" at home, and his kids were wondering what he was thinking. Bischoff thought it was an attempt at something different and comedic for entertainment. But it did not fit the nWo's vibe at all. The sexism and misogyny were, unfortunately, par for the course in wrestling then, and it would only get worse as the 1990s wore on.

The whole thing reeked of ego. The nWo was so hot, WCW was beating the WWF in the ratings war, and Bischoff felt like everything he touched would turn to gold. Ever heard of the term "heat check" in basketball—when a player chucks one up from thirty-five feet to see just how on fire he is? Bischoff's shot with Miss nWo was an airball.

Katz believed the whole thing was a "phenomenal rib," though something that did not connect at all with the audience. He thought

WCW just screwed up, and using those women in the contest was not by design, but rather a lack of preparation and organization.

"Whether you're gay or straight, everyone kind of gets the basic logic of this," said Katz, who went on to be a Hollywood producer, working on movies like *Snakes on a Plane* and *The Pope's Exorcist.* "[Bischoff's recollection] sounds like a lot of revisionist history to me."

Bischoff and DiBiase did commentary for the event. Bischoff's original idea for DiBiase in WCW was as a color commentator, because of his fantastic voice. That was before the nWo stuff took off.

On the *Souled Out* undercard, the Steiners beat The Outsiders to win the WCW tag titles. Patrick was the referee, but he got knocked out during the match. Randy Anderson, a WCW referee who had been sitting in the crowd, came in and made the three-count for the Steiners. Bischoff, on commentary, said Randy Anderson would no longer have a job come Monday morning.

Hogan walked out for his *Souled Out* title match with The Giant accompanied by Nate Newton, George Teague, and Ray Donaldson of the NFL's Dallas Cowboys. Giant hit his chokeslam finisher on Hogan, but Patrick, the nWo referee, would not count to three. Giant chokeslammed Patrick and nWo members ran down, ending an uninspired match in another anticlimactic finish. Bischoff handed Hogan a guitar and Hogan cracked Giant in the head with it.

Another nWo beatdown of The Giant ended the show. Hall wrote in graffiti on Giant's back "NWO 4 LIFE." *Souled Out* went off the air with fans chanting, "We want Sting!"

Meltzer described the nWo pay-per-view in the *Observer* as the "single worst PPV show in the history of pro wrestling" and "the brainchild of someone intoxicated by his own success to the point of all perspective being lost."

"By [the Miss nWo contest kiss] the show was about as much

fun to watch as three hours of somebody masturbating," Meltzer wrote. "In fact, I'm not sure that isn't what we were watching."

———

Hogan wrestled The Giant again two nights later on *Nitro*. And again, it was a disqualification finish. It was also announced on the show that Hogan had to defend the title at the upcoming *SuperBrawl* pay-per-view against Piper, but Piper had not committed to it.

That set up a fantastic segment on the following *Nitro*. Piper came to the ring with his then-seven-year-old son, Colt, and told Okerlund that he had already beaten Hogan, didn't care for a title shot, and had nothing to prove.

Hogan, Bischoff, DiBiase, and Vincent came out to confront him. Piper pleaded with Hogan—calling him "Terry"—to just let him go home and not do anything in front of his son. Piper used Hogan's real name as a way to make things feel more real. Hogan told him to drop to his knees and beg for mercy.

Hogan said Piper was hiding behind his kid and slapped the back of his head. Piper told Colt he was sorry and handed the visibly frightened child off to Okerlund. Piper knocked Hogan's and Bischoff's heads together and beat up Hogan. Piper then agreed to the match at *SuperBrawl* in California's Bay Area, exclaiming, "San Francisco, watch my fists go!"

Bars, as the kids say.

Hogan, though, would retain the title in the main event of *SuperBrawl*. To no one's surprise.

———

Bischoff escorted two kids and their mother into a room backstage at *Nitro* on February 10, 1997, in Jacksonville, Florida. He sat the children down and told them that what was about to happen was just part of the show. It was not real.

But the kids—the children of referee Randy Anderson—had to act like it was. WCW producers told them to think sad thoughts, as if their puppy had died. Montana, then nine years old, and Chase, then seven, were accompanied by their mother Kristy.

A week earlier, Bischoff fired Randy Anderson in storyline after he ran in to count three for the Steiners against The Outsiders at *Souled Out*. Bischoff overturned the result of the match and gave the WCW tag titles back to Hall and Nash.

To maximize the controversy on the scripted firing, WCW planted newspaper stories afterward about how Randy Anderson had just returned to the promotion after a courageous battle with cancer. Any press is good press, right? Especially when it can intensify a storyline.

On the February 10, 1997, *Nitro*, Bischoff took over the broadcast area with Hall, Nash, Syxx, and Patrick. Randy Anderson then came out with his family to ask for his job back, saying he brought his wife and kids "to see the pain caused."

Bischoff played nice, telling Randy Anderson he was right. He called the kids closer to him. Bischoff then told them, in a sweet voice: "Can do me a favor and tell your daddy he's still fired?"

Bischoff told Randy Anderson that for him to get his job back, he needed to beat Patrick in a wrestling match. Kristy said it was "crazy," because her husband was still undergoing treatment. But the ref told Bischoff that he "wrestled cancer" and he'll wrestle Patrick any time.

It was excellent heel work by Bischoff. The angle made him even more hateable as the power-mad, traitorous WCW executive. An anti-authority sentiment was rising in the mid-1990s and would later give way to films like *Fight Club* and *Office Space* later in the decade.

Bischoff's acting was perhaps a little bit too effective, though.

The next morning, Bischoff was back in his office in Atlanta, and he got a call from his boss, Turner Sports president Harvey Schiller, who requested to see him. When Bischoff got to Schiller's office, Schiller asked him if he fired a WCW employee on national television the night before. Bischoff, who was very proud of the segment, almost busted out laughing. He respected Schiller very much, but Schiller didn't know much about wrestling.

All Schiller knew was that calls came into the Turner offices, many from Randy Anderson's hometown of Rome, Georgia, complaining about how the referee was fired and humiliated in front of his family by Bischoff on TV. Human resources called Schiller about it and Schiller asked to meet with Bischoff. People were convinced that what they watched had been 100 percent real.

Bischoff told Schiller it was all part of the storyline and Randy Anderson still had a job in WCW.

"My part was pretty good," Bischoff said. "Randy sold the shit out of it. And those kids did a great job."

It was Randy Anderson's idea to use his family on TV, Kristy said. He took great pride in his job in professional wrestling. But Chase said he and his sister, because of their ages, had a difficult time parsing what was real and what was not.

"I don't know if my recollection is kind of hazy, but [Bischoff] always gave me, like, not-good vibes," said Chase, who grew up to be an actor. "Maybe this is me speaking in retrospect. I think maybe I knew he was my dad's boss and it probably just all felt a little bit too close to home, a little bit too real in the scripted reality world for a seven-year-old."

Kristy said people in their hometown approached her after the segment and gave their condolences. Most people "did assume it was real." Kristy responded to everyone who reached out that it was just for show, with varying degrees of success.

"You can talk to people and tell them, 'Hey, it was just make-believe,'" Kristy said. "But to some people, they believe it whole-heartedly."

Randy Anderson, who died in 2002 after another bout with cancer, ended up beating Patrick in a match on the following *Nitro*. Randy knocked Patrick out with one left hand, which he had wrapped up with brass knuckles underneath. Bischoff overturned the result, told Randy Anderson he was still fired, and then fired the referee for the match, Jimmy Jett, as well. Randy Anderson ended up being reinstated a month later.

———

On the very same *Nitro* as the referee versus referee match, there was another segment that pushed the boundaries of what was real and what was not. Some might argue it pushed the boundaries of good taste. But, for better or worse, it was a groundbreaking display of this new version of professional wrestling that Bischoff was cultivating.

Hall, Nash, and Waltman came out to the broadcast position and said there was some kind of car accident involving them and the Steiners. They had footage of it, and the video aired later. It showed Hall and Nash in the front seats of a car, with Waltman holding a camcorder in the back. It was Pruitt's personal camera—the same one used in the original nWo Disney MGM Studios promo shoot.

Hall and Nash spotted the Steiners getting into their car at a gas station. Nash, who was behind the wheel, decided to follow and tailgate them. Nash then bumped the Steiners' car, which swerved off the road briefly. Rick Steiner could be seen in the front seat, furious. The car holding Hall, Nash, and Waltman then seemingly hit a bump. The camera cut away and then back to a scene of the Steiners veering off the road and their car flipping over.

The commentary team had been selling the idea that the two brothers were severely injured in the crash. It was yet another story beat to show that the nWo was merciless and capable of doing anything to its opposition, even attempted murder outside the ring. And it looked extremely real. A car did actually flip over.

Of course, the Steiners weren't in it when it did. It was a stunt designed by Edwards, who was strapped into the car himself as the crash dummy. Pruitt produced the piece, which was edited into black and white and aired that way to fit the nWo motif. It was shot in a rural area outside Orlando, Florida, and WCW production had the road cleared.

The camera cut was when they switched the car out for the one Edwards was driving in postproduction. Kemper Rogers, the editor, made it look like there was continuity there and the Steiners were really the ones flipping. Edwards had installed what's called a pipe ramp on the side of the road and hit it while he was driving to flip the car over.

"I mean, he did do that for real," Pruitt said of Edwards. "He stunt-drove that and it made dust come up and grass come up and it looked like he really got ran off the road."

Just as with the Randy Anderson segment, calls from irate fans poured into the Turner switchboard about the car crash. People really thought WCW was going to get someone killed. The video of the crash never aired again, and the storyline was essentially dropped. The Steiners had a television match two weeks later, not showing any injuries.

As with the Disney MGM Studios trailer attack the previous summer, WCW was expanding what pro wrestling could be and further blurring the lines between reality and fiction. It was only a matter of time before they went too far.

"It was so good, that's what killed it," Scott Steiner said of the car crash storyline. "Because so many people believed it. You look back now, it still looks pretty damn good."

———

Dwight Manley was sitting in his office in Orange County, California, on a day in early 1997 when he got a call from Vince McMahon's son, Shane, who had been working in an office role with the WWF.

Manley, an entrepreneur and sports agent, had a client the WWF was extremely interested in bringing in: Dennis Rodman.

The fact that Rodman played in the NBA on the Chicago Bulls with Michael Jordan was one of the least interesting things about him. The tattooed, hard-partying, wedding-dress-wearing, pink-haired Rodman was an agitator, subversive in the world of sports.

Rodman was polarizing and extremely controversial. He was once suspended for headbutting players on the opposing team. He dated Madonna and frequented gay bars. Meanwhile, he was the NBA's best rebounder. *Sports Illustrated* labeled him "America's most provocative athlete."

In other words, he was perfect for 1990s professional wrestling.

Rodman had actually appeared in WCW before, without any kind of contract. He was in Hogan's corner during the *Bash at the Beach* pay-per-view in 1995. Rodman and Hogan had originally been connected through Tony Carlini, a custom motorcycle guru in Southern California, and they became friends. But more than that, Rodman was a legitimate fan of pro wrestling going back to his childhood.

According to Manley, the WWF offered Rodman $500,000 to appear at the annual *WrestleMania 13* pay-per-view. Rodman told Carlini, and Carlini went to Bischoff, who called Manley.

Rodman was comfortable with WCW and "loved" Hogan, Manley said. So Rodman gave Bischoff a chance to match the WWF offer, which he did. Rodman spurned the WWF and signed for multiple appearances with WCW.

It was only fitting that he would be joining his pal Hogan with the nWo.

Rodman appeared on video during the March 10, 1997, *Nitro*. Hogan came out to intro the clip with DiBiase, Norton, Vincent, and Sting, who had been teasing joining the nWo for several weeks. Also with them were Savage and Elizabeth, who had both turned and become nWo members.

The video showed Rodman, sporting purple hair and wearing a Kangol hat, with Hogan, who gave Rodman an nWo shirt. Rodman said the nWo is the "new team of the future."

Hogan said he and Bischoff put Rodman through the nWo "initiation" a night earlier in New York. Hogan and Bischoff attended the Bulls' game against the New York Knicks and Bischoff could be seen wearing an nWo shirt behind the Knicks' bench all game. Rick Telander of the *Chicago Sun-Times* wrote a negative column about Rodman partaking in pro wrestling, especially in the middle of the NBA season when the Bulls were trying to repeat as champions.

Rodman was in the corner of a team consisting of Hogan, Savage, Hall, and Nash in the main event of the *Uncensored* pay-per-view event six days later, in Charleston, South Carolina. Piper teamed with the Horsemen: Benoit, McMichael, and Jarrett. Luger,

Giant, and Scott Steiner made up Team WCW. Rick Steiner was supposed to be the fourth member, but the nWo took him out before the match backstage.

The stakes were high. The stipulations of the match were that if WCW won, the nWo had to return all the WCW titles and the nWo wouldn't be able to wrestle in WCW for three years; if the nWo team won, then it could challenge for any WCW title at any time or place; and if Piper's team won, he got a cage match with Hogan at a later date.

The final two men in the match were Hogan and Luger. Rodman handed Savage a spray paint can from his coat and Savage sprayed graffiti in Luger's face when Luger had Hogan up on his shoulders in his Torture Rack submission hold. Hogan escaped the hold and pinned Luger, winning the match for the nWo.

Afterward, Rodman graffitied Luger's back with "NWO" and put the boots to him before Sting rappelled down from the top of the arena with a bat. Sting took out Hall, Nash, and Savage and pointed his bat toward Hogan and Rodman. Sting punched out Hogan and hit his Scorpion Death Drop on him. The vigilante avenger showed what he stood for—not WCW, but firmly against the nWo and Hogan, specifically.

Uncensored drew an estimated 325,000 buys, the second most in promotion history at the time behind *Starrcade 1996*. That was more than *WrestleMania 13* earned, which was around 237,000 worldwide, in the same month.

It was hard to believe that one of WCW's off-brand pay-per-view shows outdid *WrestleMania*, the trademark event that started the national professional wrestling boom.

But it wasn't just Rodman's presence. Meltzer noted in the *Ob-*

server that the WCW house show business was "amazingly hot." And that wasn't because of Rodman. It was because of the nWo.

———

Nash stood in the ring on *Nitro* two weeks later and told viewers that Hall was away "taking care of business more important than pro wrestling."

The reality to that vague statement was that Hall had failed a drug test and checked himself into a rehabilitation facility for drugs and alcohol. The substance-abuse and mental-health issues he dealt with on and off through most of his life had resurfaced, this time due to the deterioration of his marriage.

One of the main reasons Hall went to WCW was because the schedule was lighter than in the WWF. That was largely because WCW wasn't nearly as profitable and couldn't sell tickets at the rate the WWF did. The success of the nWo was a double-edged sword. When business was good in wrestling, the amount of dates wrestlers had to work only increased. Hall had been away from home more than he expected and it caused his personal life to spiral. The road could be a dangerous place for him, filled with temptations.

The WCW creative team wanted Nash to insult the absent Hall on TV, to sow nWo storyline discontent. He refused to do so. Hall and Nash had become best friends and had complete loyalty toward each other. Nash was like a big brother to Hall.

Nash did imply storyline tension with Hogan and Bischoff in the interview. He threw shade at them for being at Rodman's movie premiere and not with the nWo on *Nitro*.

Some of Nash's unhappiness was real.

Hogan had done little things to get under Nash's skin. There were still feelings that Hogan was stealing some of the things that made Hall and Nash cool and unique. Perhaps a decade or so later they would have referred to Hogan as a swagger jacker.

At one point, Hogan wore boots that read "Hollywood's Wolf-pack." The Wolfpack was how Hall, Nash, and Waltman referred to themselves as a trio, almost like a subgroup of the nWo, which extended to real life. The three of them were very tight and they took exception to Hogan attempting to appropriate the phrase. They were the ones who had been doing the Turkish wolf hand gesture since the WWF days with The Kliq.

"Hulk sees [Wolfpack] getting over and motherfucker has it written on his boots," Waltman said. "We said, 'Uh uh, no.'"

For the most part, though, Hogan and the three of them were on the same side and hung out together off-screen on TV nights. Hogan, Hall, and Nash also often traveled together to shows on a private jet. Hogan and Savage were allowed to have beer in their locker rooms—Hogan was partial to Miller Lite—so Hall and Nash were frequent visitors.

With Hall in rehab, Nash had to defend the WCW tag-team titles against the Steiners by himself at the *Spring Stampede* pay-per-view April 6, 1997. That wasn't going to fly, so WCW wrote around it. Scott Steiner got himself arrested in storyline backstage during the event after trying to attack the nWo, and the match ended up being just an extremely underwhelming bout between Nash and Rick Steiner.

The main event, on a show without Hogan or Piper, was Savage taking on Diamond Dallas Page, with Page getting the victory, the biggest of his career up to that point. Page's rivalry with Savage, one of the best things on WCW programming in 1997, was what elevated Page to being a credible main-event performer, because Savage was generous in giving Page clean victories.

The aftermath of Savage vs. Page at *Spring Stampede* was intra-nWo turmoil. Patrick, who left the ring earlier disgusted by Nash's excessive beatdown of Rick Steiner, came out to count the three for Page. Nash then followed and powerbombed the ref, veritably ending Patrick's time in the nWo.

During the storyline chaos, Savage was going to strike Page's valet and real-life wife, Kimberly, but Bischoff stopped him. Savage then punched out Bischoff. Nash pulled Savage away, leading to the group holding one another back.

Hogan confronted Nash and Savage in an in-ring segment a night later on *Nitro* and largely squashed the fictional beef. Nash said "for life" isn't a catchphrase: "When you're in the nWo, it's for life." Savage and Bischoff made tentative amends, too. But the nWo was shown to still be vulnerable a week later. Sting, Luger, and Giant cleared the ring of the group with bats and *Nitro* ended with them standing tall.

That episode was a banner one for WCW. Taking place in Philadelphia, that *Nitro* drew a paid attendance of 15,132 fans with a gate of $219,816, both the second-best marks at the time in promotion history, Meltzer reported. About $143,000 in merchandise was sold, a single-event WCW record at the time. About 38 percent of that was nWo merchandise. A Sting T-shirt had become the promotion's top seller, and nothing beat plastic Sting masks when it came to profit margin.

Meanwhile, Hall sat alone in a room at a rehabilitation facility, a symbol of how the chaotic, incendiary wrestling war could have a human toll. He wouldn't be the last example.

CHAPTER 9

YOU REALLY ARE BATMAN

The burden of the nWo's success was starting to show by spring of 1997. WCW's business was and would continue to be excellent, but tension backstage began to turn physical. The wear of travel, combined with constant use of drugs and alcohol, was eroding the psyches of those backstage. Egos were beginning to drive people's actions.

Hall returned on the April 21, 1997, *Nitro* and the next pay-per-view main event, at *Slamboree*, was set up as a six-man tag-team match. Hall, Nash, and Syxx would face Flair, Piper, and then–NFL star Kevin Greene. The card was scheduled for Charlotte, North Carolina. Greene was most known for playing for the Carolina Panthers.

There was an internal conflict around that main event. Nash and Piper already didn't like each other, because of a perceived lack of selling by Nash in the *Uncensored* headliner. In wrestling, selling is acting out that you're injured or beat up by your opponent in a match or angle. Flair and Piper then took exception to Waltman being in the *Slamboree* headliner, feeling that it should be someone with a bigger name teaming with Hall and Nash.

That pissed off Hall and Nash, because Waltman was a close friend. They argued that Waltman was the one guy in the match who could really perform at a high level in the ring. He was a great athlete and could make Piper and Flair, who were older, look good.

Waltman remained in the match, despite protests from the two legends. The origin of the issues could be boiled down to a difference in generations. Piper and Flair felt like Hall and Nash, the new guard, didn't respect what they had accomplished for decades. Hall and Nash believed those two—and other older wrestlers in the promotion—didn't acknowledge what they were doing at that moment, which was helping WCW be wildly profitable for the first time and boosting salaries in the process.

Hall, Nash, and Waltman cut promos on *Nitro* saying that Piper and Flair had run the wrestling business into the ground, and they had to build it back up. Flair and Piper responded, saying they should have some appreciation for the wrestlers who got the industry to where it was.

Those interviews were part of the storyline, but largely they were "shoot" promos. Those guys actually felt that way. In wrestling, a "shoot" is something that's real. A "work" is fabricated.

The *Slamboree* match, on May 18, 1997, went off without incident. The WCW team won when Piper choked out Nash with a sleeperhold, Flair pinned Hall, and Greene pinned Waltman. It was an acknowledgment by Hall, Nash, and Waltman that even though things were shaky behind the scenes, they were willing to do their jobs and "put over" the babyfaces overwhelmingly.

The frustrations—and the storyline—should have been over at that point. They were not.

Flair said in a *Nitro* interview that he had won more world titles than Waltman had "pieces of ass" in his life, which angered people backstage. Waltman, in another segment a night after *Slamboree*, hauled off and slapped Flair hard in the face with full force. Flair then chased Waltman down the entranceway to the backstage area at the arena in Asheville, North Carolina. Waltman said Flair had actual intentions of kicking his ass if he caught him, though he did not.

Things came to a head after the June 9, 1997, *Nitro* in Boston. The main event was Piper and Flair taking on The Outsiders with Syxx in their corner. Flair and Piper started the match out quickly, which Hall and Nash did not want. They had time to fill before a big ending with Sting, and there was a rematch scheduled for the next pay-per-view, *Great American Bash*. Hall and Nash didn't want to waste that early intensity when they were going to be doing the same match shortly after on a bigger stage.

But the *Nitro* match started out with a big melee and ended too early. WCW had to fill time afterward with a giant brawl with multiple men—nWo and random WCW wrestlers—running down to ringside.

In the chaos, Nash tweaked his knee and the whole mess made him furious. After the show, Hall, Nash, and Waltman were in the locker room and Nash screamed "motherfucker" and hit a locker. Without saying anything, he left that room and went to where Piper and Flair were getting dressed. Hall and Waltman followed him. The door was locked, but all nearly seven feet of Nash kicked it in, and he got in Piper's face. Piper tried to kick Nash in the knee, but Nash took his giant hand and shoved Piper in the face.

On his podcast years later, Piper said he charged Nash, "leg-dived him," and threw him out of the dressing room. That's certainly a completely different version of events from the one Nash and Waltman had, but hey—that's pro wrestling. Waltman said Piper was "out of his mind."

The *Nitro* in Boston set WCW records for attendance (18,003 with 16,025 paid) and gate ($243,946), Meltzer reported.

———

The nWo wasn't just getting big domestically. It was blowing up in Japan, too.

Chono was the first Japanese wrestler in the nWo and he became the de facto leader of nWo Japan. Norton, Bagwell, and Farmer, as the fake nWo Sting, were frequently on tour there, courtesy of WCW's relationship with New Japan Pro-Wrestling. The Great Muta joined with Chono as part of nWo Japan in the spring of 1997, sending the group to a new level of popularity.

Chono and Muta were two of the most popular wrestlers in Japan and had the kind of cool factor there that Hall and Nash had in the United States. Muta's case was particularly interesting, because it was his alter ego. He also played a character under his real name, Keiji Muto. And in the storyline, the sneering, painted-face Muta was a heel member of the nWo and the clean-shaven Muto was a babyface representing New Japan Pro-Wrestling—sometimes on the same shows.

Tokyo-based Japanese wrestling historian Fumi Saito worked as an editor for Japan's *Weekly Pro-Wrestling* for three decades and covered WCW for the publication, making frequent trips back and forth between the United States and Japan during the nWo era. The popularity necessitated it, he said.

Saito said the nWo brand got so big in Japan that it became part of pop culture, specifically urban streetwear culture. If you were riding on the subway in Tokyo in 1997 to 1998, there was a likelihood you would see young Japanese people wearing the black nWo shirts with the white lettering. And they might not have even known a thing about wrestling or what the nWo was. It was just the "it" thing. Like Supreme or Fear of God today.

The Japanese-born Onoo, Bischoff's friend who worked in WCW as an on-screen manager and liaison to Japan, said there was one show at Tokyo's Sumo Hall where he noticed fans would walk up, buy an nWo T-shirt at a vendor outside the building, and then leave. Onoo told New Japan officials to move those merchandise stands inside, so at least fans had to buy a ticket in order to get a shirt.

"So people buy the ticket, walk inside, and buy like two dozen nWo T-shirts—and leave," Onoo said. "And they were not wrestling fans."

One of the issues in Japan was similar to what was happening in the United States. The nWo merchandise was selling like crazy, but the wrestlers in the nWo (except for Hogan) were not getting a cut of the action. Chono broached the issue many times with New Japan management, who blamed WCW. It eventually led to Chono dropping the nWo and starting his own group called Team 2000 with its own merchandise, the trademarks to which he owned.

An argument over T-shirt money got physical at a bar in Osaka. Bischoff and Onoo had accompanied WCW wrestlers to a massive New Japan show on May 3, 1997, at Osaka Dome. About 53,000 were in attendance. Hall and Nash made the trip, teaming with Chono in a six-man tag match against Muto and the Steiners. Waltman teamed with nWo Sting and Bagwell and Norton faced Luger and Giant.

After the show, several wrestlers and officials went out to an *izakaya* and Bischoff and Tiger Hattori, a referee who also worked in New Japan's office, started to exchange some trash talk, centered around the lack of money going to wrestlers (and presumably Hattori himself) from the nWo merchandise. It started out friendly and escalated.

Hattori ended up challenging Bischoff to an amateur-style wrestling match right there at the bar with a few hundred dollars on the line. Hattori was an AAU champion wrestler decades earlier in the United States. But Bischoff was bigger and ten years younger than Hattori. They cleared the tables to the sides at the bar and went at it. Hattori couldn't take Bischoff down, so Bischoff won the bet.

"That got him hot, oh man," Bischoff said. "Because he was this wrestling champion. Now, he was smaller than me, so that had a lot to do with it. But still, his ego—he just went batshit after that."

———

Bischoff felt like Hogan needed his own theme song to differentiate himself from the rest of the nWo. How many times could the regular nWo entrance music play during one episode of *Nitro* before people started getting sick of it?

Bischoff had long been a fan of Jimi Hendrix and the nWo theme was basically a modified mashup of several Hendrix songs. There was one Hendrix song—the bluesy, electric guitar–charged "Voodoo Child (Slight Return)"—that Bischoff felt would exemplify Hogan and his presentation in front of the audience.

He took a shot and reached out to Hendrix's stepsister Janie, who controlled the late musician's estate, to see if they could work out a deal. Bischoff was shocked to learn the asking price for the rights was $100,000. WCW was doing excellent business and that was more than affordable for such an epochal song.

The contract brokered gave WCW worldwide rights to use "Voodoo Child," but only two minutes of the song, which ran up to five minutes long. WCW would play it on a loop when Hogan came out, and he made it his own by pantomiming guitar riffs on the championship belt to the tune. Bischoff said they could only use it once or twice per show, but it was money well spent.

The first time WCW used "Voodoo Child" was an all-time-great entrance.

A black limo was shown to start *Nitro* in Chicago a week after the Boston show. Hall, Nash, Hogan, Bischoff, Savage, Waltman, and Rodman came out of it. Rodman was wearing an nWo shirt with "BITE ME" on it. That was one of the catchphrases the group, especially Bischoff, adopted in another example of their thumbing their noses at wrestling tradition. Rodman's Bulls had just beaten the Utah Jazz in the NBA Finals three days earlier.

The announced main event of the episode was Hogan and Rodman against Luger and Giant, but it descended into chaos before any kind of match could happen.

WCW promised the rematch—an actual match—would headline the next pay-per-view, *Bash at the Beach*. It would be the one-year anniversary of Hogan breaking bad and joining the nWo.

Bash at the Beach took place July 13, 1997, in Daytona Beach, Florida. Rodman came out for his first wrestling match wearing black jeans, a cut-up nWo shirt, a do-rag, and orange sunglasses. He also had cat whiskers painted on his cheeks. Rodman's hair was pink and yellow with some green and blue mixed in.

The crowd chanted "Rodman sucks!" but he stunned them into cheering when he downed Luger with an arm-drag technique. Rodman was also able to leapfrog over Luger three times when Luger was running toward him from the ropes, a very athletic maneuver for a six-foot-seven man. Behind the scenes, Rodman trained in wrestling with Diamond Dallas Page and went over the match with Hogan, Giant, and Luger beforehand.

The finish of the match came when a very tall man dressed like Sting (obviously Nash in a Sting mask) walked down and hit Giant with a baseball bat. Hogan then hit Rodman by accident and Luger picked Hogan up onto his well-muscled shoulders into his Torture Rack submission hold. Hogan gave up.

It was clear WCW was behind Luger as a top babyface. Hogan had let Luger beat him cleanly five weeks earlier on *Nitro* via submission—Hogan's first submission loss since 1981 in Japan.

Rodman made $750,000 for the match, making it at the time one of the largest one-off appearance fees in wrestling history. But Rodman was well worth the money. Not only was he pretty capable and entertaining in the ring, his presence got WCW the media attention it was craving. WCW might have been winning the ratings war, but the WWF was still pro wrestling's top name brand. Having Rodman associated with WCW helped the promotion from a mainstream perspective more than any other matches or storylines could.

Bash at the Beach sold an estimated 325,000 pay-per-view units. That tied it with *Uncensored* four months earlier as the second-biggest WCW pay-per-views ever at the time, behind *Starrcade 1996*.

Manley, Rodman's agent, said the NBA rogue "got off" on the crowd reaction, though he was shocked they were booing him so much.

———

Page walked a few doors down from his suburban Georgia home and entered Bischoff's garage on a weekend afternoon in June 1997. The two cracked open some beers and shot the shit about what was going on with WCW and in each other's lives. Then Bischoff got serious.

He told Page he was going to be part of a big segment on the next *Nitro*. Page would get beaten up by the entire nWo and Sting would rappel down from the arena ceiling and save him.

OK, great, Page thought. Those were the kinds of situations he wanted his character to be in, mixing with the hottest acts in the company. Beatdowns and saves were run-of-the-mill wrestling segments, though. So why was Bischoff so stern all of a sudden?

That's when Bischoff let on exactly how Sting was going to save Page. He was going to pull Page up and ascend back to the rafters with him on his wire. Bischoff knew Page was afraid of heights, so he was surprised when Page agreed without any further discussion.

Maybe it was the beer being consumed. But Page was open to the idea, because the environment in wrestling at the time was so ultra-competitive that opportunities couldn't just be turned down. Every wrestler believed he was just one red-hot segment away from getting more popular with the crowd, which would inevitably lead to a fatter paycheck.

Before the *Nitro* in Boston—the one where Nash and Piper got into it in the locker room afterward—Edwards affixed a harness around Page's waist for a test run. Sting was going to rappel down, hook Page's harness with a carabiner, and both Sting and Page would be pulled up by Edwards and Brazell. During the rehearsal, they got Page about ten feet off the ground, and everyone was satisfied with the safety of the stunt.

Then Edwards told Page he wanted him to do a trial run all the way up to the top. Page told Edwards that he was going to be Frank Sinatra that night—he'd do it in one take, live on *Nitro*. They could get him to agree to the stunt once, but he sure as hell wasn't going to do it twice.

For the segment, Page wore a long black leather duster jacket, so the harness would be completely obscured. He got completely destroyed by the nWo during that chaotic brawl that went way too long. Sting rappelled down and fought off the nWo with his baseball bat over a prone Page outside the ring.

The whole scene was frenzied, and there had to be some ad-libbing because things didn't go exactly as planned. The nWo was not supposed to attack Sting, but they did in the confusion and to fill time. Live television doesn't always run smoothly. Because things were going slightly off script, Page started to hyperventilate while he was facedown waiting for Sting to hook him up.

Sting was able to crouch down and hook Page's hidden harness to a rope attached to his own harness and the two got pulled up together.

Page went up horizontally with Sting on top of him, straddling Page like a horse. Bischoff had wanted Savage to do something similar earlier that year—get pulled up to the rafters by Sting—but Savage didn't like the idea, because of that positioning. Savage told Bischoff and Edwards he thought it would look "gay." As if sweaty, shirtless men wearing spandex, wrestling around a ring was the most heteronormative thing in the world.

When Sting and Page got all the way up, about 250 feet, to the catwalk, Page quickly grabbed the railing "like a cat trying to get out of a tub," as Edwards recalled. He was hanging upside down, still attached to Sting, before Edwards and Brazell could unhook him. When they did, Edwards tied him to the other side of the rail. Page was relieved and excited—and moving around way too much in a small area high above the FleetCenter.

"I got scared he was gonna pull us off," Edwards said. "He wanted to hug me and Barry, because it was such a dramatic moment in his life."

When Page got a hold of himself and everyone was safe, he

looked up at Sting, who had a white light behind him. It was just the lighting equipment Edwards and Brazell carried with them so they could see what they were doing up at the top of those arenas. But in the moment, for the adrenaline-fueled Page, it was profound.

"Oh my God!" Page exclaimed to Sting. "You really are Batman!"

And that really was how the Sting character was being presented by WCW at the time. Like wrestling's own Dark Knight, a shadowy figure who would show up unexpectedly from the sky and fight off the evil nWo despite being outnumbered. He was also the only good guy WCW had coming close to the nWo's cool factor. It was a lesson that when the bad guys go dark and gritty, the only way for a babyface to succeed is to match that energy. At least in the mid-to-late 1990s.

"I was a WCW kid through and through," current WWE star Cody Rhodes, the son of Dusty Rhodes, said. "And if you really looked at it, WCW sucked compared to the nWo. Like really, it was [just] Sting."

While Page's status was being elevated in his program with Savage and Luger was getting a chance to impress against Hogan, it was clear to everyone that the endgame—or at least the end of the current nWo story arc—was going to be Sting taking on Hogan, likely at *Starrcade*, the biggest WCW show of the year, in December.

Sting still had not spoken a word nor wrestled on television since he declared himself a free agent and started appearing in the rafters in white face paint and all-black attire. The original idea was not to drag out the big Hogan vs. Sting match until the end of 1997—more than a year after Sting's character change—but the silent bad-ass swooping in with his baseball bat was undeniably popular.

And Bischoff wanted to see how far he could take it. That was risky, because WCW was in the middle of the ratings war with the

WWF and trying to wage it without one of its biggest stars wrestling in money-drawing matches on television and pay-per-view.

"My ego was invested in this," Bischoff said. "This is what this story was born out of—my ego. I wanted my long-term story, and I wanted mine to be the best there ever was."

It was. Until it wasn't.

———

With many of the main-event storylines in 1997 revolving around Sting, there were several instances of Sting impersonators other than Farmer, the nWo Sting. Nash donned a Sting mask at *Bash at the Beach*, there was an army of men dressed like Sting on a *Nitro* sent by Sting himself, and, on several occasions, Sting would appear in the rafters only for another Sting to be getting into the action near the ring area. Edwards donned the Sting outfit on the catwalk for those occurrences. The nWo beat up a fake Sting doll that crash-landed in the ring at one point, too.

Perhaps the best impersonation in WCW that year, though, wasn't a Sting doppelgänger at all. It was Page dressed up like the Mexican *luchador* La Parka (Adolfo Tapia Ibarra), who wore a black-and-white skeleton-like outfit with a skull mask.

Before the July 7, 1997, *Nitro*, Bischoff and Sullivan got Page backstage and told him the idea. Savage had a match on the episode against La Parka. Except it wouldn't actually be La Parka under the mask—it would be Page. La Parka, with some Spanish interpretation by Konnan because he did not speak English, was able to school Page a bit on his mannerisms, including his trademark dance, which was kind of like the Robot mixed with a bit of salsa.

Page got dressed in Tapia Ibarra's La Parka outfit in the ice-skating rink adjacent to the arena in Memphis that was hosting

Nitro. WCW brass didn't want anyone seeing it was Page in the getup. During this era, Bischoff and others felt it was just as important at times to fool the wrestlers as it was to trick the audience. They didn't want any information getting out. Savage was the only other person who knew what was going to happen.

In the match, Page acted exactly like La Parka, and no one was the wiser until he hit Savage with his Diamond Cutter finishing move, which brought the crowd to its feet. That's when they knew. Page then ripped off the mask, revealing himself before pinning Savage. Hall came out to try and get to Page, but he escaped through the crowd.

"That was a magical fucking wrestling moment," Page said.

———

The one hundredth episode of *Nitro* took place on August 4, 1997, at the Palace at Auburn Hills outside Detroit. It was one of the most memorable WCW shows of the era, though somewhat tarnished by what happened six days later.

J. J. Dillon had been brought in by WCW that year as a promotion official behind the scenes and as an on-screen authority figure, the chairman of the fictional WCW executive committee. He was previously the manager of the Four Horsemen in the 1980s and more recently one of McMahon's top lieutenants overseeing WWF talent relations. He did an interview with Okerlund on the one hundredth episode formally announcing that WCW would do everything in its power to get Sting back on board. The buildup to *Starrcade* at the end of the year had begun.

In the main event of the show, that path to *Starrcade* got sent a little off course. Luger challenged Hogan for the WCW World Heavyweight championship—and beat him cleanly with the Torture Rack to win the title. Hogan had been champion for almost a full year, going back to *Hog Wild 1996*.

It was something of a full-circle moment. When *Nitro* debuted in 1995, Luger's surprise appearance after being with the WWF just days earlier set the tone for what the program would become. While he wasn't the most well-liked person behind the scenes and was limited in the ring, Luger worked hard and connected with the audience as a babyface in 1997.

When Luger beat Hogan, the 17,616 fans in the building went ballistic. The Giant, the Steiners, Page, and other WCW wrestlers came out to celebrate with him.

With a physique straight out of a bodybuilding magazine, Luger looked like a million bucks. His Torture Rack submission was extremely popular with the crowd, so much so that fans would rise to their feet when he picked opponents up for it. WCW did a nice job of drawing that reaction out of crowds by previously having Luger pick up enormous, 300- and 400-pound-plus opponents with the strongman move.

The attendance and gate ($240,519) for the milestone episode were the second biggest in WCW history, per Meltzer. The *Nitro* replay, which aired after the special three-hour show at 11 p.m. ET, did a record 2.31 rating, which was more than some first-run *Raw* ratings during that time. *Nitro* would make a permanent change from two hours to three hours weekly a few months later.

Head-to-head, the live *Nitro* beat the live *Raw*, 4.4 to 2.7. WCW had won forty-seven straight weeks against a first-run *Raw*. The combined numbers of the two shows represented a record total of 5,065,000 total homes in the United States watching pro wrestling that Monday night, Meltzer reported.

Hogan has said in interviews over the years that the nWo was so wildly over with fans that he didn't need the title to maintain his and the group's momentum. However, just six days later, in a rematch between Hogan and Luger, Hogan won the title back at the *Road Wild* pay-per-view in Sturgis, South Dakota.

The finish of the match came when a man dressed like Sting hit Luger in the back with a baseball bat. Commentary was still selling it as if it were the actual Sting, even though everyone was long past the point of being deceived by that trope.

Afterward, cameras cut to the nWo celebrating backstage with Rodman, who took a black spray paint can and tagged the title all over again with "NWO." Hogan said he loved "sharing" the belt with his fellow nWo members.

The celebration segment took place backstage rather than in the ring, because Hogan got hit in the head with a rock thrown by a fan. The trend of people in the crowd tossing things (including themselves) in the direction of the performers started the night Hogan turned at *Bash at the Beach 1996*. It was encouraged by WCW indirectly (and sometimes directly), but had clearly reached a dangerous point.

Bischoff felt like giving Hogan the title right back after Luger's historic win was done to create more "heat." In other words, to get fans angry that Hogan once again had the belt—and make them even more invested in his losing it for good. It was a way to make the future Hogan vs. Sting match even bigger, because no one seemed to be able to get the championship off Hogan for the long term. Not Flair, not Savage, not Piper, and now not Luger.

Bischoff, in hindsight, regretted moving too fast to get the belt back on Hogan when there could have been more meat on the bone with Luger as champion. There's no doubt the crowd was behind Luger.

"It was a poor decision on everybody's part, mostly mine," Bischoff said. "I greenlit that shit. There's no other way to look at it. I know what the thinking was then. It was, 'It'll be so much heat, because people want Lex to be the champion.' We knew it was gonna get heat and it did, but maybe the wrong kind of heat. Maybe not."

———

The nWo was grittier and rawer than wrestling had seen at that point. That irreverence was what appealed to the teenage and young male adults that WCW wanted to court. In 1997, there were some lines crossed that made Turner, WCW's parent company, uncomfortable. Turner had just merged with Time Warner in late 1996 and the effects of that deal were starting to be felt by WCW in the fall of 1997. Bischoff had several meetings with the wrestlers about toning down some of the bad language, vulgarity, and sexual double entendre.

Waltman was one of the worst offenders. He was chewed out during his storyline with Flair for pulling Flair's tights down, exposing Flair's ass, in one segment. Waltman was nearly fired for that, combined with a cumulative amount of toilet humor.

No better example was the gesture that Waltman made famous: the crotch chop.

Waltman said he saw another wrestler do a taunt that consisted mainly of him pointing to his genital area years earlier. He doesn't remember exactly who it was, but he started doing something similar, putting his own spin on it during his run as 1-2-3 Kid in the WWF. Waltman would stretch both of his hands into a karate chop posture. Then he would take both extended hands and quickly chop his inner-thigh region—with his tights- or jeans-covered groin area on showcase in the middle.

The Kliq started doing the crotch chop, much like the Turkish wolf gesture, when all the members were in the WWF. When Waltman signed with WCW, he brought the unique sleight of hand with him, debuting the crotch chop on the October 21, 1996, *Nitro*.

Others in the nWo would adopt it, as well, including Hogan. Hall, in particular, used the taunt liberally. On the September 15, 1997, *Nitro*, the entire group did it as part of a gag Hall would do, which consisted of him saying something was "down here," to which whoever he was with would ask, "Down where?" And Hall would do the crotch chop.

Over in the WWF, Michaels and Levesque started a group on August 11, 1997, called D-Generation X, which was the promotion's answer to the nWo, though even more sophomoric when it came to sexual references. The WWF was starting to push the envelope of good taste further than WCW was able to. Michaels and Levesque made the crotch chop the signature gesture of D-Generation X, later shortened to D-X.

There was a slight difference in the technique by the Kliq members remaining in the WWF. Michaels and Levesque made the crotch chop into an X for D-X. They also added a phrase to it: "suck it."

That was surely a bridge too far for a WCW that was attempting to get more family-friendly. The inappropriate hand signal—and the aforementioned boorish phrase—became wildly popular, especially with boys and college-aged men, getting many a teen suspended at school. D-X developed a following that has made it one of the most influential factions in pro-wrestling history, right behind the nWo.

The crotch chop has lived on, long past the expiration date of both the nWo and D-X. Pete Weber, the bowling Hall of Famer known as the bad boy of the sport, borrowed it from wrestling and started using it in his own celebrations. A high-school football coach in Texas was suspended for doing the gesture in the direction of the opposing team's bench in 2011. Several UFC fighters in recent years have used it to celebrate victories, including Jon Jones, who is regarded as the greatest mixed martial arts fighter of all time. Joel Embiid of the Philadelphia 76ers has been fined multiple times for doing the crotch chop during NBA games.

The crotch chop, oddly enough, has become somewhat of a timeless nod to pro wrestling, though it has transcended the medium. Three decades later, many purveyors of the perverted gesticulation don't even know where it came from.

"It's pretty fucking cool," Waltman said of the lasting power of the gesture he innovated. "It's a little lowbrow or whatever. I guess there's probably things you would more like to be remembered for, but still. It's pretty cool, right? Like you had that kind of impact on pop culture, not just wrestling."

———

The Four Horsemen had a memorable segment on the *Nitro* two weeks after Hogan regained the title. The Horsemen were going to face the nWo at the *Fall Brawl* pay-per-view in a War Games match and they were trying to convince Curt Hennig, WCW's newest signing, to join the group and fight alongside them.

Arn Anderson, who had been essentially retired due to a badly injured neck, was a tremendous wordsmith on the microphone and cut a moving promo offering Hennig a spot in the Horsemen. Not just any spot, Arn said—"my spot," as the Horsemen's enforcer. Hennig accepted and would team with Flair, Benoit, and McMichael in the cage match.

The following week, the nWo came out during what was advertised as a Horsemen interview with Okerlund. The group did a parody of the segment from seven days earlier. Waltman dressed like Flair, complete with a fake big nose, and Konnan, who had recently joined the nWo, impersonated McMichael. Bagwell, who by then was going by "Buff" in front of his last name, walked out looking like Hennig.

Then Nash came out wearing glasses, a wig of thinning hair, and a big fake belly. He was supposed to be Arn. Nash was also wearing glasses and a neck brace and carried with him a big Styrofoam cooler. Waltman shouted "woo!" after every two words, mocking Flair's famous catchphrase. Nash mocked Arn's speech to Hennig, saying he was offering Bagwell "not a liver spot, not your dog Spot, but my spot."

It was humorous and effective in hammering home the storyline bad feelings between the Horsemen and the nWo. Arn was fine with the depiction at first until he talked to his wife and children, who were furious. Which made him change his mind about the whole thing.

What pissed Anderson off the most was the Styrofoam cooler. That was an inside joke that only people in WCW would get. Arn carried a cooler full of beer with him on the road. And Nash arranged for someone to actually go and get the exact cooler Arn used for the parody segment. Arn didn't want people to think he was an alcoholic, though at that time it wasn't uncommon for wrestlers to drink heavily and use drugs.

Arn confronted Nash after the show and Nash said it wasn't anything personal, just a way to get more heat on the match at *Fall Brawl*. Arn said he believed him. But he still couldn't stand the segment and found out years later that it was actually the idea of Terry Taylor, who recently had replaced Sullivan as WCW's head of creative.

"I'm never gonna say, 'Well, I never drank anything [or] I didn't drink a dozen beers every night after working out during the day and wrestling at night,'" Arn said. "Well, of course I did. There was probably a couple nights I had two dozen. Not the point. The point is don't bring it into the workplace."

This wasn't just an isolated incident, either. There was still heat between Flair and the nWo, especially Waltman and Bischoff, who Flair believed was allowing the nWo to run wild behind the scenes, as well as on the air. The whole plot line that the nWo represented the new wave of pro wrestling and Flair, Piper, Arn, and others were part of the old generation wasn't just playing out on television. It manifested itself in real life, as well.

In that way, the nWo wasn't just a pro-wrestling group or storyline—it had become an idea.

"[Bischoff] would rather climb a tree and tell a lie than tell the truth, and that's how he ran the business," Flair said. "I can't see why they created animosity, because for a company to be success-ful, you've all got to work together and be on the same page. . . . [Bischoff] literally created animosity. Like, he wanted those people to have animosity with each other."

Hennig would end up turning on the Horsemen at *Fall Brawl* on September 14, 1997. He threatened to slam Flair's head in the cage door during the War Games match unless one of the other Horse-men surrendered. McMichael gave in, giving the nWo the victory in the match. Hennig shut the chain-link fence door on Flair's head anyway. The next night on *Nitro*, Hennig officially joined the nWo.

Hennig became the thirteenth active member of the bloated group, and he was joined in November 1997 by his real-life good friend Rick Rude, who became Hennig's manager. Rude was unable to wrestle due to a bad back injury he sustained in the early 1990s, but became another mouthpiece for the nWo.

By then, DiBiase, the stable's original mouthpiece and money-man, had been purged from the nWo. He and Ray Traylor turned babyface, joining Patrick and Giant as former nWo members still in WCW.

Bischoff referred to DiBiase, Traylor, and Giant as "bad casting." He didn't feel like they fit with the group. None of them had that fresh, different element that the nWo represented.

"You could put a great actor in a horrible script and the movie is still going to suck—and the actor is going to get the blame," Bischoff said. "But it was bad casting. And that was on me."

———

Piper returned to WCW in the fall of 1997 to reignite his feud with Hogan. The two met in a cage match in the main event of *Halloween Havoc* on October 26 in Las Vegas. In a nontitle contest, of course. Once again, Piper didn't want to lose to Hogan and Hogan didn't want to lose the belt. WCW didn't want the latter, either, because Hogan vs. Sting was still being built heavily for *Starrcade.*

Speaking of Sting, several men dressed like him appeared during the Hogan vs. Piper cage match, as a storyline way for Sting to get in Hogan's head. Hogan called Savage out for help and Savage climbed up onto the cage and hit a double axe handle (both hands with fingers interlocked coming down onto an opponent's head) from the top of it.

How Savage's then-forty-four-year-old knees didn't explode upon landing from the sixteen-foot cage was a marvel in itself. But he did miss his mark, which was part of the script, hitting Hogan rather than Piper. Then Piper choked Hogan unconscious yet again with his sleeperhold.

Hogan and Savage began a beatdown on Piper after the match with help from Bischoff. They handcuffed Piper to the cage. Hogan put on one of the errant plastic Sting masks and started whipping Piper with his belt.

A "fan" wearing a Sting mask then climbed up the side of the cage and entered the battleground. Hogan and Savage grabbed the "fan" and started beating him up before security got inside to remove him.

He wasn't a fan at all. He was a plant—someone scripted to become part of the action. In actuality, he was a stuntman that Edwards brought in to be part of the pay-per-view ending.

Bischoff liked the idea of fan interaction. After garbage filled the ring at *Bash at the Beach* in 1996 when Hogan turned heel, he wanted his promotion to lean into the crowd's bad behavior. Sometimes, WCW plants would throw things to try and spark that reaction. Bischoff's theory was that wrestling promotions could teach people how to act via a manipulated mob mentality.

WCW did the same thing with *Nitro* parties on college campuses. The promotion started manufacturing them, recruiting students and sending an interviewer and the Nitro Girls dance team to a school. They threw a fake party that could be used on the air to demonstrate the enthusiasm the show was creating with young people. The strangest thing then started happening. Fraternities and other college students started throwing legitimate *Nitro* parties on Monday nights.

Throwing water bottles and junk-food wrappers into the ring just became something fans did at WCW shows. The spectators had no idea they were manipulated into doing that by the promotion, the same way college students were manipulated into holding *Nitro* parties.

Halloween Havoc 1997 was a step even further, though. Having a stuntman pretending to be a fan entering the cage was encouraging the type of conduct that could have been dangerous for the talent and spectators.

People throwing stuff had gotten bad enough, because many fans in the front rows would get hit with debris from people behind them. It looked captivating on TV when someone like Hall got hit with a full cup of soda and then slicked his hair back in one motion, like he was the coolest guy in the world. But Hogan got hit with a rock at *Road Wild* in 1997 and there were other examples like that. Randy Anderson and Okerlund had also been hit with flying objects over the years, as had just about every member of the nWo.

Bischoff said the worst thing he got hit by while performing was a cup filled with used chewing tobacco. The chew got stuck in his thick, dyed jet-black hair. He said it was "the most disgusting thing" that's ever happened to him. But it did not convince him to have officials ask fans to tone things down.

That was another incident afterward, though he doesn't remember exactly when.

"As I'm walking out doing my bullshit, out of the corner of my eye I see something from way the fuck up—almost from the rafters— coming at us," Bischoff said. "And I looked, and it was a full bottle of beer with the cap on, and it came down about six inches in front of me. Hit the floor and exploded. And I went, 'All right, we got to quit encouraging bad behavior. Because this is getting scary.' Not only for us as talent, but people start throwing shit at the ring and they overshoot it, undershoot, whatever. Now we're hitting kids in the audience.

"So that actually started out as being very cool, but evolved into being very dangerous."

CHAPTER 10

NO, MAN—IT'S CHRISTMAS

Sting was alone.

Week after week for more than a year, he stood on the catwalk looking down on a sold-out arena. His painted-white face was hollow and emotionless. He appeared aloof, disenchanted with the ways of the world.

The real-life Steve Borden was a hell of a professional wrestler, but he was hardly an award-winning actor. That emptiness that emanated from Sting wasn't a performance. Borden himself was a mere husk of a human being by late 1997.

"I don't know if it was the facepaint or the fact that I was silent for a lot of the nWo era, but fans seemed to be able to connect with me just through the look in my eyes," Sting said. "I can look at pictures of me from that time . . . and I can see the complete hopelessness and despair in my eyes. It was not an act. It was not a character. I was lost."

Beginning in 1996, the same year the nWo storyline began, Sting struggled with painkillers, muscle relaxers, and alcohol. He had been a steroid user previously, but he had held out a long time from the other stuff. He was having trouble sleeping, and once he started popping the pills, everything else just snowballed.

Sting was going through marital issues at the time with his wife,

Sue, stemming from his addiction. Unlike with Hall, who was outgoing and belligerent when under the influence, Sting was more subdued. He wasn't a big party guy, so much of his drug consumption was in private.

Borden, the man, was every bit as isolated as Sting was up in the rafters, though few realized it.

WCW was building Sting up as the biggest threat to the nWo, the savior of the promotion. His plastic masks were the company's top seller from a profit-margin standpoint. No one was getting a bigger reaction from the crowd. Rightly, Bischoff and the WCW creative team had more than a year's worth of storyline hinging on Sting, the vigilante antihero.

They all missed the point of what made Sting so popular. It wasn't because he was WCW's Batman, as Page had exclaimed. It was because Sting was so relatable to WCW's young-male demographic.

Sting had been ostracized and cast out like many young men felt like they were in the 1990s, the decade when Kurt Cobain and Marilyn Manson took hold. The nWo were the arrogant, wisecracking high-school bullies who thought they could get away with everything, and Sting was a victim of their aggressions. WCW fans couldn't wait for him to strike back with his baseball bat, because many of them saw themselves in him. Hogan was the perfect avatar of the muscled-up high-school jock who always got his way.

Sting's wardrobe—black pants, black boots, black trench coat—fit the entire misfit motif. It was the fashion of those who perceived themselves to be outcasts. In a tragedy unrelated to Sting and his character, a pair of teenagers named Eric Harris and Dylan Klebold donned black trench coats and perpetrated the most infamous school shooting in American history at Columbine High School in Colorado less than two years later.

WCW didn't quite envision the Sting character in that way, as a symbol of simmering young-male rage. But Bischoff and the creative team did understand its creepy, marginalized nature.

The nWo was in the ring, celebrating a win for Hall and Savage over Luger and Page in the main event of *Clash of the Champions* on August 21, 1997, when the lights inside the Nashville Municipal Auditorium started to pulse and ominous music played over the PA system.

The camera cut to the top of the building. Sting was there—with a live vulture perched on his left arm. A child's voice could then be heard over the arena speakers.

"We look to the skies for a vindicator," the voice said. "Someone to strike fear into the black heart of the same man who created him. The battle of good and evil has begun. Against an army of shadows comes a dark warrior, the purveyor of good with the voice of silence and a mission of justice. This. Is. Sting."

The lights then went out. After nearly forty seconds, they came back on, and the vulture was perched on the top rope of the ring. Bischoff got closer and looked terrified. Hall held him back. Bischoff tried to grab something at the bird's feet, but there was nothing there. It started flapping its wings when Bischoff reached over. Nash then raised his WCW tag-team title belt to his shoulder as if he was going to swing it like a bat at the vulture.

The bird was supposed to carry a note down to the nWo that read, "Hogan's soul." Somewhere between the catwalk and the ring, the note had fallen, so Bischoff had nothing to reach out and grab. The segment ended up being more comical than disturbing, but the effort was there.

On the following *Nitro*, four days later, Dillon interrupted a Bischoff interview via phone. Dillon, in his role as on-screen authority figure, said WCW had understood Sting's request loud and clear and he was "committed" to making Hogan vs. Sting happen.

Meanwhile, Sting walked out through the entranceway and sneaked behind Bischoff. He grabbed Bischoff's leather jacket and Bischoff got on his knees, begging. Sting draped a Hollywood Hogan T-shirt over Bischoff's head and pushed Bischoff with the sole of his boot. Sting took the shirt and put it in Bischoff's mouth.

That *Nitro* episode ran unopposed. *Raw* was preempted due to the U.S. Open tennis tournament. And WCW pulled in a monster number: 3,549,000 homes watching, the most to ever watch a pro-wrestling show on cable at the time, per Meltzer.

The wrestling business in general, and WCW specifically, was reaching an all-time level.

Nitro nearly doubled *Raw*'s rating head-to-head on September 8, 1997. On October 20, 1997, *Nitro* and *Raw* combined for a record 5,398,000 homes watching. *Halloween Havoc* on October 26, 1997, set the all-time ticket sales record for WCW ($297,508), which was then topped by the *World War 3* pay-per-view ($395,831) the following month.

Halloween Havoc, with Hogan vs. Piper in a cage match as the headliner, became the most-purchased WCW pay-per-view ever at the time with an estimated 405,000 buys. Compared with November 1995, *Nitro* ticket sales were up 892 percent in November 1997, according to an internal WCW report.

Wrestling on cable was hotter than ever. WCW was more popular than it had ever been. And everything was pointing toward the end of the year: *Starrcade*. It would be the biggest pay-per-view in WCW history. And Hogan vs. Sting would be the biggest match in WCW history.

Pro wrestling, led by WCW and the Hogan-Sting feud, led to a

10 percent ratings decline in *Monday Night Football* that year, Meltzer reported. *Starrcade 1997* would break the WCW ticket sales record on the first day of purchases.

———

There was another impending development. WCW had announced that it would be starting a second prime-time television show, on a different night, to go along with *Nitro*. Initially, the plan was to have one show that would be branded WCW and another branded as nWo. That idea had been scrapped, in part because of the failure of *Souled Out*. But the implication it would happen was used, of course, as part of a storyline.

Starting in the summer of 1997 into the fall and winter, Hall and Bischoff would talk trash at the broadcast position during *Nitros* with commentator Larry Zbyszko. Hall and Zbyszko went back to their days in the AWA, and Zbyszko and was a mentor to Hall. Zbyszko was an accomplished wrestler in his day, though he turned forty-six years old in 1997 and had not wrestled in two years. But Hall wanted to give back to someone who helped him on his way up, so they conjured up the kayfabe beef.

The match that was agreed to was Zbyszko taking on not Hall, but Bischoff. And the stipulation that got Bischoff to agree to the match was that *Nitro* would be on the line. If Bischoff won, *Nitro* would belong to the nWo. If Zbyszko won, the show would stay with WCW. That would be the *Starrcade* co-headliner right underneath Hogan vs. Sting.

To up the ante, the special referee for the match was announced as Bret Hart.

That's right, one of the WWF's biggest stars had jumped ship, signing with WCW and starting there in December 1997. McMahon had told Bret he could not fulfill the contract that was promised a year earlier, and Bret took a massive deal from Bischoff that would pay him more than $5 million combined over 1998 and 1999.

Bret left the WWF under the most bizarre of circumstances. McMahon and his confidants double-crossed Bret, having him lose a match and the WWF championship to Michaels at *Survivor Series* on November 9, 1997, in Montreal, even though Hart did not agree to do that. Bret had vowed to not drop the belt to his real-life enemy, Michaels, and McMahon pulled a fast one, having referee Earl Hebner call for the bell and say Bret submitted during the match when he did not.

With Bret departing for WCW, McMahon and the WWF used the legitimate and controversial incident, dubbed the Montreal Screwjob, to their advantage. They made it into a storyline and McMahon, who had largely just been featured as a play-by-play announcer on television, became Mr. McMahon, the tyrannical boss who just cheated the beloved Bret Hart. Gerald Brisco, one of McMahon's right-hand men, said he believes this was the beginning of the WWF's Attitude Era, the red-hot period when the promotion became as close to an R-rated product as it could get and broke through the pop culture zeitgeist like never before.

Bischoff, though, was technically doing the heel boss character more than a year before McMahon did it. It was representative of the counterculture 1990s when the idea of knocking your boss on his ass with a punch was very in vogue. Bischoff's real-life role as WCW executive led to his being the only exec to really beat McMahon and the WWF for an extended period of time.

On screen, Bischoff's character was incredibly obnoxious, by design, as the megalomaniacal authoritarian of the nWo and WCW. He would mock fans by telling them how much he loved everyone in the arena in an over-the-top, grating way. Bischoff also made life hell for the babyfaces, like Luger and Giant. As much as fans wanted to cheer the charisma of Hall and Nash, they had absolutely no problem booing Bischoff lustily.

Zbyszko, the protégé of WWF legend Bruno Sammartino, was the man tasked with giving Bischoff his comeuppance. Bischoff was a legitimate black belt in karate and had been in professional kickboxing matches about a decade and a half earlier. He knew how to fight for real. But he did not know how to perform in a professional wrestling match. In other words, he didn't know how to make it look like he was hurting someone when he actually was not.

Leading into the match, Bischoff went to shoot a video to promote it at the WCW's Power Plant training facility. The vignette would air on *Nitro*. Bischoff ended up kicking one of his training partners right in the face and busted his nose, leaving him bloody. It was the first kick he threw during the session. Bischoff said he did warn the wrestlers he was training with, and they wore headgear.

"It's either hurt people or look like it missed by a mile," Bischoff said. "I was still fairly capable at the time, and I could do it for real, but I wasn't good at doing it for 'not real.' I couldn't work it."

As an appetizer to what could potentially happen if Bischoff won, the nWo commandeered *Nitro* the episode before *Starrcade*. The group took over the broadcast position and recruited behind-the-scenes workers, giving them nWo shirts. Konnan, Bagwell, and Rude invaded the production truck, where Konnan said it was a "hostile takeover" and asked producer Craig Leathers directly if he was with the nWo or not.

Workers on ladders took down the WCW MONDAY NITRO sign above the entrance and key grips started taking down the giant letters "WCW" on either side of the aisleway. The commentary table was affixed with a sign that said "NWO Monday Nitro" and a new banner was unfurled saying the same. A giant NWO Monday Nitro metal sign was lowered in front of the top of the curtain. The ring was spraypainted in the center with "NWO."

The rest of the show was all nWo, with Bischoff, Rude, and Nash taking over on commentary and only matches involving nWo members. Bobby Heenan, the weaselly heel color commentator, slithered back to the broadcast position to kiss Bischoff's ass in an effort to get a job in the nWo. Heenan told Bischoff he was the "Donald Trump of wrestling." That sure took on a new meaning decades later.

Throughout the episode, Bischoff and the nWo had Christmas gifts for Hogan. At the end of the show, a random guy brought Hogan one last present. Bischoff said he didn't arrange for that one. Hogan opened the box and inside was a head. A facsimile Hollywood Hogan head, that is.

The camera then cut to Sting standing on top of the entranceway. He started to zipline toward the ring as Hogan fled. That's how the last show before *Starrcade* went off the air.

———

Another big match scheduled for *Starrcade* was Nash taking on The Giant in what was billed as a giant-versus-giant matchup. It never happened.

Nash had a holiday gathering for family and friends and ended up eating several brownies infused with marijuana. Nash also had an issue during that time with Xanax, muscle relaxers, and alcohol—like many other wrestlers—and that cocktail mixed with the weed was foreseeably detrimental to his health. He said he started sweating, thought he was having a heart attack, and called 911. Nash's family also had a history of heart issues.

"There's an Australian guy ... [he] was one of the EMTs," Nash said. "He says, 'So what have you ingested?' And I said, 'Well, I had some bourbon, I drank a bottle of wine, I had a couple beers, I had some somas, I ate some pot brownies.' He goes, 'Oh, so this is a suicide attempt.' I said, 'No, man—it's Christmas.'"

Nash was taken to the hospital, where they concluded he did have a heart attack, though he believes it was just a combination of the things he drank and ate and a hard workout he had earlier that morning.

Critics have speculated that Nash avoided the match because he didn't want to lose to The Giant. But Nash legitimately was in the hospital. Nash's heart ended up being fine, but it was a genuine scare.

––––––

Starrcade was held December 28, 1997, in Washington, D.C. The bout between Zbyszko and Bischoff was called a "mixed martial arts type of matchup" by Mike Tenay on commentary.

"Mixed martial arts," abbreviated later as MMA, wasn't even being officially used by the UFC until the following year (the sport was then mainly called "no holds barred" or ultimate fighting), though the phrase had originated decades earlier. Bischoff came out wearing black karate pants, a black belt, black boots, and gloves similar to what UFC fighters wore.

Hall accompanied Bischoff to the ring and played a part in the messy finish. He slipped a steel plate into Bischoff's knee pad and Bischoff knocked Zbyszko out with a kick. But Bret Hart, the special ref, saw the whole thing. He punched Bischoff and put Hall in his Sharpshooter submission. Zbyszko choked Bischoff out with his own belt and Bret declared Zbyszko the winner. *Nitro* would remain with WCW.

Then came the main event: Hogan vs. Sting. It could have been the match that put WCW over the top, the one that cemented the promotion as the top dog ahead of the WWF. Instead, it has become one of the most discussed wrestling matches in pro-wrestling history—for all the wrong reasons.

Sting would be having his first real, televised match since September 1996. WCW had gone all in on the storyline of Sting being the character who would finally put an end to Hogan's reign, and perhaps the nWo itself. The creative team and people like Edwards took the time and care to build Sting up into this mythical figure. It was risky to invest in such a long-term play in the middle of a heated ratings battle on Monday nights. But there arguably wasn't a more popular person in wrestling than Sting, with the possible exception of "Stone Cold" Steve Austin, who had risen to top-star status in the WWF.

The only thing that made sense was for Sting to win and dethrone Hogan, fair and square. It was predictable, but sometimes the best stories end in a predictable manner. In movies and comic books and television shows, with some exceptions, the good guys—however dark and brooding they might be—usually win in the end. And that was the plan for Sting, for him to get a clean pin or submission over Hogan and go into 1998 as the WCW World Heavyweight champion.

That was not exactly what went down.

Buffer did the ring announcing, and capped it with his "Let's get ready to rumble!" catchphrase. There was a feeling of gravity at the MCI Center in D.C. Sting came out through the entrance for his first match in fifteen months after a special effects lightning strike inside the arena with that same, unsettling voice of a child welcoming him. He carried his signature baseball bat and wore a black leather coat and black pants with a scorpion on the leg. Hogan was greeted by chants of "Hogan sucks!"

After about ten minutes of fairly rudimentary action, with the crowd very much engaged, Hogan landed his finishing move, the leg drop, and pinned Sting cleanly.

One, two, three. No interference, no cheating. No malfeasance from Patrick, the referee. No count that was too fast. Just what appeared to be a win by Hogan, completely on the up-and-up.

Then, Bret Hart came out inexplicably. He stopped Penzer, the other ring announcer, from ringing the bell and said, "It's not gonna happen again." Bret punched out Patrick, chased down Hogan, and threw him back in the ring. nWo members Bagwell and Norton came out, but Sting fought them off and put Hogan in the Scorpion Death Lock submission hold.

Hogan gave up. The match was over, again. This time, Sting was the new champion.

Just about all the wrestlers affiliated with WCW came running out to celebrate, led by Luger. Sting jumped into Luger's arms. The crowd roared. Sting said something mostly unintelligible into the camera—his first words on air in more than a year—and ended the rambling by shouting *"mamacita!"*

On commentary, Dusty Rhodes said the long wait was worth it and Sting's win was "breathtaking."

But really, it was more confusing.

Ultimately, WCW and the fans got what they wanted: Sting beating Hogan to win the belt. But how it got there was mind-numbing. Hogan did nothing nefarious when he pinned Sting moments earlier, yet Bret Hart came out angry about some kind of screwjob, as if it were similar to the real-life one he dealt with in Montreal. The match restarted for no good reason.

It was clear something was amiss. But what exactly went down, why, and what was the original plan? It depends on who you ask.

Bischoff said the idea was always for Sting to win with no funny business and "everybody was on board" with that plan. Why else would WCW prolong the match for so long and build it up to such an extent? But things changed the afternoon of *Starrcade*.

Bischoff had a meeting with Hogan in his makeshift office inside the bowels of the arena and Sting came in. Both Bischoff and Hogan felt like something was wrong with Sting. He wasn't drunk or high, or anything like that. But he seemed out of it, mentally.

Bischoff didn't think Sting looked to be in great physical shape, at least for a top-tier pro wrestler, and had not even bothered to tan. Bischoff said the latter was more a euphemism that Sting just didn't appear to have it together on several levels. Wrestlers typically bronzed themselves via a tanning bed or spray to gain a better aesthetic under the arena lights.

Others could tell something was up with Sting, too. Meltzer wrote in the *Observer* that "16 months of work was exposed halfway through Sting's walk down the aisle" and "the mythical superhero turned human right before the fans' very eyes." He added that Sting "looked really small compared to the past," referencing his physique.

Hogan noticed the issues more than Bischoff did, and Hogan did not believe that night was the right time to put the title on Sting given his apparent mental or emotional condition. That's when they "shifted gears" and changed the finish of the match.

Where things got dicey, Bischoff said, was that Sting was supposed to kick out of the pin after Hogan hit the leg drop. Patrick was going to count to three despite Sting kicking out, a call back to his time as the nWo referee, and that's when Bret was going to come out to right the injustice.

There is still plenty of confusion on how everything went down from those involved decades later.

"I just know there were a lot of changes that were happening that very day, and we didn't know for sure how we were going to handle the deal, how we were going to do the finish, until literally when we walked through the curtain," Sting said. "And as far as the count goes, to this day I don't know what happened."

When Bischoff told Hogan that he wanted Hogan to lose the title to Sting, Hogan asked Bischoff why and what the plan was after that. Hogan felt like he never got a real answer from Bischoff on the latter question.

Hogan might have been having some flashbacks to the WWF and McMahon trying to phase him out of the top spot when he knew in his heart that he could still carry a company. Hogan was correct that time years earlier and he felt he was correct again in 1997.

If he was going to lose to Sting, Hogan wanted some kind of finish that would make him come out looking just as strong, if not stronger than if he had won, because "this is about making money."

"There has to be some type of out, you just don't beat somebody and kick him to the curb and say, 'Well, I don't know what's next,'" Hogan said. "And I've already been through that once. So I said, 'Well, what's the storyline moving forward?' And Eric really wasn't sure where we were going with this thing."

Hogan felt so much tension about the finish of the match that he agreed to let Sting beat him. In Hogan's perspective, Sting just simply did not kick out when he was supposed to, and he does not recall being informed of Bret Hart's intervention in the match beforehand.

Patrick has a different recollection of things. He said when he arrived at the arena in D.C. that afternoon before the show, Bischoff saw him and pulled him aside. Bischoff told him to just count to three with nothing funky, a normal count for the main event.

Later, Patrick said he ran into Hogan, who told him to make the count "nice and slow." About thirty minutes later, Patrick saw Sting. And Sting told him to "rapid fire" the count—make it fast.

Everyone's wires seemed to be crossed. Or there were other agendas at play. Maybe both.

"So now I'm like, 'All right, so I've got this guy here who is considered the franchise [in Sting] and I got this other guy over here [Hogan], who is also considered the franchise, and I'm stuck in the middle of this headbutting, who's-gonna-do-what-in-the-finish, almost Montreal Screwjob type of shit," Patrick said.

Patrick looked for Bischoff backstage for some clarification, but Bischoff "didn't want to be found—he didn't want to answer that question." Patrick felt like he was being set up, like no matter what he did he'd come back through the curtain after the main event and he'd be fired on the spot. Patrick thought he was the scapegoat of some internal political battle. So he just did what Bischoff, his boss, told him to do, but admitted to making the count slightly quicker than usual. No one really noticed, because it wasn't a markedly fast count by any stretch.

Afterward, Patrick's fears were quelled. He said no one ever brought the situation up to him. And he himself didn't talk about it publicly for decades.

"Nobody said shit to me," Patrick said. "They're just like, 'Move on.' It's like, 'Oh, thank God we got past that moment.'"

The messy finish didn't make anyone look good. Not Hogan, not Sting, not Patrick. And especially not Bret Hart, who was a major star coming from the WWF and had a massive amount of sympathetic fan interest after being betrayed by McMahon.

Bret said he had been told it would be a fast count by Patrick and he would come out to make sure Sting wasn't getting swindled the way Bret did in real life. Instead, what ended up happening made Bret look foolish, since there was no skullduggery by Patrick to speak of.

"It just was a dumb, very flat, empty kind of idea that somebody that had no real brains tossed out," Bret Hart said. "And you just knew that nobody put any thought into this idea. It's nothing, and it's not going to blow anybody's mind. It's not worthy of what I represented at the time."

According to Hogan, the next day Sting got in Hogan's face at a gym and accused him of underhandedness regarding the finish of the match.

"I said, 'Bro, I didn't screw you on the finish—you didn't kick out,'" Hogan said. "Sting goes, 'Well, you're putting me over . . . on *Nitro*.' I said, 'Fine, no problem.'"

Bischoff said he had to perform "reconstructive surgery" to get the storyline back to making some semblance of sense. Had he been a doctor, he would have gotten sued for medical malpractice.

The next night on *Nitro*, the commentary team was hammering home the idea that Patrick made a fast count—which, of course, it was not—and that's why Bret Hart came out to intervene. Hogan and Bischoff did an interview during the show saying that Hogan had won honestly, and Bret Hart stuck his nose in where it didn't belong.

Dillon said later in the show that the final result of the *Starrcade* main event—Sting winning and getting the title—would stand. He said if Hogan and Bischoff had an issue, Sting was willing to defend the belt against anyone from the nWo in that night's main event.

So the rematch was on. Sting took on Hogan again, and the end result was not necessarily easier for anyone to wrap their heads around. *Nitro* went off the air as Sting landed a second Stinger Splash on Hogan in the corner and referee Randy Anderson got caught in the move, sending the ref to the ground.

The viewers at home never saw the finish to the match, and it was by design—a ploy for future ratings on a new show that would premiere more than a week later. Turner received many calls with complaints afterward. The whole thing was turning off all the fans they gained over the last year and a half.

On the first *Nitro* of 1998, Dillon said in an interview with Okerlund that Sting was still WCW champion at that very moment, and he apologized for *Nitro* the previous week going off the air before fans could see what happened in the match. He said the result was under investigation and WCW was not able to show it at that time, because the tape was in a judge's chambers.

And then came the hook. Dillon said the tape would be aired three days later, on WCW's new show, called *Thunder*.

The finish of Hogan vs. Sting from *Nitro* was finally shown on the *Thunder* premiere. After Randy Anderson was knocked out, Patrick ran in while Sting had Hogan in his Scorpion Death Lock submission. Sting dropped the hold and went after Patrick. Hogan then hit Sting with a foreign object and pinned him, while grabbing a handful of Sting's tights for leverage. Patrick gave Hogan the title belt and Sting went after Patrick again, clotheslining him.

The match seemed to then restart with Randy Anderson coming to. Sting put Hogan in the Scorpion Death Lock again and

Randy Anderson called for the bell, saying Hogan had given up and Sting was the winner.

Get all that? Even with a second chance to get things right and have the story make sense, WCW could not pull it off. There was more mess to come.

Dillon came out and took the belt. Bischoff followed him and grabbed the title, resulting in a tug of war. Bischoff kicked Dillon and Sting came from behind Bischoff and hit him with the Scorpion Death Drop. Hall and the rest of the nWo came down to the ring to beat up Sting before WCW wrestlers, led by Bret Hart, saved him. Randy Anderson held up Sting's arm as the apparent winner.

The camera then cut back live to *Thunder* with Dillon in the ring for an interview with commentator Mike Tenay. Dillon called out Sting and Hogan, who came out with Bischoff, Nash, Konnan, and Vincent. Dillon declared the title vacant. He asked for Sting to hand him the belt. Instead, Sting threw the title down on the floor in front of Dillon. Sting told Dillon, "You've got no guts," and told Hogan, "You, you're a dead man." That's how *Thunder* went off the air.

So after all that buildup, all that time and effort invested into Sting—and Hogan vs. Sting—the outcome was convoluted, at the most generous, and disastrous when it came to having any amount of credibility with the fanbase.

Starrcade 1997 was still an overwhelming business success. Ticket sales added up to a WCW record $543,000, and $161,961 of merchandise was sold, another record, Meltzer reported. The show was sold out and the paid attendance (16,052) was the most ever for a WCW show. The estimated pay-per-view buys were 700,000, which made it the highest-selling professional wrestling pay-per-view of all time at that point.

WCW had an all-time-high amount of people watching and delivered to them an all-time blunder.

"Just the fact that Sting doesn't speak for a year and a half and the first thing out of his mouth is something in Spanish—'*mamacita*,'" Nash said. "I mean, that's what he yells to the hard mic when he goes over. I'm just thinking to myself, 'Could you imagine if Neil Armstrong just took that step down [onto the moon] and was in it for himself, and said something about Coca-Cola?'

"[Hogan] had creative control. You can't give a wrestler creative control. Can't happen. Just can't happen. He doesn't have to do anything he doesn't want to do."

For nineteen months, going back to when Hall showed up on *Nitro* to start the nWo storyline, WCW had fans enraptured by how it was skillfully blurring the lines of reality and fiction, and making its product feel more adult.

And after building all that creative capital and credibility, the biggest night in company history ended with something so ridiculously farcical that it was almost like all that work was for naught.

Starrcade 1997 surely wasn't the end of the nWo's run of success—there were more record-setting shows and ratings numbers to come—but it could easily be labeled as the beginning of that inevitable end.

PART III

CHAPTER 11

THAT WAS THE DOWNFALL OF IT

Inside the Lawrence Joel Veterans Memorial Coliseum in Winston-Salem, North Carolina, Nash stomped down a hallway. Hall was right behind him. The two of them looked for Bischoff's makeshift office, which he had set up in the bowels of every arena for television shows. And they found it.

Nash didn't even knock. He kicked open the door. Bischoff was there behind a desk. Hall followed Nash into the room, closed the door behind him, and leaned on it so no one else could come in.

Hours earlier, on March 9, 1998, Bischoff had fired Waltman—via FedEx—while Waltman was home nursing a fractured vertebra.

"Fire our friend, why don't you fire us, too, motherfucker?" Nash said.

Hall and Nash believed Waltman's firing reeked of a political play, a way for Bischoff (and Hogan) to show them who the boss was.

Bischoff claimed it was something different. WCW and Waltman had a deal memo in place for a contract extension while Turner legal put together a finalized contract. Bischoff felt the agreement was done, a dead issue. Waltman disagreed and was hoping Barry Bloom, his agent, could get him more money.

Hall and Nash both got big raises going into the new year. Nash earned a base salary of $1,518,979 in 1998, and Hall made a base salary of $1,423,194. Waltman wanted to cash in on WCW's incredible business success.

Only Savage (thanks to Slim Jim), Bret Hart, and, of course, Hogan made more than Hall and Nash in WCW that year.

In 1998, Hogan's base salary was $3,788,061 plus a $2 million signing bonus. Hogan's contract also gave him 15 percent (or $675,000) of WCW pay-per-view sales for events he was on. Hogan got 25 percent of the gross ticket sales revenue for *Nitro* and *Thunder* episodes he appeared on, a figure that could not drop below $25,000 per appearance. The same applied for nontelevised house shows (without the $25,000 per appearance caveat). Hogan got 50 percent of merchandise sales on products using his name or likeness and $20,000 per month promoting the nWo as long as he remained a member of the group.

So one couldn't blame Waltman for trying to get a piece of the action. His annual salary was only $244,620 and he was a key member of the nWo. Waltman was a former WCW cruiserweight champion and important to the versatility of the group because of his considerable in-ring skills and willingness to take pins.

But Bischoff took Bloom's continued negotiations as an affront. There were also personal issues between Bischoff and Bloom. Bischoff believed he had an understanding with the agent that if Bischoff sent clients his way, he wouldn't try to drag him over the coals in negotiations.

Bischoff saw it as a betrayal, so he fired Waltman.

In an online Prodigy chat, Bischoff wrote that he only signed Waltman to make Hall and Nash happy, yet the two of them were still "negative and disruptive," therefore he didn't see any need in keeping Waltman around.

Was that something he said in character to sow storyline tension, or was it sincere? Hall and Nash thought the latter. Bischoff said it was likely the former, though he doesn't recall writing it.

"I was very guilty of merging work and reality," Bischoff said.

Throughout the early part of 1998, the big story on WCW television was internal division in the nWo. It started off with Nash and Savage at each other's throats and shifted into a beef between Hogan and Savage, which led to a full-fledged turn by Savage against Hogan.

Savage feuding with Hogan again in storyline was a meaningful twist. It showed who Hogan trusted to work opposite him at that stage and who Bischoff had faith in to carry a main-event program.

A few months prior, Bischoff had a meeting with all the wrestlers backstage and said, among other things, that the only people in the locker room who could bring in money were Hogan, Savage, and Piper.

That pissed several wrestlers off, like Hall and Nash, who felt the nWo's financial success was because of them. But Bischoff's remarks were indicative to many of where things were politically.

In on-air, storyline interviews during this time, Hogan and Bischoff downplayed that there was infighting going on in the nWo. They referred to it as a "right-wing conspiracy," making several references to Ken Starr's investigation at the time into then-president Bill Clinton's Whitewater scandal.

When Waltman was fired, things completely boiled over in real life. Hall and Nash stopped contributing creatively to WCW. Hall was off television shortly after due to more issues with his personal life and addictions. At one point, Hall and Nash wore WWF T-shirts under their clothes with the implied threat of The Outsiders revealing them on *Nitro*.

"That was the downfall of it," Hall said of Waltman's firing.

Nash added: "We took our ball and went home."

Bischoff said there were never any legitimate threats of quitting made by Hall and Nash, despite their anger.

"I mean, at the end of the day, if [Hall and Nash] would've failed to perform under the contract, I would have sued them for breach of contract," Bischoff said.

To no one's surprise, WCW took the political turmoil backstage and made it part of the storyline. There had always been plans for an nWo vs. nWo internal feud, but the battle lines were now being drawn somewhat along real-life lines. It was difficult to decipher whether the things being said on television were legitimate or in-character.

The *Uncensored* pay-per-view took place six days after Waltman's firing, in Mobile, Alabama, with Hogan vs. Savage in a steel cage as the main event. On the undercard, Giant beat Nash by disqualification when Brian Adams ran in to interfere. Adams was another recent addition to the nWo, coming over from the WWF where he played the character Crush. Hall got a title shot against Sting in the semi-main event, losing despite interference from Dusty Rhodes, who had also recently joined the nWo.

It was telling that Hogan vs. Savage was the headliner, not the WCW championship match, which was Sting vs. Hall. Sting had finally beaten Hogan to win the title a month earlier at *SuperBrawl*.

During the cage match, Hogan's old friend Ed Leslie, now playing a new character Hogan brought into the nWo called The Disciple, dragged Hogan to safety when Savage attempted an elbow drop off the top of the cage. The match ended in a no contest.

Leslie being back in the fold was an example of Hogan wanting to feature his pals and surround himself with allies, which was in sharp contrast to WCW dismissing Waltman. Hogan got his buddy back and Hall and Nash lost theirs.

———

Bischoff saw Hall before *Nitro* the next night. It was WCW's annual spring break episode at Club La Vela in Panama City Beach, Florida. Club La Vela was a gigantic outdoor nightclub with a pool inside it. The ring was placed in the middle of an island with water all around the ringside area, plus a bridge so wrestlers could get from the entranceway to their matches.

Bischoff asked Hall if he was "going in" before the show. Hall responded that he was—there was a plan for The Giant to pick him up and toss him into the pool during a segment.

Bischoff wasn't talking about the water. Bischoff was asking Hall if he was "going in" to rehab, which Hall did end up doing again for the second straight year.

There were some direct catalysts to Hall's condition in early 1998.

Hall had taken a wrestler named Louie Spicolli under his wing, in storyline and reality. Before a match with Spicolli, Hall gave one of his "survey time" promos that had gotten over big with audiences. He would ask the fans if they were there to see the nWo or WCW, which inevitably led to more cheers for the nWo. Spicolli told Hall that he was "here for the nWo," which led to Hall adopting him as his storyline "go-for."

Spicolli was a unique addition to the nWo. Though he wouldn't have been considered fat by regular standards, he was quite the contrast to Hall and Nash, two six-feet-five-and-up Adonises. Spicolli was a good wrestler and had spent some time working in the WWF,

ECW, and Mexico. He didn't get to show much of his in-ring skills in WCW, playing more of a comedy character—kind of like the wrestling version of Chris Farley.

There was a funny segment on *Thunder* where Spicolli stole Zbyszko's golf clubs and broke them during a Hall promo. A couple weeks later, Spicolli told Hall that he would fight his matches for him until Hall could get the title shot he earned. On the February 9, 1998, *Nitro*, Spicolli took Zbyszko's place on the broadcast team, saying the two had made up and Zbyszko had asked him to bring Zbyszko's bags to the arena. Zbyszko showed up later, chased Spicolli around the ring, and said he broke into his room, stole his stuff, and put him in the wrong car.

Six days after those segments and a week before what would have been a potentially huge career breakthrough in a scheduled match against Zbyszko at *SuperBrawl*, Spicolli died at the age of twenty-seven.

The official cause of death was an enlarged heart that brought on a heart attack, according to his sister Tina Mucciolo Peters. Spicolli was reportedly found by investigators at his Los Angeles home with an empty vial of testosterone, pain pills, and an anxiety-reducing drug at his bedside.

"It was a little frustrating to hear people say that he died of a drug overdose," Mucciolo Peters said. "But, after a while, it's like, I almost would rather people think that and use that as a cautionary tale than to say, 'Oh, it was not drug-related.' Because really it was."

Mucciolo Peters said her brother was going to go into rehab in the summer of 1997 when he got a call from Terry Taylor, the WCW official, about a job. The opportunity was too good to pass up for Spicolli, so he decided against rehab and signed with WCW.

To start *Nitro* the day after his death, a graphic was shown on screen acknowledging Spicolli's passing. Outside of an offhand remark by Schiavone on commentary later in the show, Spicolli was never mentioned in WCW again. Meltzer reported that everyone in the company was explicitly told not to bring his name up.

———

Nash walked out to the ring and interrupted Hogan's promo with Bischoff on the March 26, 1998, episode of *Thunder*. The segment blurred all lines between fiction and reality.

"You come out here week after week as the self-proclaimed leader of the nWo," Nash said to Hogan. "You're the man. But everybody knows that the heart and soul of the nWo is the Wolfpack. So I want to know, if you're the boss, why doesn't my buddy Syxx have a job anymore here? Why isn't Scott Hall on TV? What's up with that?"

Hogan replied: "As far as your little teeny buddy Syxx-Pac goes, it's not my fault that he can't cut the mustard and run with the rest of the nWo. And as far as your man Scott Hall goes, I don't have a clue where he's at. I thought maybe since you were like his best friend and stuff that you could let me in on the inside scoop."

Hogan and Nash teamed up at the next pay-per-view, *Spring Stampede*, three weeks later, in Denver. Their opponents were Piper and The Giant and the stipulation was that, in order to win, someone had to climb up a pole in the corner of the ring and grab a bat that was affixed there. Once one of the wrestlers wielded the bat, he could use it on his foes.

Hogan didn't end up making the climb. But he did use a bat given to him by The Disciple to hit Piper and get the win.

Afterward, Hogan tried to make peace with Nash—and then hit him in the back with the bat.

The *Spring Stampede* main event was Savage vs. Sting for the WCW title. Nash came out, powerbombed Sting, and put Savage on top of him while the referee was knocked out. Savage won to become champion. Hogan and The Disciple came down to the ring after the match, with Hogan saying to the camera that Nash couldn't do that and "that's my belt."

That action mostly marked the end of the first nWo story arc, at least the spirit of it. The nWo's goal was to take over WCW and it worked toward that goal for nearly two years. Ultimately, the nWo failed in storyline—with Sting getting the better of Hogan twice and winning the title and Hogan and Nash turning on each other.

With Hogan and Nash not seeing eye to eye behind the scenes, this could have been a good point to begin the endgame of the nWo story, to write a proper finale for the iconic group. But WCW was still hot, records were still being set, and there was more money to be squeezed out of those three letters graffitied on a black background.

The next night on *Nitro*, Savage did an interview in the ring and introduced Nash as the true leader of the nWo. The main event was Savage vs. Hogan for the belt and, sure enough, Hogan won to win the championship back with help from Bret Hart, who had apparently (and inexplicably) turned bad and joined the nWo. Nash tried to help Savage, but Bret Hart took him out.

Things were starting to get a bit confusing. But the following week brought some clarity.

Nash and Savage did a promo in the ring and referred to themselves as the Wolfpac. They still considered themselves part of the nWo, but this was a splinter group, one that was clearly going to be the babyface to counter Hogan's heel nWo. Nash was the leader of the Wolfpac and Konnan was introduced as the newest member.

A week later on *Nitro*, Nash, Savage, and Konnan came through the crowd during a match wearing nWo t-shirts. Except they didn't have the traditional white lettering on the black backdrop. These shirts were red and black, the new colors of the Wolfpac. Nash, Savage, and Konnan added another member in that segment: Hennig, who pulled off his white and black nWo shirt to reveal the red and black.

The crowd reacted very positively to the Wolfpac as good guys. There were now two nWo factions plus WCW, all battling one another. Jimmy Hart was actually one of the producers behind the Wolfpac theme music, which was completely different from the original nWo entrance. The Wolfpac song, fittingly, was a rap by hip-hop artist C-Murder. The chorus was: "Don't turn your back on the Wolfpac, you might wind up in a body bag."

"Wolfpac is back causin' mass destruction," the rap went. "Guess who's here? The bad boys of wrestling."

Konnan, who played an inner-city cholo character despite being born in Cuba, was one of the breakout stars of the Wolfpac. He was at least legitimately Latino, unlike Hall, and came off authentically urban and cool. Konnan would come out to the ring with a microphone and start chants in Spanish with catchphrases like "*¡Órale!*" and "*¡Arriba la raza!*"

His popularity was underrated. Konnan had white people in places like Kentucky and West Virginia chanting along with him in Spanish. WCW even got him his own music video where Konnan rapped himself, with the artist Mad One. At one point, Konnan was trying to make a phrase about "tossing salad" catch on, with the meaning evading censors and, largely, the fans.

"It was crazy," said Ross Forman, who worked for *WCW Magazine* and the promotion's creative team. "It was all for his work on the mic, whatever he would say. Half of it, the public probably didn't even understand because he'd be talking Spanish. Some of it he probably shouldn't have been saying. I can only imagine if there were subtitles. We probably would have been pulled off the air with some of the stuff he said."

––––––

The nWo splitting into separate Hollywood and Wolfpac groups was as much by necessity as it was due to creative decisions. David Crockett, a longtime WCW producer and the son of Jim Crockett of WCW predecessor Jim Crockett Promotions, said the fracture was more due to "personalities than storylines."

"You had some very powerful egos and personalities, and there was one [Hogan] that thought he should be the very best," Crockett said. "[Hall and Nash] didn't want to be second bananas to him. They wanted it to be the nWo, not Hogan's nWo. . . . Hogan had [Bischoff] in his pocket."

Bischoff admitted he could be guilty of erring on the side of Hogan at times. Because it was Hulk Hogan, after all—the biggest financial draw in pro-wrestling history. The pissing contest Nash and Hogan seemed to be in—over the soul and spiritual ownership of the nWo—he chalked up to something else.

"It's kind of like a marriage," Bischoff said. "It starts out great. You're dating, going on that first date and going on that second date. Things are going really good. Sex is awesome. You're having fun, have a lot of things in common. Life is great. And then it gets to real life.

"Kevin and Hulk, [it's like] once the new car smell of the nWo wore off, then it became what? 'It's all about me. What's in it for me?' Because that's the nature of the business. How do you keep yourself over? How do you keep yourself from being overshadowed by somebody else, so that you can keep your equity right at a high level, so that if you have to go somewhere else, you can? That's the nature of the business that people don't really understand completely."

Hogan and Nash came to something of a détente, leading two separate nWo factions. The idea of an nWo civil war had promise, even if it was a departure from the group's original motivations.

There was big money and real-life bad blood in a potential Hogan vs. Nash match—if the two were able to set their egos aside and work together.

CHAPTER 12

BLEEP BOB COSTAS

Triple H stood in the ring during *WWF Monday Night Raw* with Chyna, his female bodyguard character, behind him. He said he was ushering in a new era of the D-Generation X group by starting an army.

And when you start an army, Triple H said, "the first thing you do is you look to your blood, you look to your buddies, you look to your friends. You look . . . to The Kliq."

The D-X music hit and Waltman walked out, wearing a black leather jacket and bandana, looking very much like his character Syxx in WCW. Back in the WWF, just three weeks after Bischoff fired him, Waltman would take the name X-Pac.

Triple H handed Waltman the microphone, saying he had been an "indentured servant for two years." Waltman took it and looked into the camera.

"I heard Hulk Hogan come out on television, saying I couldn't cut the mustard," Waltman said. "Well, Hulk Hogan—you suck, pal. So I don't think you have any room to talk about anybody cutting any kind of mustard. And Hulk, I got some more advice for you. You better not stop short, or Eric Bischoff will go so far up your ass he'll know what you had for breakfast."

Waltman continued: "Kevin Nash and Scott Hall would be standing here with us if they weren't being held hostage by World

Championship Wrestling. And that's a fact, Eric Bischoff. So put that in your pipe and smoke it."

The crowd went crazy, because it felt like they were listening in on something they weren't supposed to be hearing. Waltman had gone on what was supposed to be a scripted WWF television show and blasted Hogan, Bischoff, and WCW, stunning viewers and further adding fuel to the still-simmering backstage feud between Hogan and Nash.

The fourth wall hadn't just been knocked down, it had been eviscerated. To the delight of fans.

Waltman was called in for a deposition in the lawsuit between the WWF and WCW after the promo. He was asked why he made that statement about Hall and Nash, and Waltman responded: "Well, I was talking to Kev the night before and he told me it would be a good idea if I said that."

Waltman was speaking completely from the heart on *Raw*. And now the WWF had turned the tables on WCW, using real-life situations and blending them with wrestling storylines the way Bischoff had when he countered the Billionaire Ted skits with the nWo. It was unabashedly successful, too.

Since the Montreal Screwjob, McMahon had become an evil authority figure character on screen, a caricature of himself. He was opposed mainly by Steve Austin, the goateed, bald-headed, beer-swilling, ass-whupping everyman who fans could not wait to see give the bullying boss his retribution. Austin had the same anti-establishment chops the nWo did and he took things to another level. His trademark gesture wasn't a Turkish wolf or demonstrating "4" and "life" with his hands. It was a pair of middle fingers.

Austin said one night before *Raw*, McMahon came to him and

said Diamond Dallas Page in WCW was using the diamond sign gesture with his hands, putting together his pointer fingers and thumbs and holding it up. McMahon asked if there was anything Austin could do like that, rather than giving people essentially a "fuck you" every Monday.

"I looked at him, I thought about it for two seconds and I said, 'No,'" Austin said. "I kept flying the middle finger, and it worked."

The difference was the nWo were the bad guys; Austin was very much supposed to be the good guy, yet he was every bit as violent and profane as the heels, if not more so. This was a cultural touchstone. Austin wasn't the first disrespectful asshole in entertainment that people rooted for. But he was representative of what was starting to become the norm. The Punisher had become the new Captain America. American audiences had rejected political correctness and embraced the insolent, in a similar way that many believe they are rejecting "woke culture" decades later.

Journalists at the time wrote that pro wrestling was no longer entertainment for the whole family, as it had been in the 1980s. Kirk Johnson penned a *New York Times* article in March 1998 with the headline "PROFESSIONAL WRESTLING CUTS GOOD GUYS FROM THE SCRIPT."

There were no heroes anymore in the WWF and WCW. Just antiheroes and villains and the line was even blurry between which was which half the time. The nWo was the catalyst to it all.

"The crowds that go to see the top stars, whether they be Austin, Hulk Hogan, Kevin Nash & Scott Hall, Shawn Michaels or whomever else, are going to see their heroes that have been popularized in both companies by doing weekly anti-social behavior and getting away with it," Meltzer wrote. "No rules and no limits. Fans who rally behind those wrestling cultural symbols, whether they be young kids, or more violence prone older teens and early 20s males, are going to emulate that behavior."

The only man in sports or entertainment at the time to embody that culture more than pro-wrestling stars was controversial boxer Mike Tyson. So of course, in 1998 the WWF brought in Tyson, the king of pay-per-view who was less than a year removed from biting Evander Holyfield's ear during a fight. Tyson, who previously had spent three years in prison on rape charges, was suspended at the time from boxing due to that incident, but he was cleared by the Nevada State Athletic Commission (NSAC) to perform in wrestling.

The *WrestleMania XIV* main event on March 29, 1998, in Boston, had Michaels defending the WWF championship against Austin with Tyson as the special referee. Austin won the title, Tyson punched out Michaels, and Tyson held up Austin's arm as the show went off the air.

The bad boy of boxing had helped christen Austin, pop culture's next bad boy. Meltzer referred to it in the *Observer* as "the coronation of Steve Austin as the new Hulk Hogan," the WWF's leading man. But boy, the messaging of 1980s Hogan and 1990s Austin could not have been more different.

Off the momentum from *WrestleMania* (which did monster numbers at the box office and on pay-per-view), Waltman's barbs, and, primarily, the work of Austin and McMahon, *Raw* snapped *Nitro*'s eighty-three-week ratings winning streak on April 13, 1998. The entire episode teased a match between Austin and McMahon, though ultimately it never actually happened when Dude Love (Mick Foley) attacked Austin to close the show.

Two weeks later on *Raw*, the newly restructured D-X—Triple H, Waltman, the New Age Outlaws (Road Dogg and Billy Gunn), and Chyna—"invaded" *Nitro*.

They piled into a military jeep that had a rocket launcher in the back and caused some chaos outside the arena where WCW was holding its show in Norfolk, Virginia. All five were wearing military paraphernalia, including camouflage and helmets. *Raw* was being held just twenty-five minutes down the road in Hampton.

Triple H had a megaphone and yelled things like "WCW sucks." The group asked fans outside if they had gotten free tickets and got them to chant "D-X, D-X!"

At one point, D-X drove the jeep down toward the loading dock of the Norfolk Scope, where WCW was holding its show, but the large metal door came down before they could get inside. At the entrance, Triple H and Waltman called for Hall and Nash. Triple H boomed into the megaphone, "Let my people go!"

In reality, D-X invaded in the afternoon before the show—it was still light outside. But the taped skit got the point across. A few weeks later, D-X did something similar outside the WCW office building in the Atlanta suburbs and the cops were called.

The WWF had become the daring promotion, the one willing to take things to a different, unseen level in pro wrestling. The WWF, led by Austin, Tyson, and D-X, had become the cooler, edgier product.

Bischoff and the nWo might have started that movement, but McMahon upped the ante.

"I always say, we built the Saturn V [rocket] and we all sat there, and we were getting ready to take off to the moon," Nash said. "And Vince showed up on the top there and before they all got in the capsule, Vince gave them a boot over the side and goes, 'I got it from here.'"

Of course, Bischoff wasn't going to let that stand. Being the martial artist he was, he had a counter to the counterpunch.

On the May 11, 1998, *Nitro*, Bischoff came to the ring alone. He said the D-X "wannabes" were just doing the bidding of McMahon. Bischoff called Waltman a "little puppet" and said he wasn't going to apologize for firing him.

To cap it off, Bischoff said he would be in the WWF's backyard that following Sunday. The WCW pay-per-view *Slamboree* was going to take place in Worcester, Massachusetts, not far from the WWF's Connecticut headquarters. Bischoff challenged McMahon to a match: "You and me in the ring, how about it, Vinny?" Bischoff said he'd be waiting and "I'm gonna knock you out."

The Turner legal team had been breathing down Bischoff's neck since the WWF sued WCW in 1996, but Bischoff got that challenge cleared, as ridiculous as it was. Three days after calling out McMahon, Bischoff did another promo on *Thunder*, reading from a legal letter sent to WCW that said Bischoff had no authority to suggest McMahon would be at the pay-per-view. Bischoff said McMahon didn't have the guts to show up.

At *Slamboree*, on May 17, 1998, Bischoff came out wearing a cutoff black nWo shirt and wrapped hands. Buffer did the ring introductions, including for McMahon, calling him "the man who considers himself the most important star in the WWF." McMahon, obviously, did not come out. Referee Mickey Jay counted to ten and Buffer announced Bischoff as the winner by forfeit and disqualification.

McMahon did respond to Bischoff's callout in a statement on the WWF website, spelling Bischoff's name wrong twice.

"I consider Eric Bichoff's [sic] Challenge a cheap and desperate tactic to increase WCW PPV Buys," McMahon wrote. "I will not do anything to help WCW increase their PPV Buys. Therefore, I will not appear at Turner's next PPV as invited. However, if Mr. Bichoff [sic] is hell bent on fighting me, then such a fight can be arranged at any time, in any parking lot in the country, void of television cameras, photographers and public announcement."

Bischoff wasn't sure what McMahon would do when he called him out. Hogan and Savage both told him they thought McMahon would answer the challenge. Bischoff said he actually had a strategy if McMahon did show up and fight him. McMahon was six-foot-two and well over 200 pounds of muscle. He had been lifting weights for years. Bischoff was around five-foot-ten and 190 pounds, but he was a decade younger—forty-two years old to McMahon's fifty-two then—and a black belt despite not having trained for some time.

"My goal was to stay away from him and tire him out, because he was so big, and he probably didn't have great cardio," Bischoff said. "Because he put all his emphasis on building his body. If you don't build your cardio to go along with it, you're going to gas out in about two minutes. So I would've just moved around, moved around, and then I would've gone for his legs first. Chopped them down, chopped them down, and then take them out."

Bischoff said back then he was "pretty sure" he would have beaten McMahon had they fought. Decades later, after having gotten to know McMahon, he's not quite as confident. McMahon might not have had a martial arts pedigree, but his tenacity and toughness stood out to Bischoff.

"Occasionally you come across real street fighters," Bischoff said. "And Vince is one of those. And, technically, I was probably pretty capable at the time, but Vince is enough of a street animal that he might have overcome that."

———

The nWo civil war was heating up in the spring of 1998 into the summer. The battle lines had been drawn, and consumed almost every major player in WCW. Sting and Luger had joined up with Nash, Savage, Konnan, Hennig, and Rude as part of the nWo Wolf-pac. Both got huge ovations when they put on their red and black shirts for the first time.

For Hogan's black-and-white team, The Giant made a surprising turn out of a storyline hatred for Nash. Bischoff, Disciple, Scott Steiner, Bagwell, Adams, Norton, Vincent, and Rhodes rolled with nWo Hollywood, which also inexplicably added Hall at *Slamboree* when Hall turned on Nash. Bret Hart had become an associate member of the nWo, but even he wasn't sure decades later if he was ever a full-fledged member of the group due to the creative disarray.

It made sense that top babyfaces like Sting and Luger would be positioned opposite Hogan, but it left very few stars to represent WCW.

At the time, Flair was being sued by the promotion for missing dates. Diamond Dallas Page was a stalwart and Bill Goldberg, a former University of Georgia and Atlanta Falcons football player, had become insanely popular starting in early 1998. Goldberg was kind of WCW's answer to Austin—all business, intense, goateed and baldheaded, wearing only black trunks and black boots to wrestle. He had a legit badass aura about him and raw charisma.

WCW had built Goldberg up with a long undefeated streak and it was working, so much so that Meltzer believes if Goldberg had not gotten so hot in 1998, then WCW's decline would have come sooner.

But no one really wanted to see Hall and Nash in opposing factions, let alone feuding with each other. An intra-nWo battle could have worked. Hogan and Savage—the Mega Powers—against The Outsiders would have made money. But WCW's choice—and the speculation among many behind the scenes was that it was Hogan's choice—was to split Hall and Nash up. "The Wolfpack" was a name Hall came up with for himself, Nash, and Waltman. And now Hall wasn't even in the storyline Wolfpac group to start.

Nash felt that Hall picking Hogan over him "would have never happened" in actuality, so WCW had lost the tie to realism it had tried to cultivate for two years. Fans just simply did not buy the idea that Hall and Nash would be against each other without a compelling reason given to them.

Hogan got paid based on pay-per-view buys and where he was on the card, which Nash was not aware of until much later. That explained in part some of the chaotic machinations behind the scenes. Hogan was looking out for his paycheck, which Nash did not get at the time.

"Well, it would've been nice if he would've told me fucking years ago and I wouldn't have tried to wrap my brain around why we couldn't get anything done," Nash said. "And why you kept saying 'doesn't work for me, brother,' when you should have said 'doesn't work for me financially, brother.' It would've made a big difference."

———

Michael Jordan took a jump shot from the three-point line that caromed off the rim into the hands of Dennis Rodman. It was Game 6 of the NBA Finals on June 14, 1998, and the Bulls were on the road against the Utah Jazz.

Rodman tried to dribble away, but Jazz star Karl Malone reached in and knocked the ball loose. He and Rodman got tangled up and both men fell to the floor as the ball came out. Rodman and Malone tried getting up, but their limbs became intertwined again, sending them back down. Then it happened a third time.

When they finally got up, Malone started running toward the

other side of the court and Rodman got in his way. The two collided, sending both down to the hardwood again. Rodman was called for a foul.

Mark Madden, the wrestling journalist who became a WCW Hotline host, said he got a call from a friend who worked at WCW after the game who told him: "Look, the boys did it."

Did what? Madden responded. His friend told him about Rodman and Malone, who had brought their impending professional wrestling storyline to what ended up being the deciding game of the NBA's championship series.

"We compromised the NBA Finals," Madden said.

Earlier in the basketball season, the Jazz were playing a game in Houston against the Rockets. Diamond Dallas Page was in the city for an autograph signing, and someone hooked him and Ross Forman up with tickets to the game. Malone saw Page in the stands and threw up the diamond sign with his hands as an acknowledgment. The two had never met before and Page and Forman were shocked Malone knew who Page was. Malone, then one of the NBA's biggest stars, was a massive pro-wrestling fan.

"Ross Forman shit his pants," Page said.

Page and Malone met after the game, exchanged numbers, and started talking on the phone regularly. Malone got Page tickets to the All-Star Game that year. After Bischoff told him that Rodman was coming back to WCW, Page started recruiting Malone.

"I told [Malone], 'I know you want to do this shit,'" Page said. "I said, 'What about me and you against Rodman and Hogan?' I said, 'Would you have a problem with that?' He goes, 'No.' He goes, 'That might be interesting.' I go, 'Well, think about it. I'm gonna run it by Eric, but I didn't want to do it without your blessing.' He's like, 'No, go ahead and run it by him. We'll see what happens.'"

Bischoff was able to broker the deal during a meeting with Malone and his wife, Kay Kinsey, in the kitchen of their Salt Lake City home.

Rodman returned on the June 8, 1998, *Nitro* in Auburn Hills, Michigan. He was part of a segment with Hogan, Bischoff, and Bret Hart where he hit a button with the Wolfpac in the ring that set off pyro fireworks from the four corner turnbuckles. Later on the show, Rodman was with Hogan and Bischoff and a few women in a VIP suite where it appeared that they were drinking champagne. Nash had a promo after that, asking Rodman why he was hanging out with "White Boys 'R' Us." To cap the episode, Hogan and Rodman, who was wearing plaid pajama pants, attacked Page with chairs.

The story with Rodman, though, wasn't so much about where he was and what he was doing. It was about where he was supposed to be and what he was supposed to be doing.

Rodman showed up on *Nitro* with the nWo right smack in the middle of the NBA Finals. A day earlier, the Bulls defeated the Jazz in Game 3. And the next day, after hanging out with Hogan on TV, Rodman "overslept" and missed practice, according to Manley, his then-agent.

Manley said Rodman had permission from Bulls general manager Jerry Krause and Bulls coach Phil Jackson to appear on *Nitro*. But he did not have permission to miss the following day's practice. Manley said Rodman "had too much fun the night before." Rodman was fined $10,000 by the NBA for missing practice and an undisclosed amount by the Bulls.

For WCW, it was another publicity coup. Rodman's shenanigans on *Nitro* made every major television sports segment and all the big newspapers. And then, with Rodman and Hogan versus Malone and Page set for the upcoming *Bash at the Beach* pay-per-view, Bischoff had the idea to use the NBA Finals as a means to promote the match.

It was a tricky situation. Turner was one of the NBA's broadcast partners, and Bischoff's direct boss, Harvey Schiller, was the head of Turner Sports. Had Schiller known what Bischoff wanted to do, "Harvey might have shot me in his office," Bischoff said.

So Bischoff spoke to Rodman and Malone before the game. He made it clear that he didn't want them to do anything that would affect the outcome. (The Bulls ended up winning the decisive Game 6 to capture the NBA title.) But if there was an opportunity after a whistle when the ball was dead, Bischoff told them, "Don't hit each other, just let us know you don't like each other."

"That's all I said," Bischoff said. "And they took it from there."

Many would argue that Rodman and Malone got physical with each other down low in the paint just about every game. But while that was true, Manley acknowledged that Bischoff's recollection has validity.

"[The wrestling storyline] 100 percent changed the dynamic between them," Manley said. "Look at the other eleven games [they played against one another]. Never had it like that."

Legendary sports broadcaster Bob Costas, on commentary during the game, took a dig at Rodman and Malone, saying they are "regrettably scheduled to wrestle in one of those bogus events next month.

"Why Malone wants to lower himself to that is anyone's guess," Costas said. "And Rodman apparently wants to start the wrestling now."

There was nothing Costas could do. "Bogus" pro wrestling had affixed itself to a game that included Jordan, one of the most culturally significant human beings of the 1990s or any other decade.

Hogan and Rodman versus Page and Malone was officially announced at a press conference in mid-June 1998. Malone called
Hogan a "coward" for hitting Page from behind. Hogan said Rodman
was going to beat Malone "in the ring like he beat him on the court."

Malone made his first WCW television appearance on the
June 29, 1998, *Nitro*. He and Page rode on one of Malone's semi
trucks, a big rig, into the arena in Tampa, sending waiting nWo
members fleeing.

Malone and Page hit the ring, where Hogan and Bischoff were
waiting, with chairs. Malone and Hogan had a stare-down. Hogan
went for a handshake and Malone slapped his hand away. The two
men locked up. Malone tied Hogan in a choke and then slammed
Hogan down. The crowd went crazy. Malone, clearly an exceptional athlete, followed with two clotheslines, sending Hogan out
of the ring.

Behind the scenes, things weren't nearly as acrimonious, of
course. Malone had come to Atlanta to train to wrestle at the WCW
Power Plant facility. Page, along with two wrestlers Page respected
for their ability to put on good matches in the ring, Chris Kanyon
and Billy Kidman, coached the basketball star. Before the pay-per-
view, Page, Malone, and those two flew to Southern California to
work out the match with Hogan and Rodman. Manley said Bischoff
sent out a truck with a wrestling ring in it that got put together in a
building for rehearsals.

Hogan's philosophy was always to call matches in the ring. In
other words, he didn't like to script or choreograph things too much.
He preferred to listen to the crowd and adapt on the fly while out
there. Hogan simply could not do that with two novices in Malone
and Rodman, otherwise everyone was risking injury.

Page, on the other hand, always laid out his matches move for move, hold for hold. So Hogan told Page what he wanted to do in the match and Page wrote it all out for the four of them to practice, which didn't go over perfectly well.

"I really liked Dennis, but he was a different cat," Page said. "He did not like to practice."

The *Nitro* before the pay-per-view, a week after Malone's first appearance, was one of the biggest ones ever, in front of 41,412 people at the Georgia Dome. Not only was WCW pointing toward the big *Bash at the Beach* main event, but Hogan was going to defend his WCW title against the red-hot Goldberg.

First, Goldberg had to beat Hall to earn the challenge, which he did—something Hall wasn't very happy about, given how green Goldberg was. He had not even been wrestling on television for a year yet at that point.

In the main event, Hennig, who had turned on the Wolfpac and joined up with nWo Hollywood, came down to ringside to help Hogan. Page and Malone came out behind Hennig. Malone gave Hennig a Diamond Cutter, Page's finishing move, where you grab an opponent by the back of their head over your own shoulder and pull their body down to the mat.

Goldberg landed a Spear tackle on Hogan, who was distracted by what was happening outside the ring. Goldberg then lifted Hogan up for a Jackhammer, a suplex-powerslam hybrid, and pinned him cleanly to become WCW champion. The crowd in Atlanta came unglued.

Goldberg's wrestling record moved to 108-0 with the victory, it was announced on commentary, which was a completely made-up number. But the undefeated streak, an idea partly thought up by WCW broadcaster Mike Tenay, was a genius marketing strategy.

That *Nitro* was perhaps the most significant one of all time. It set the WCW records for attendance, ticket sales ($906,330), and merchandise sales (around $300,000), Meltzer reported. But the criticism was that Hogan losing the title like that and crowning Goldberg as the new potential face of WCW could have made a whole lot more money on pay-per-view with a more defined storyline.

Critics felt like it was a hasty move as a result of *Raw* starting to win the Monday ratings battle. Bischoff said such assessments didn't make sense.

"We're already making money hand over fist," Bischoff said. "It wasn't like we were desperate for revenue. And the core mission of WCW was to deliver television ratings for the network. It should be so fucking obvious to people."

Bash at the Beach took place July 12, 1998, in San Diego. The morning of the show, Manley had breakfast with Malone and asked how much Malone was getting paid to do the match. Malone told him $900,000, a figure he was proud of getting. Malone didn't have an agent at the time, but negotiated with Bischoff with the help of Jazz owner Larry Miller. Manley told Malone that Rodman was getting $1,500,000 and Malone ended up hiring Manley as his agent.

"He would have [wrestled] for free," Manley said of Malone. "He loved it. He would watch it at home. He'd have vanilla cream waffle cookies and watch it from home—he loved it."

The match itself was not as impressive as Rodman's debut a year earlier, but it didn't have to be. Rodman wore a white "Rodzilla" T-shirt that had his head on it and the nWo logo stamped onto his blond hair. The shirt was still popular three decades later. Top boxer Devin Haney wore it during media interviews in 2023. Malone, meanwhile, wore purple spandex pants, similar to the ones worn by Page. He looked like a real wrestler and comported himself quite well.

Hogan and Rodman beat on Page for a good portion of the match before Malone got the hot tag—a fresh babyface finally getting into the match to help his ailing partner—and cleaned house. Malone clotheslined Hogan twice, clotheslined Rodman, and body-slammed both of them pretty easily. In an old-school sequence, Malone grabbed the heads of Rodman and Hogan and cracked them into each other, to the delight of the crowd.

The finish of the match wasn't as satisfying for the fans. The Disciple hit his finishing move on Page with the referee distracted and Hogan got the pin for the victory.

Malone, not knowing what happened, hit Disciple with the Diamond Cutter, Page's finisher, and raised his hand like he won. Charles Robinson, the referee, took umbrage at that, so Malone gave him a Diamond Cutter as well.

Rodman did not do much in the match. Some speculated that he might have been under the influence of something recreational. He was partying quite a bit during that time period. But Bischoff said Rodman was neither drunk nor high.

"He might have been hungover," Bischoff said.

The action might not have been anything memorable, but the business was. *Bash at the Beach 1998* sold an estimated 580,000 pay-per-view units, making it the second-biggest WCW pay-per-view ever, behind *Starrcade 1997*.

Rodman and Malone having a match against each other garnered a ton of mainstream press. Most major newspapers picked up the story, including the New York *Daily News*, which ran a quote from Malone referencing how a certain famous sports broadcaster chided him for getting involved with pro wrestling.

"Excuse my French, but bleep Bob Costas," Malone told journalist Bob Raissman. "I say bleep him."

CHAPTER 13

ONE OF THEM, I KNEW, HAD A GUN

While WCW and the WWF were in a back-and-forth brawl for ratings on Monday nights, Jay Leno was in a similar position in late-night television.

Leno, a New York–born standup comic, took over as host of *The Tonight Show* on NBC from Johnny Carson in 1992. Carson had built the program into one of the most prestigious on American television and himself into the king of late-night TV. *The Tonight Show*, hosted by Carson, helped launch the careers of many influential 1990s small-screen stars like Jerry Seinfeld, Ellen DeGeneres, and Roseanne Barr.

Carson, a quick-witted comedian and talented interviewer, gave way to Leno after thirty years as host in a surprise passing of the torch. Many figured David Letterman, whose late-night show followed Carson's on NBC, was the heir apparent. Letterman, spurned by his longtime network, jumped to CBS to start a new program, *Late Show with David Letterman*.

Late Show went head-to-head with *The Tonight Show* hosted by Leno, beginning a multidecade battle for late-night ratings supremacy.

The battle was one-sided after 1994, though always close. Leno, who averaged around five million viewers per night, emerged as the new champion of the 11:35 p.m. Eastern time slot with the key eighteen-to-forty-nine demographic.

Leno and his producers understood what 1990s audiences wanted. Letterman, detractors said, was too highbrow, an elitist. Leno, a frumpy everyman with a memorably large chin, connected better with the average American. His humor wasn't necessarily lowbrow, but his *Tonight Show* went to places others might not have. It was Leno's interview with English actor Hugh Grant following Grant's arrest for soliciting a prostitute for oral sex that helped launch his dominance over Letterman.

Gary Considine was the executive producer of NBC Studios in the 1990s. He was a longtime pro-wrestling fan. When he was a producer for Carson's *Tonight Show* in the eighties, Considine was partly responsible for Hogan's appearance as a guest, even before his rise to stardom at *WrestleMania I*. Considine was such a fan that he looked out the window of his Burbank, California, office every five minutes that afternoon to try and catch a glimpse of the statuesque Hogan.

In the mid-to-late-1990s, with Leno as host, several wrestlers, mostly from WCW, were guests on the highly rated late-night show. Hogan, Savage, Page, and Bret Hart were among the names to appear. Leno enjoyed chatting with them, never talking down to the wrestlers by suggesting that what they did for a living was fake. And more important for NBC, the ratings would spike when a WCW star came on, beginning in 1996. That was the power of pro wrestling during the nWo era. Fans would follow their favorites to whatever program they might have been on.

Seeing that trend, Considine reached out to Bischoff and proposed the idea of a more formal partnership between WCW and *The Tonight Show*. That meant more wrestlers would come on more frequently. Bischoff agreed, and some of the promotion for Hogan and Rodman versus Page and Malone took place on the program.

As Considine had hoped, *The Tonight Show* benefited from the ratings. That prompted him and producer Debbie Vickers to sit down and try to come up with an idea to further expand the relationship.

Considine doesn't remember if it was he or Vickers, but one of them blurted out the question: "Do you think Jay will wrestle?"

Considine brought the idea to Bischoff first, and the WCW exec "loved it," Considine said. Then the producer pitched it to Leno himself. Somewhat to Considine's surprise, Leno went for it without hesitation.

"I said, 'Oh yeah, let's do it. It'll be funny—it'd be fun, you know?'" Leno recalled. "There wasn't [anything] like, 'Well, as host, it might be beneath me.' No, shut up. No, it's funny. I think it's something Carson might even have done back in the day."

Rodman and Malone wrestling was such a great success for WCW that Bischoff was happy to go to the celebrity well again one month later.

The storyline was set up by Bischoff's character having a make-shift talk-show set constructed, complete with a desk, sofas for guests, and a band beginning in the summer of 1998. Bischoff would crack obnoxious, cringe-worthy jokes, many of them directed at Leno on these *Nitro* segments. The attacks, according to the story WCW was telling, got under Leno's skin so much that he, one of the most recognized men in the country, had to come out from behind his own desk and deal with things in the squared circle.

Leno was not an athlete and obviously had no prior wrestling training. He would not have been able to have a one-on-one match. At least not a good one. Bischoff came up with the idea of doing Page and Leno against Hogan and Bischoff himself. All the parties agreed, and it was booked for the main event of the *Road Wild* pay-per-view show.

Leno did not appear at all on *Nitro* to promote the match, like Rodman and Malone did. He didn't really need to since he had his own show and following. Two months earlier, *The Tonight Show* had nearly fifteen million viewers tune in for an interview with Jerry Seinfeld.

A week before the pay-per-view, Leno and his bandleader, Kevin Eubanks, had a discussion on *The Tonight Show* about Hogan and Bischoff talking trash about Leno on *Nitro*. Leno brought out a short man dressed like Hogan, complete with a dyed-blond Fu Manchu, black bandana, and nWo tank top. The faux Hogan left the set on a kid's bicycle that was dressed up like a motorcycle. But then the real Hogan and Bischoff came storming onto the stage.

Hogan said Leno crossed the line with his jokes and shoved Leno. Eubanks came over to hold Leno back. But Leno took a swipe at Bischoff. Eubanks took Leno off the set and Bischoff and Hogan took over *The Tonight Show*.

The show came back from commercial with Bischoff sitting in Leno's host chair and his feet up on the desk. Hogan was in the primary guest's seat with his feet up on a stool. The nWo had taken over the country's most popular late-night show.

Leno and Eubanks came back onto the set with cops and then Page appeared and jumped Hogan from behind. Hogan and Bischoff were eventually taken away. Page stuck around, said he would train Leno—"Who do you think trained Malone?"—and Leno eventually agreed to the match, which in reality was already planned.

The Tonight Show featuring the nWo's takeover was one of Leno's biggest margins of victory against Letterman: two whole ratings points, 4.8 to 2.8.

Obviously, Leno wasn't going to do much in the match, but he still needed to train, or he'd hurt himself or someone else. Page had Kanyon, Kidman, Erik Watts, and Shane Helms stay out in Los Angeles in the weeks leading up to *Road Wild*. Leno trained twice or three times a week for about a month. WCW rented out a space and put up a ring for the sessions. Leno didn't get hurt at all during training, and Page said the plan was never for him to take any real falls.

"I got bounced around a little bit, but that's OK," Leno said. "Please. It was show business."

Eubanks, who was going to be in the corner of Page and Leno for the match with the plan for him to get physical, was not as lucky. The wrestlers were teaching him how to do Page's Diamond Cutter, and Eubanks didn't kick his legs out enough to land flat on his back. Eubanks said he didn't tell anyone he was hurt, but when he was driving home he wasn't able to turn his neck.

"On that side of it, you've got to take it seriously," Eubanks said. "What I did, though, was mess myself up a little bit, but it went away after a few days. So it wasn't serious or anything. But I knew better. Whenever I do that again: kick your legs out."

Leno had his own mishap, just not in the ring. The *Road Wild* pay-per-view took place every year at the huge motorcycle rally in Sturgis, South Dakota. Leno was an avid motorcycle rider, but didn't bring his own bike. He was flown out by WCW on a Gulfstream jet. The morning of the show, a bunch of WCW people went out riding their bikes around the city with a Hells Angels escort. Edwards, the stunt coordinator, let Leno and his wife, Mavis, use one of his bikes.

"We didn't get fucking two hundred feet down the strip and everybody's going crazy," said Edwards, who was riding another motorcycle in front of the Lenos. "So I think [fans] see who he is. No, he fell off my motorcycle. He put the brakes on, and it fell over."

Edwards said Leno "can ride the shit out of a motorcycle," but he just wasn't used to the high-performance bikes Edwards had with him. Edwards dropped his own motorcycle immediately—didn't even put the kickstand on—and ran back to Leno and Mavis.

"I'm like, 'Eric's gonna fucking kill me,'" Edwards said. "And I don't really give a shit about Eric as much as I'm just so concerned about [the Lenos]."

They were fine. Leno, Edwards said, offered to write him a check for any damage to the bike, but Edwards declined. They were all sponsored motorcycles anyway.

Road Wild took place August 8, 1998. Leno came out for the main-event match holding a coffee cup and wearing a light blue *Tonight Show* T-shirt, dark blue track pants, and a bomber jacket. Eubanks wore a white tuxedo shirt. He asked WCW's wardrobe people to cut off the sleeves. Those who didn't know who he was could have taken him for one of the wrestlers. Eubanks worked out quite a bit and had surprisingly large, muscular arms.

Leno did basic things in the bout. He twisted Hogan's arm, got some punches in on Bischoff, and threw Bischoff into the corner turnbuckle repeatedly. Eubanks factored heavily into the finish of the match. He landed a Diamond Cutter on Bischoff—as rehearsed—and Page put Leno on top of Bischoff for the pin and victory.

Hogan and Bischoff attacked Page, Leno, and Eubanks afterward, but Goldberg came in for the save and speared Hogan and Bischoff. Goldberg raised the hands of Page, Leno, and Eubanks to cap the event.

There were no paid tickets to the event, because it was part of the annual Sturgis rally. But the pay-per-view numbers were strong again, an estimated 365,000 buys. It was one of the ten biggest WCW pay-per-views of all time. But it was also the night when things in WCW started to come apart at the seams.

———

Hogan and Nash had a lot in common aside from being larger-than-life pro-wrestling stars.

While they might have had an affinity for the art as kids, neither man dreamed of being a pro wrestler. They had other, more prominent loves. Hogan played the bass and wanted to be in a rock band. Nash was a basketball player, good enough (and dedicated enough) to earn a Division I scholarship.

As adults, pro wrestling became a means to an end for both of them. And that end was money.

Professional wrestling was purely a capitalistic endeavor for Hogan and Nash. They treated it like a business and told anyone else who would listen that was how wrestling should be treated. They surely fell in love with wrestling, but the business of wrestling above all else. Keeping things in that context was more than a small part of both of their successes.

The problem with that philosophy is there is an inherent selfishness that has to exist. And wrestling, if nothing else, is a collaborative endeavor. Every night, wrestlers trust their opponents—their coworkers—with their bodies in the ring. Something can go wrong at any time, leading to long-term injury, paralysis, or worse. Wrestlers have died in the ring.

Hogan and Nash had similar ideologies about wrestling, but they were coming from very different places in terms of experience.

Hogan was the aging icon clinging to his top spot with every muscle in his giant, bronzed arms. He felt he had been wronged before and was going to do everything in his power to make sure it wouldn't happen again.

Nash's backstage power in the WWF had come from his group of friends. He subscribed more to the rising-tides-lift-all-boats mentality, as long as his and his friends' boat rose the highest.

At its very foundation, the beef between the two of them could be boiled down to one thing.

Nash and Hall felt like they were the real nWo—the younger, charismatic guys who gave the group its cool factor, the ones who spoke directly (and irreverently) to the coveted teen and twenty-something male demographic.

"Was it frustrating for them?" Mark Madden said. "Put it this way, if it wasn't, I was frustrated for them. . . . The minute Hogan turned, [the nWo] began to get worse—not bad, but worse. Because then Hogan could Bigfoot everything and did, like he always did. Everywhere."

Hogan, though, felt like the nWo would not have worked had it not been for his long-established star power and the shock of his heel turn. Hall and Nash might have been hip and captivating talents, but Hogan was the biggest financial draw in the history of the business.

"If you look at team members, you always have one person that stands out, no matter what," Jimmy Hart said. "Everybody's got equal time—interview time, wrestling time, and everything. . . . Well, the same thing with Nash, Hall, and Hulk. All three of them had the TV times and stuff together. But who stood out? It was Hulk. Because there was something special about him."

Of course, it's obvious that the nWo would not have worked if not for all three of those men. But in the middle of a wrestling war, spending weeks on the road in hotel rooms and driving rental cars, everyone was exhausted and, in some cases, chemically altered. That can be a dangerous brew, chased with a double shot of ego.

"I hate saying this shit: Drugs and alcohol do fucked-up shit to people," Bischoff said. "The drain being away from your family. It stresses you in ways that creates behavior that is not really who you are. It just brings out the worst in you."

And the worst possible thing nearly happened on August 5, 1998, in Casper, Wyoming. It was the final WCW TV taping—an episode of *Thunder*—before the *Road Wild* pay-per-view. After months of tension and public and private shots taken at each other, Hogan and Nash, with Hall also involved, had a "fucking heated argument," according to Bischoff.

"One of them, I knew, had a gun in their bag," Bischoff said. "And I was the referee."

Meltzer reported at the time that Nash felt like Hogan and Bischoff were doing everything they could to make the Wolfpac group look bad, like fodder for Hogan's Hollywood sect of the nWo. There were even questions about whether or not Nash would show up for *Road Wild*, which he did, or even quit the company. Nash was an afterthought on the show, despite he and the Wolfpac being wildly popular with the crowd.

"They actually came pretty close to blows," Scott Steiner said of Nash and Hall's standoff with Hogan.

Bischoff said the confrontation between the three core members of the nWo was ultimately just "posturing."

"Nobody was going to stab or shoot anybody," Bischoff said. "Nobody was really going to get in a fight, but man, it felt like it for a minute."

Within a matter of weeks, Hogan and Nash called another truce, albeit somewhat begrudgingly. There was money to be made, after all.

"Kevin always was a professional, was able to always put any personal things on the side and to keep the business [flowing]," Barry Bloom said.

Ironically enough, Hogan said decades later that one of the reasons for the fall of the nWo was that Bischoff had become a "mark" for Hall and Nash. In other words, he was acting more like a fan of those two than an executive.

Nash had become a key member of the creative team by early 1999. But the conventional belief among those who were in WCW then—and something Bischoff has acknowledged—is that Bischoff almost always sided with Hogan.

"Here's the truth," Bischoff said. "Here's the thing I've never said to anybody: Hulk had a bigger, broader vision and the experience to back it up. Kevin and Scott had an organic feel that Hulk never had, because Hulk was created. He was created in the Hulk Hogan machine, the WWE machine. The fact that he was such a unique character. He was so special at that point in time. That character was created because, not to sound crazy, but the universe needed that character at that point in time. Scott and Kevin came along when it was street cred. It was in the street, it was in the alley. It was built from the ground up. And they brought a gritty reality to this Marvel-like creation and that combination was magic.

"It wasn't that one was more valuable than the other, or I valued one more than another. It was managing, 'How the fuck do I keep this shit together?'"

———

Hall, though, did not have his stuff together throughout 1998. In addition to time spent in rehab, Hall was arrested on several occasions. He allegedly groped a woman inside a car in front of a hotel in August 1998 and, in October 1998, he allegedly scratched up a white limo with keys to the tune of thousands in damages.

Hall was incredibly self-destructive. He drove drunk often and flipped or rolled several cars while driving. Hall totaled eight Cadillacs during that time period and didn't get "even a scratch" on him.

Despite the groans of many, WCW ended up using Hall's real-life struggles as a storyline. He started stumbling to the ring holding a cocktail cup, acting like he was drunk on television. Or maybe he actually was drunk. At that point, it hardly mattered.

Hall and Nash were in a storyline against each other, Hall with Hogan's nWo Hollywood and Nash with the Wolfpac. On the October 5, 1998, *Nitro*, Nash tried to seek out Hall, with cameras following him, by going to local dive bars in Columbia, South Carolina, where the show was being held. He found Hall in one and proceeded to beat him up in the bathroom. Hall ended up facedown in the toilet, which is where that story should have remained.

Even with the WWF featuring Austin's middle fingers, D-X genital references, a porn-star character named Val Venis, and banter about female wrestlers' "puppies" (color commentator Jerry "The King" Lawler's pet name for breasts), the alcoholic Hall storyline was particularly tawdry. It was Bischoff's idea, because of his continued desire to blur the lines between real and fake.

Hall thought it was a "bad idea" to do that story, but Bischoff was the boss. He said eventually Turner pulled the plug on it.

"I ain't proud of my behavior," Hall said. "I'm ashamed of some of the things I've done. I hurt some people's feelings who didn't need their feelings hurt."

Hall tried to look at some positives about it, that maybe kids would see consuming alcohol and drugs isn't the way to live.

"It's fun," Hall said. "But it ain't the answer."

In October 1998, Hall's ex-wife, Dana Burgio, posted two letters on a website called NWO Central. Burgio wrote that WCW had "decided to exploit [Hall's] very real problem with his addiction to drugs and alcohol as a means of entertainment of the fans for profit and ratings, only to stand by and watch him destroy himself."

Bischoff acknowledges now that it was a bad idea. He was trying to "take reality" and "weave it into . . . fiction," as he had so many times successfully over the two-plus years prior.

"But I stepped over the line on that one," Bischoff said. "I fucked that one up. That was too much."

There were other examples during this period of WCW making light of serious, real-life subjects. Bagwell legitimately injured his neck severely in a tag-team match on the April 22, 1998, *Thunder*, spiking his head into the mat taking a move from Rick Steiner. Bagwell said he was paralyzed for seven or eight minutes.

Bagwell ended up having a bruised spinal cord and needed surgery before regaining full function in his arms and legs. When he returned to television, WCW used the injury as part of a storyline. In one segment, Hogan pushed Bagwell down, out of a wheelchair. In the fall of 1998, Bagwell faked another neck injury and paralysis in storyline several times to dupe Rick Steiner when Bagwell and Scott Steiner were feuding with Rick.

"That was the one that was too much, I thought," Bagwell said. "I had to call my parents at home [before the show] and let them know I wasn't gonna be hurt again. That would have been devastating, you know? Again, to other people that didn't know, it probably was devastating. And when I faked it, it just pissed them off."

———

Early in 1998, it appeared like WCW was teasing a match down the road between Hogan and Bret Hart. Perhaps it would be another long-term plotline that ended with the two of them going head-to-head at *Starrcade*, like Hogan vs. Sting the year prior. Hogan and Bret had real-life tension between them, stemming from when Hogan wanted to drop the WWF title to Yokozuna and not Bret in 1993, which Hogan has denied.

That was the kind of storyline Bischoff could no doubt sink his teeth into, since there was an element of reality. And Hogan vs. Bret was the "obvious" plan, Bischoff said. But Bret could never build any momentum in WCW, and it's one of the more confounding things about this era of wrestling.

Bret was one of the greatest of all time. He was a phenomenal in-ring wrestler and a red-hot act coming off the Montreal Screwjob, getting big-time babyface reactions from the fans. Bret could have been someone used to continue and sustain WCW's momentum. It didn't happen, even as the WWF was pulling away late in 1998.

In hindsight, the Bret Hart character never really recovered from the *Starrcade 1997* mess. Had there actually been something devious done by Patrick, Bret would have been the no-nonsense hero who made sure Sting got a fair shake against Hogan. But the fiasco finish of that match had a domino effect.

"It fucked Hogan, and it fucked Sting, and it fucked Bret," Bischoff said. "It was like an orgy."

Bischoff's take is that the chemistry between Bret and Hogan "never materialized" and Bret didn't ever really want to be in WCW. McMahon said he could no longer afford him, so Bret didn't have many other options.

There was also the matter that Bret didn't get along with many, if any, of the power brokers in WCW. He had a beef with Hogan and had just come from a very public, real-life feud with Michaels, who was close friends with Hall and Nash.

"He had nowhere else to go," Bischoff said. "So he showed up on our doorstep. And when he showed up on our doorstep, he was surrounded by people that, in his mind, didn't want him even to be there. So I understand why he came in with a less-than-enthusiastic attitude, but he did. And a lot of what didn't happen with Bret I have to take a responsibility for ultimately, because I was the guy. There was no one else there but me at the top. But a lot of it had to do with him, because this is a collaborative business."

Bret pushed back on the idea that he wasn't motivated coming into WCW. He said he was hungry to prove himself there and help WCW beat McMahon, who had just performed the most brazen double-cross in pro-wrestling history with Bret as the victim. Bret said he believes he was undercut in WCW from the beginning, and it was entirely "political."

Nash and Bret formed a friendship decades later, but Bret said that Nash then had "every intention to make sure that I didn't go anywhere" in terms of stardom in WCW. Bret was told by behind-the-scenes people that Hogan would also work against him in booking meetings.

"Hogan would always just kill everything with me," Bret said. "Whatever they had in mind for me, or somebody thought to do with me, he would put a line through it. Almost just shoot the whole thing down and make sure it didn't happen. And I [heard from people] who were in the room that 'Hogan made sure they killed your name every time your name came up' during the TV tapings or the shows or whatever, when they write the shows. So I didn't find that out until years later."

Bret said it was "clear as day" that he should have opposed Hogan in the storyline right away and that match would have been "money in the bank." Instead, WCW had him spinning his wheels in relatively meaningless undercard programs.

Rather than finally tabbing Bret as a headliner in the fall of 1998, Hogan and WCW dipped back into Hogan's past as they had before with Savage and Piper. Hogan felt like he could make himself and the company money with a reboot of his early 1990s storyline with the Ultimate Warrior.

And, initially, Hogan was right. The man formerly known as Jim Hellwig debuted in WCW on the August 17, 1998, *Nitro* to confront Hogan and reignite their rivalry. The WWF owned the rights to the "Ultimate Warrior" moniker, but Hellwig changed his name legally to "Warrior," and Warrior was what he used in WCW.

With the anticipation of Warrior's debut, *Nitro* beat *Raw* seven out of eight weeks, though two of those weeks *Nitro* was unopposed with *Raw* preempted due to the U.S. Open tennis tournament. One of those unopposed episodes, August 31, 1998, *Nitro* had what was then the most watched pro-wrestling show in the history of cable, a 6.03 rating or 4,485,333 homes per average minute, Meltzer reported.

Things faded quickly, though, kind of like the hokey special effects WCW provided Warrior with, including fog spewing into the ring from all corners when Warrior would appear or disappear. Producers didn't enjoy working with him, because he'd frequently miss his time cues during meandering, incoherent promos. And the then-thirty-nine-year-old, ridiculously shredded Warrior got hurt quickly, tearing his bicep and straining his ankle.

Warrior participated in the double-cage War Games match at *Fall Brawl* on September 13, 1998, in Winston-Salem, North Carolina. He was on the WCW team with Piper and Page. Nash, Luger, and Sting made up the Wolfpac team. And the nWo black and white had Hogan, Bret, and Stevie Ray (Lash Huffman). The latter had been in the Harlem Heat tag team with his real-life brother Booker T (Booker Huffman), but had turned on him to join the nWo.

Ray, during this period, became the de facto leader of what had become known as the nWo B-team, with the likes of Adams, Norton, Vincent, and later Horace, the actual nephew of Hogan.

The nWo had gotten incredibly bloated and those lower-card wrestlers were treated more like a comedy act, soiling what it had once meant to be part of the nWo.

To sum up the state of things in WCW then, this is how Ray responded to an email request for an interview for this book: "No offense but I got better things to do with my time than talk about that bull shit, so I'd rather not. But I appreciate you reaching out."

Despite the injuries, Warrior stayed around for a big *Halloween Havoc* main event against Hogan on October 25, 1998, in Las Vegas. It was a disaster. A bloody Hogan tried to throw a fireball at Warrior (using flash paper, an old wrestling trick), but it took forever for him to do it and once he did, it missed. Hogan pinned Warrior, getting back his loss from *WrestleMania VI* in 1990, with the help of Horace.

Warrior made just two more appearances for WCW and then disappeared again. No fog machines necessary.

Hogan went away soon after, too, announcing on the *Nitro* two weeks after *Halloween Havoc* that he would be running for president of the United States in 2000. This was something of a play on the fact that longtime wrestler and commentator Jesse Ventura had been elected governor of Minnesota a few days earlier. Hogan and Bischoff did not like Ventura. Hogan announced that Bischoff would be his campaign manager.

Then Hogan went on *The Tonight Show*, with his former wrestling adversary Leno, to announce that he was retiring from wrestling to focus on his campaign. Hogan ended the interview saying, "We are going to get back on track in the year 2000." He did not say he would make America great again, but it wasn't far off.

A few months later, Hogan did an interview on *Larry King Live*, where Hogan said of a presidential run: "It's something that's not out of the question, because with everybody having a different agenda and everybody owing everybody something in the political arena, it would be nice to have somebody that could put America first."

Scott Steiner was tabbed as Hogan's successor as the leader of nWo Hollywood. That didn't last long. Hogan would be back sooner than people thought.

With no Hogan, the main event of *Starrcade* on December 27, 1998, in Washington, D.C., was Goldberg defending his WCW title against Nash. That was not the headliner anyone could have imagined at the beginning of the year. But Goldberg was red hot and still on his undefeated streak. Nash was a cool, antihero babyface leading the Wolfpac.

The ending of the match left a bad taste in the mouths of many.

After months of feuding with Nash, Hall came out to help his former-best-friend-turned-enemy-turned-seemingly-friend-again. He zapped Goldberg with a cattle prod. Nash hit his Jackknife powerbomb and pinned Goldberg to end his undefeated streak at (a totally fabricated) 173-1. Nash was the new WCW champion.

Even without Hogan, *Starrcade 1998* did an impressive business number, an estimated 460,000 pay-per-view buys, making it the third-biggest WCW pay-per-view event at the time. Though Nash ending 1998 as champion made all the sense in the world from a storyline perspective, the circumstances of Goldberg's streak ending were less than ideal.

Nash beating Hogan for the title and nWo supremacy at *Starrcade* was where the money was, but that did not happen. Politics got in the way.

No, not American politics. Wrestling politics.

———

There did end up being a match between Hogan and Nash. And it was among the most infamous in the history of professional wrestling.

The January 4, 1999, *Nitro* took place at the Georgia Dome in front of 38,309. The advertised main event was a rematch between Nash and Goldberg for the WCW title. But early in the show, Goldberg was arrested in storyline and taken from the stadium to a police precinct. Later, it was explained that Elizabeth, who had long been a member of the nWo, had accused him of sexual harassment.

Nash was shown outside the stadium complaining that he had a match with Goldberg later in the night and Goldberg was headed to a police precinct. Hogan, in his return to *Nitro*, could be seen coming into the building, laughing at Nash. Hogan said Goldberg was guilty.

In an interview a few segments later, Nash said he knew Hogan was behind Goldberg's arrest and if Goldberg couldn't make it back to the building in time, he wanted to put the belt on the line against Hogan. Flair, who had become the president of WCW with a win over Bischoff at *Starrcade*, cosigned that idea. Hogan said in an interview that it would be his final match and he'd win and retire with the belt. He said he had only come to *Nitro* to announce his vice-presidential running mate.

Goldberg was unable to make it back to the Georgia Dome and so, finally, for the first time, Hogan would face Nash in a one-on-one match in front of a giant crowd, the second-largest ever for a *Nitro* after the last Georgia Dome show, where Hogan lost to Goldberg.

Hogan came out with Scott Steiner. Nash had Hall in his corner. Hogan and Nash circled each other to start the match as Schiavone said, on commentary, that "this is what pro wrestling—World Championship Wrestling—is all about."

Seconds later, Hogan faked a punch and poked Nash lightly in the upper chest with his right pointer finger. Nash fell to the canvas as if he had been shot.

Hogan pinned Nash and the referee counted to three. Hogan was the WCW champion yet again, because Nash simply lay down for him.

It was all a storyline double-cross. After the pin, Hogan, Hall, Nash, and Scott Steiner all celebrated together. Goldberg finally made it back to the building and ran into the ring, but he was beaten down by a newly reunited nWo.

Hogan spraypainted "NWO 4 LIFE" in red graffiti on Goldberg's back. Nash held the title up, so Hogan could tag it "NWO" in red. Nash said into the camera: "Can you say déjà vu?"

The nWo had reformed together under the name the nWo Wolfpac Elite. And the whole scene did not go over well with fans.

The finishing sequence between Hogan and Nash has become known as the "finger poke of doom," and is considered a death-knell moment for the nWo, if not for WCW as a whole. The idea was to hit the reset button on the nWo, get the group back to its foundation with Hogan, Hall, and Nash when things in WCW were at their hottest.

On the surface, that wasn't such a bad idea, but the execution—

deviating from what had been an advertised main event and replacing it with a non-match—just served to upset people. And not in the way that makes bad guys effective in wrestling. The nWo, which had been built on the feeling of realism, had degenerated into just another phony professional wrestling storyline.

"[The finger poke of doom is the] most despised thing, perhaps, that was ever done [in wrestling]," Ross Forman said. "I knew where we were going directionally, but that certainly just seemed to backfire."

The new group, wearing black and red, lasted a few more months and produced some more big business numbers. But by the spring of 1999, due to injuries and ponderous creative choices, it had basically fizzled out. The nWo never recovered from the infamous poke and neither did WCW, which declined rapidly in 1999 and 2000, and then was sold to the WWF in 2001.

"Wrong," Hogan said of the poke. "Makes no sense. Embarrassing. Sorry I was a part of it. Can I please take it back? I mean, I got no words for it. It was just a completely wrong thing to do. I don't remember much other than how bad it was and what a bad decision it was. I don't know whose decision it was or don't remember how we got there. I really don't. But all I know is it was a horrible mistake."

Meltzer saw it as a compromise rooted in behind-the-scenes dick-swinging, rather than creative ingenuity. Neither Hogan nor Nash wanted to lose to the other, but Hogan got to get the belt back and Nash was able to stop Goldberg's streak in the *Starrcade* main event.

"I thought it was political, in the sense of a power thing," the journalist said.

Bischoff and Nash have downplayed the negative impact of the moment.

"It was a plot twist or a swerve depending on what genre of television you're talking about," Bischoff said. "That's all."

Bischoff said the real pivotal moment where things took a downward turn was the previous summer. Turner and Time Warner had merged in 1995 and the new company was on the verge of merging again, with AOL in 2000. Those talks were already happening in the summer of 1998 when Bischoff said he was told by executives in a meeting that he had to make *Nitro* "family-friendly."

By the end of 1998, Bischoff said he was so burned out between merger talks and the ongoing lawsuit with the WWF that he essentially removed himself from the creative process outside of simply greenlighting ideas. He could see things circling the drain and knew it was too late to stop it.

"We were going to go back to what WWE did when I beat their ass," Bischoff said. "That was the beginning of the end. The finger poke of doom was the manifestation of it."

PART IV

CHAPTER 14

I COULD HAVE
CALLED HIM
PORKY THE PIG

Bischoff sat in a conference room inside an office building in the upscale Buckhead neighborhood of Atlanta. Across from him was Jerry McDevitt, attorney for WWF parent company Titan Sports. It was the morning of April 29, 1998, and Bischoff was in the middle of his fourth deposition in Titan's lawsuit against Turner Broadcasting, WCW, and Bischoff himself.

Much of the civil case revolved around what WCW's intentions were when it debuted Hall on *Nitro* less than a month before the case was filed on June 21, 1996. Titan's argument and belief was that WCW wanted fans to think of Hall as Razor Ramon, a WWF-owned character who was coming down to invade WCW on behalf of the WWF. That, McDevitt argued, would be tortious and WCW would be liable for damages.

Hall was not given a name on WCW programming initially, for several weeks. And that was one of the threads McDevitt was attempting to pull on that day in Buckhead, nearly two years after the case had begun. It wasn't the first time McDevitt had asked Bischoff about that topic, and would not be the last.

On his first night back with WCW, Hall famously said, "You know who I am, but you don't know why I'm here." In a previous deposition, McDevitt asked Bischoff what he thought that line would communicate to the wrestling audience. Bischoff replied: "That they knew who he was, and they weren't exactly sure why he was there."

McDevitt referenced that again on April 29, 1998, asking Bischoff if that was a truthful answer. Bischoff said it was.

The rest of the exchange could have been something out of one of the WWF or WCW scripts.

McDevitt: "And that was the impression you wanted to create?"

Bischoff: "Yes."

McDevitt: "That they knew who he was?"

Bischoff: "They knew who he was."

McDevitt: "Who was he?"

Bischoff: "Scott Hall."

McDevitt: "And that was the impression you wanted to create, that that was Scott Hall?"

Bischoff: "Yes."

McDevitt: "But you didn't use the name 'Scott Hall,' correct?"

Bischoff: "No."

McDevitt: "You didn't use any name, right?"

Bischoff: "That's correct."

McDevitt: "And as you sit there today, you can think of no legal reason whatsoever why you couldn't have said, 'Y'all know who I am, I'm Scott Hall, but you don't know why I'm here,' right?"

At that point WCW attorney David Dunn objected. But McDevitt—and Bischoff—pressed on.

Bischoff: "I'm not a lawyer. It wasn't a legal issue."

McDevitt: "You could have said that, right?"

Dunn: "Objection."

Bischoff: "I could have called him Porky the Pig, could have called him anything, but I didn't."

The lawsuit went on—kind of like that, with back-and-forth jockeying for internal documents—for more than four years and included WCW countersuing the WWF in 1998 for defamatory trade practices, based on the Billionaire Ted skits.

It was in some ways a proxy war between McMahon and Bischoff (and Turner), as the two sides duked it out in courts and conference rooms while *Raw* and *Nitro* went blow for blow on Monday nights. One of the claims was that WCW violated the Lanham Act, which prohibits trademark infringement and dilution and false advertisement.

WCW was instructed by the court in 1996 to not use the names "Razor Ramon" or "Diesel," nor have them referred to as being from the WWF, which was being alluded to on the WCW 900 Hotline. Ultimately, WCW settled out of court on July 18, 2000.

Terms of the settlement were not disclosed, but McDevitt said it was "a lot of money," enough for the WWF to buy a struggling WCW eight months later for $4.2 million.

It was also an influential case when it came to copyright laws. It turns out, the nWo had an impact on the legal battlefield, too.

"[The case] really laid the foundation for creativity to be protected by law, which is the way it should be," McDevitt said. "As much work goes into creating some of the characters—once you're familiar with the process with which they do it—it's very sophisticated. The idea that we invest in that, spend all that money, and do that, you can't come and rip off our [intellectual property]."

Titan v. Turner was a fascinating case in that it examined professional wrestling, its storylines, and its characters through a legal lens. Wrestling is an entertainment medium unlike any other. For decades, pro wrestlers stayed in character even when they were out of the ring and off-screen. Promoters did not want babyfaces and heels to spend time with one another socially, at bars or restaurants or anywhere else, so as to not break kayfabe. Those ideals were antiquated in the 1990s, but still existed to a degree.

All of that begs the question: If a wrestler is in character while at work, as well as when he or she gets off work, where does the character end and the actual person begin? And if the human being and the character are largely one and the same, which can be the case at times, can any one company make a claim to owning that character?

In movies or television shows, it's easy and logical to separate the actor from the character. When Tom Cruise gets spotted out in public, no one is going to call him Pete "Maverick" Mitchell or Ethan Hunt. Those are just roles he played in the *Top Gun* and *Mission: Impossible* franchises, respectively. But when Hogan is out at his bar or shop in Clearwater, Florida, he's not going to be referred to as Terry Bollea. Everyone knows him as Hulk Hogan.

So when Hall played the character Razor Ramon, how much of that was the creative strategies of McMahon and WWF writers, and how much was it just an extension of Hall himself? That's one of the many things WCW argued, not to mention that many of the characteristics of the Ramon character came from when Hall played The Diamond Studd in WCW, including the slicked-back dark hair and toothpick perpetually in his teeth.

"Charles Dickens, if he were alive today and writing *Oliver Twist*, would have a copyright in Oliver Twist," Dunn said. "But [author] Erik Larson does not have a copyright in Winston Churchill because he wrote *The Splendid and the Vile*. Winston Churchill is a real person, and the real things he did, and the real characteristics of him, are in the public domain and cannot be copyrighted."

McDevitt argued basically that once a man or woman appears

in a role on a scripted pro-wrestling show, that person becomes a character on that show. Pictures of Hall when he used the character name "Big" Scott Hall in AWA were submitted into evidence with McDevitt pointing out that "Big" Scott Hall looked nothing like the Hall that appeared on *Nitro* in May 1996.

In the 1980s, Hall had curly blond hair, was significantly more muscular, and had a mustache. Hall even acknowledged in a deposition that friends he knew for decades did not recognize him after he changed his look to play The Diamond Studd. That character had long, wet black hair, dark stubble, and was much leaner. Razor Ramon had similar characteristics. McDevitt's point was how could anyone think the man who came out on *Nitro* was the character Scott Hall since that 1980s character looked nothing like the 1996 Hall.

McDevitt felt like it was obvious Hall and WCW were trying to portray Hall as Razor Ramon in WCW, complete with the phony Cuban accent Hall used as Razor.

"Fans were smart to know," McDevitt said. "If Batman is brought down in costume, but they didn't call him Batman, you'd still know it's Batman."

WCW argued that Hall wasn't dressed like Razor Ramon at all. He wore a denim vest and jeans, not tights with a razor on them like the Ramon character did. There was, though, an instance early in Hall's run with the nWo where he had the word *chico* on his trunks, which could have been interpreted as a reference to the Razor character.

During a March 30, 1998, deposition, Hall told McDevitt that he didn't think there was a problem with using that word on his gear. But then he saw WCW attorney Nick Lambros after the show. Lambros told Hall that Lambros's wife said *chico* meant "little boy" in Spanish and Hall looked "kind of funny wearing 'little boy' on your crotch." Hall said he never wore *chico* on his ring attire again, but not because he feared legal repercussions.

"Because Mr. Lambros made fun of me," Hall said in the deposition.

WCW ended up calling Hall and Nash by their real names, further blurring the lines of fictional character and actual human being. It worked perfectly for what Bischoff was going for with the nWo. But other options were explored.

It was revealed in lawsuit documents that WCW had done trademark searches on potential character names to be used for each before settling on just using Scott Hall and Kevin Nash.

Beginning June 12, 1996, two days after Nash's debut, WCW began looking, via Turner's legal team, into the federal trademark registry for potential monikers for Nash that were adjacent to his WWF character name Diesel: "Axcel," "Axzel," and "Axle." For Hall, WCW had Turner attorneys do a federal trademark search for "The Bad Guy," which was a WWF nickname for Razor Ramon.

According to documents, Turner legal got back to WCW director of business affairs Gary Juster, writing that outside counsel recommended not using "The Bad Guy" because of a pending application for "Wrestling Bad Guys" for magazines relating to wrestling owned by London Publishing Co., plus a registration for "Bad Guys" for clothing owned by Bad Boys Every Wear B.V.

Lambros wrote in an affidavit that Hall wanted to use "The Bad Guy," because it was a nickname he used while previously with WCW.

"In light of the threat of litigation against WCW made by Mr. McDavitt [sic], I had a question as to whether WCW could utilize the names 'Axzel' or 'The Bad Guy' without becoming embroiled in a lawsuit with Titan," Lambros wrote in a May 2, 1997, declaration. "Trademark searches were part of the process of resolving that question."

In essence, WCW's attorneys put the kibosh on "Axzel" (or one of the other spellings) and, especially, "The Bad Guy," out of concern that the WWF would sue, which happened anyway.

McDevitt's first letter threatening legal action was sent June 7, 1996, three days before Nash showed up on *Nitro*. Before that, McDevitt penned a letter to Turner senior counsel David Payne on March 20, 1996—two months before Hall even appeared—warning WCW not to use WWF intellectual property, including the wrestlers' trade dress or wrestling gear.

WCW, interestingly enough, didn't launch a trademark search on "New World Order" until July 23, 1996, more than two weeks after the group was christened at *Bash at the Beach*, such was the knee-jerk nature of the organization at that time.

————

During the early appearances of Hall and Nash on *Nitro*, Mark Madden was saying on the WCW Hotline that those two were "non-WCW wrestlers" about to have a match with WCW-contracted wrestlers. He was also making claims about the WWF's financial woes and the promotion's potential impending bankruptcy in 1995 and 1996.

During a deposition, Madden said he was told by Bischoff to treat the storyline with Hall and Nash on the 900 line "as a shoot," wrestling parlance for real or legitimate. The hotlines at that time were an odd hybrid of actual news, gossip, storylines, and complete bullshit.

Madden was subpoenaed to testify as to where he got his

information for the 900 line, but he invoked journalistic privilege, saying he did not have to reveal his sources. That spawned an entirely new legal proceeding by McDevitt to get Madden to give up that information.

Ultimately, it was ruled by the United States Court of Appeals, Third Circuit, that Madden might have been a professional journalist but while talking on the WCW Hotline he was doing so as an entertainer. This separate lawsuit was written about in *The New York Times* in 1998 with the headline "WRESTLING INSULTS FUEL FREE SPEECH CASE."

It was a groundbreaking case, well ahead of its time—long before the advent of wannabe "journalists" on social media. Madden's situation established at the time the legal precedent of who constitutes a journalist, in so far as how one can assert the privilege to not reveal his or her sources.

"We hold that individuals are journalists when engaged in investigative reporting, gathering news, and have the intent at the beginning of the news-gathering process to disseminate this information to the public," Judge Richard Lowell Nygaard wrote in the August 6, 1998, opinion. "Madden does not pass this test."

Madden said in an interview for this book that he had forgotten who gave him that information by the time the final decision was handed down. What he was saying on the WCW 900 number, Madden said, really just amounted to smack talk and was not meant to be taken at face value, not unlike what pro wrestling is known for in the first place.

"The hotline was generally banter," Madden said. "Stuff like that wasn't taken as seriously, like it is now on the internet and the blogs and the podcasts. . . . It wasn't an obsession with people like it is now."

On television, WCW never used the names "Razor Ramon" or "The Bad Guy" or "Diesel," and attempted early on to establish that neither Hall nor Nash was under contract to the WWF. But the lawsuit turned up on multiple occasions when WCW referred to them internally as the names of their former characters and mentioned the WWF by name.

One of the most damning pieces of evidence were logs of *Nitro* in May and June 1996, which were written out after the show as a summary of what happened for the promotion to keep on record.

According to court documents, the pre-show formats were written, by hand, by Kevin Sullivan, the head of the creative committee. The formats were then typed up on a computer by producer Annette Yother. After the show, associate producer Michele Bayens would write out a log of the episode "by adding very specific time-coded descriptions, in the post-production phase."

For the May 26, 1996, *Nitro*, Hall's debut, the log read that it was apparent that the "large man" in the ring making references to the Billionaire Ted skits "is (was) a wrestler from WWF. He declares war w/ WCW/WWF—ref gets him to leave."

In the log for the June 3, 1996, *Nitro*, the "large man from last week's broadcast" was referred to as "razor ramone" and "RR" twice, all in parentheses. Nash debuted on the June 10, 1996, *Nitro*. In that log, Hall is again called "Razor Ramone" and "RR." Nash is simply called Nash.

Titan argued that those internal documents showed that WCW intended to portray Hall as Razor Ramon, while WCW countered that the logs were not seen by any fans nor anyone from the public.

That was not the case, however, with other documents entered into evidence. On June 19, 1997, an affidavit from Titan's vice president of sales, James A. Rothschild, was filed with the court. In the affidavit, Rothschild wrote that he attended the National Association of Television Program Executives (NATPE) convention in New Orleans in January 1997. It was basically a place where TV producers and networks could meet with advertisers and sell time on their shows or stations.

While at the convention, Rothschild wrote that he visited the Time Warner sales area, where there was a section dedicated to selling WCW programming to advertisers. Rothschild picked up a promotional packet being distributed there, he wrote.

In the packet, which became evidence, Hall and Nash were mentioned with the description that they were "formerly Razor Ramon and Diesel in the WWF." The packet also had written that Syxx was formerly the 1-2-3 Kid and Vincent used to be Virgil, both WWF's intellectual properties.

WCW denied that this packet was handed out at the NATPE convention, that it was simply an internal draft and TBS subsidiary Turner Broadcasting Sales, Inc. (TBSI) compiled the deck without the promotion's knowledge. McDevitt argued that the use of those trademarks and the WWF by name was a violation of the 1996 consent order from the court that prohibited WCW from making any statements referring to Hall as Razor Ramon or Nash as Diesel.

"It is a bald-faced and brazen violation of the Order made in the most damaging forum imaginable," McDevitt wrote in a motion for order of civil contempt, which was denied pending further discovery and depositions. "There is no reason to include the references to Titan's characters whatsoever other than to pass off on the reputation of Titan's characters and to tell television executives that Titan's popular characters now appear on WCW."

McDevitt said he and the WWF's legal team "laughed" when WCW filed its countersuit, which claimed, among other things, that the WWF defamed Turner in its Billionaire Ted skits. McDevitt said the counterclaim by WCW allowed him to depose Turner, which he did.

Transcripts from Turner's deposition, as well as McMahon's deposition, never made it into the public court records, because the case never went to trial. For this book, more than four thousand pages from the lawsuit were obtained, though more than one thousand still remain under seal.

McDevitt said Turner was "very charming" and "very charismatic" when he sat for the deposition. McDevitt said he had Turner watch every single Billionaire Ted skit and asked him after every one what he believed in each was defamatory.

McDevitt said Turner was noticeably irritated watching them. He mentioned something about his character in the parody wearing a cheap suit and "literally stormed out of the room," after the final skit was played. McDevitt described it as "like life imitating art."

As for McMahon, Dunn said he was a "challenging and difficult witness." McDevitt was a "character" himself, Dunn said, very much "simpatico" with his client McMahon, who he said was similar to the character he played on screen, though not completely the same.

"Vince played Vince McMahon on TV," Dunn said. "Ted didn't play Ted Turner on TV. So there were differences, certainly. But I think Vince McMahon wanted to make this a fight between him and Ted Turner. I don't think it really was. Ted Turner was running a conglomerate media corporation, and Vince McMahon's business was heavily focused on WWF."

Dunn said *Titan v. Turner* wasn't necessarily any more heated compared with other civil cases he has worked on involving competitors in the same industry. And it wasn't necessarily more colorful of a case than others he has experienced in entertainment. But it was unique, in its own way.

"It's really all combined in the whole issue of, 'Where do you draw the line between the individuals and the persona, and what's real and what's fictional?'" Dunn said. "And a lot of that is a line that's deliberately blurred in professional wrestling."

CHAPTER 15

BAD TIMES DON'T LAST, BUT BAD GUYS DO

McMahon sat at a desk wearing a blue dress shirt, open at the collar, and a black sports jacket. He had a bandage on his forehead, covering up a self-inflicted cut from a match four days earlier.

It was the January 24, 2002, edition of the WWF television show *SmackDown*, which had joined *Raw* on prime time three years earlier. McMahon was in a feud with Flair, who had risen in the story to be co-owner of the WWF.

McMahon had bought WCW in real life one year earlier, but in storyline his son, Shane, swooped in and purchased the wrestling promotion under his father's nose. Shane teamed up with his sister, Stephanie, who was in control of ECW, another company the WWF had just acquired. When McMahon's WWF defeated the alliance between his children's promotions to take full control, he fired Shane and Stephanie. But, in the story, his kids then sold their shares of the WWF to an ownership group led by Flair.

In several pre-taped vignettes on the *SmackDown* episode, McMahon explained that he needed to exact revenge on Flair, who he said would only destroy the WWF with the direction he was taking it in.

McMahon said that Flair was leading the WWF to its death,

but McMahon himself was going to beat him to it. He was going to "inject the WWF with a lethal dose of poison."

"If anybody is going to kill my creation, I'm gonna do it," McMahon said.

The camera zoomed out to capture a mirror behind McMahon. In the mirror could be seen the back of McMahon's black chair with three letters written on it, in white.

"Me," McMahon rasped, "and the nWo!"

———

The lights went down inside Toronto's SkyDome and a familiar tune blared over the PA system.

Hogan walked out to the entranceway wearing a black and white feather boa around his neck and strumming the air guitar to the nWo theme song. The crowd of 68,237 went crazy.

It was *WrestleMania X8* on March 18, 2002. The nWo was in the WWF and Hogan was making his first appearance at a *WrestleMania* in nine years. His opponent? The Rock, who had become one of the biggest stars in the industry. The dream match, which no one could have even imagined a few years prior, was billed as Icon vs. Icon.

It was a true passing-of-the-torch moment. Hogan was wrestling's biggest crossover star of the 1980s into the 1990s. The Rock was on his way to being one of the most recognizable people in the world.

And then something unexpected happened.

Hogan and the nWo were heels when they came into the WWF. Hall faced Austin, the WWF's biggest babyface, on the *WrestleMania X8* card. The Rock was also a good guy, one of the headliners trying to keep the nWo from killing the WWF, as McMahon had intended in the storyline.

The Toronto crowd saw things differently. This was Hogan's homecoming. They started cheering him over The Rock.

Hogan and The Rock stood face to face to begin the match as the crowd showered them with cheers. They didn't touch for more than two minutes as the noise grew louder and louder. The Rock turned his head to the right, as if to acknowledge the crowd. Hogan turned his to the left. Then the two alternated. The sound was deafening.

The fans exploded further when Hogan mounted a 1980s-like comeback, no-selling The Rock's punches and then hitting his big boot and leg drop. The Rock kicked out. Hogan missed another leg drop and The Rock hit his Rock Bottom finisher twice, followed by the People's Elbow. The Rock pinned Hogan, who stayed down for the three count.

The Rock won the match, but Hogan had won back the people like it was 1985 all over again.

That weekend, with everyone seeing the way things were heading, McMahon asked Hogan if he had packed his red-and-yellow ring attire. Hogan said he had not. McMahon lent him his private jet and Hogan flew home to Florida, got his gear, and flew back to Canada in time for *Raw* in Montreal.

Hollywood Hogan was no more. It had been a nineties fad. The heroic babyface Hogan returned for the first time in more than six years to a resounding welcome back from the fans, leaving Hall and Nash and the nWo behind.

After departing the WWF in 1993 with his reputation besmirched by admitting to steroid use and his relationship with the promotion dead, Hogan was once again in the good graces of the fans. The boos and indifference toward Hulkamania were gone. It was running wild again. All it took was Hogan to be a dastardly son of a bitch for several years before fans wanted to see the old him again.

The nWo would hang around a little while longer, adding Waltman, The Big Show (formerly The Giant), Michaels, and others. But Nash had injuries and Hall's personal issues crept up again and he requested his release. This iteration of the group had a short shelf life, similar to nWo 2000, which was created in late 1999 WCW and consisted of Hall, Nash, Bret Hart, and Jeff Jarrett before falling apart.

McMahon officially announced that the nWo had been disbanded on the July 15, 2002, *Raw*—during the same promo in which he announced the new storyline general manager of his flagship television show.

Bischoff.

McMahon introduced his former hated rival to the crowd. Bischoff came out onstage and he and McMahon embraced each other twice in one of the most surreal moments in the history of the industry.

Bischoff would work for WWE (the WWF name was gone later in 2002 after a lawsuit from the World Wildlife Fund) as an on-screen character on several occasions. He also had a short stint as the behind-the-scenes executive director of *SmackDown* in 2019.

Hogan, Hall, Nash, Waltman, and Bischoff would all work together again in Total Nonstop Action (TNA) wrestling beginning in 2010. Hall, Nash, and Waltman had a few months that year in an nWo-like group called The Band, and they also called themselves the Wolfpac, complete with the old nWo Wolfpac theme music. Sting was briefly a member, too.

In 2020, the nWo—specifically the core four of Hogan, Hall, Nash, and Waltman—was inducted into the WWE Hall of Fame. They didn't get to give their speech until a year later due to the

COVID-19 pandemic, and when they did it was in front of fans on screens rather than in person.

The WWE Hall of Fame induction was equally as ironic as it was deserving. This was the group of guys who left the WWF in the 1990s, when the promotion was struggling financially, and helped WCW became the top dog for a time.

"I mean, you got four guys that were basically going at Vince as a shoot, pushing hard to actually try to take over—not put him out of business, but basically take his spot and be the number one company," Hogan said. "So all of a sudden you're inducting four guys in the Hall of Fame that twenty years ago were trying to stab you in the back."

———

Leno was recovering from injuries after a stretch of bad luck. It was February 2023. Three months prior, the longtime former host of *The Tonight Show* sustained severe burns on his face after one of his prized cars caught on fire in his Los Angeles garage. Two months after that, in January 2023, Leno broke his collarbone and two ribs and cracked both of his kneecaps in a motorcycle accident.

Leno was walking in LA, still on the mend, when a fan approached him. The man wanted to talk to Leno about his only pro-wrestling match, back in 1998. In Leno's recollection, the dialogue went something like this.

Fan: "Hey man, look, I know wrestling is fake. But that time you wrestled Hogan, I could tell—you were really pissed."

Leno: "No, no. I wasn't pissed."

Fan: "No, no. You were mad!"

Leno: "Look, I'm the guy. I was the one in the ring. If I was pissed, I'd say I was pissed."

Fan: "You really went after him!"

Leno, haplessly: "No, I didn't."

This is the exact scenario that Bischoff has talked about ad nauseam. Professional wrestling is "fake." It's predetermined, a story. Just about everyone knows that. But if you can bend someone's mind and make them believe just one aspect of the show is real, they'll achieve a new level of engagement with the product. That was the entire idea behind the nWo, why it worked so well and why it changed the pro-wrestling industry forever.

Leno couldn't help but laugh about that particular interaction. He's done so many things in his career, most notably hosting the No. 1 late-night show in the United States for more than twenty years. Yet there are people who come up to him and only want to talk about a few weeks of his life from three decades ago.

"This guy was convinced it was real," Leno said. "I said, 'Sir, I'm the guy. I know Hulk, we're friends.' It was a lot of fun. I enjoyed training with him. It was the 'you go left, I go right, you come this way, I go that way.' I mean, we rehearsed it. It was a lot of fun to do, I enjoyed the crowd. But I wasn't mad. [He said], 'Oh, no. You were really pissed.' OK. All right. Thank you."

Teens, young adults, and twenty- or thirty-somethings—mostly men—were hooked on the decade's pro-wrestling boom, which was ignited by the nWo. In late 1998, an article in *TV Guide*, then one of the most widely circulated magazines in the country, chronicled the phenomenon, writing that "younger viewers have been abandoning the broadcast networks" for *Nitro* and *Raw* to the tune of "almost 10 million viewers" weekly, which had even cut into the ratings of American sporting institution *Monday Night Football*.

Time magazine did a major story on pro wrestling in June 1998, reporting that about 34 million people were watching wrestling at the time, factoring in all of the shows and pay-per-views. Merchandise sales, the magazine reported, were "well over a billion dollars" combined between WCW and the WWF.

"In the old days there was a fairly simple distinction to be made between the good guys, or 'baby faces' in the carny lingo of wrestling, and bad guys, or 'heels,'" wrote the piece's scribe, James Collins. "Now no one is reliably good. The emphasis is all on rebellion and arrogance, black leather and shades."

Those younger viewers watching then have all grown up and are a part of the workforce—your bankers, lawyers, doctors, and laborers. But also, your writers, artists, musicians, athletes, producers, actors, and politicians.

Andrew Yang grew up watching pro wrestling as a kid in New York and was enamored with the nWo, which he said "seemed much more real than a normal wrestling storyline." In 2020, Yang ran for president of the United States and later started his own political party, called the Forward Party. He found himself, while campaigning during the Democratic primary, somewhat mimicking what he saw back then.

"I often channeled my inner pro wrestler when I was making these speeches," Yang said.

During the 1990s and earlier, there were people worried about kids or even adults imitating wrestling moves and potentially hurting someone else. Who knew that what people would end up imitating wasn't the moves, but the ability to manipulate the masses?

Had Yang won the primary, he would have faced off in the general election with then-President Trump, the incumbent. Yang said he believed he had a leg up on understanding Trump compared to the other candidates, because he understood pro wrestling—and Trump was pro wrestling.

Trump had been involved with wrestling since his Atlantic City casino sponsored *WrestleMania IV* and *WrestleMania V* in the 1980s. He was a longtime friend of McMahon's and even took part in a WWE storyline against McMahon in 2007. McMahon's wife, Linda, the former WWE CEO, ended up being in Trump's first presidential cabinet, the head of the Small Business Administration.

The cornerstone of Trump's multiple presidential campaigns were his rallies. And those rallies resembled pro-wrestling shows, complete with "fans" bringing signs and Trump leading them in chants like "Lock Her Up" in reference to throwing political rival Hillary Clinton in jail. The red MAKE AMERICA GREAT AGAIN hats became the recognizable symbol of Trump's fandom, like the nWo and Austin 3:16 T-shirts of the 1990s.

"The Trump playbook is pro wrestling and so many people are trying to copy it," Waltman said.

Yang said Trump touched on something "deeper and more primal." He broke down the fourth wall like the nWo did and, in some cases, blended reality with fiction. Trump felt more raw and real than his peers with the way he spoke, even if he was selling everyone a line of bullshit.

University of Pennsylvania professor R. Tyson Smith, who has a PhD in sociology and has written academically about professional wrestling, said the appeal has grown in recent decades for "the type of cult of personality, the type of televised spectacle that captures your attention," which can be applied to pro wrestling or Trump.

"I think that a lot of political figures actually would benefit greatly from watching pro wrestling and becoming a fan, because you'd understand how to work a crowd," Yang said.

Meltzer has written about wrestling going back to the early 1970s. He said witnessing Trump made him feel like he was watching the very thing he has covered for so many decades: "The speeches and the attitude and the defiance, always running down his enemies so bad." Trump came up with demeaning nicknames for his opponents—"Sleepy" Joe Biden and "Pocahontas" for Elizabeth Warren, as examples—the way that Hogan and others did for wrestling foes.

"I think I understood the rise of Trump way better from knowing wrestling," Meltzer said.

Hogan, in that 1998 *Time* article, said aptly of his heel persona: "Now I'm the worst bad guy around. I can't win a match unless I cheat. And people love me."

When asked about pro wrestling's hold on the United States, sociologist and pop-culture expert Dustin Kidd brought up *The Seven Lively Arts*, written by culture historian Gilbert Seldes in 1924. In the book, Seldes mentions motion pictures, the stage, radio, popular music, comic strips, popular art, and dance as the things that capture the zeitgeist, that shape cultural identity.

Seldes did not mention pro wrestling. But there are elements of many of those seven things in wrestling, especially "the stage." Kidd said professional wrestling is "in some ways" America's version of Shakespeare. Seldes, Kidd said, specifically wrote about how American interests differ from those in Europe and how Americans want our arts to be "especially lively."

"I think that pro wrestling is a great example of the lively arts— maybe the greatest example of the lively arts, in that sense," said Kidd, a sociology professor at Temple University.

German filmmaker Werner Herzog said in a 2007 interview on *Fresh Air* with Terry Gross that he watches wrestling because "the poet must not avert his eyes from what's going on in the world. In order to understand what's going on, you have to face it."

"*WrestleMania* has a couple of strange and interesting sides," Herzog said during a 2010 press junket. "And my main take on it is apparently a new, very crude form of drama is emerging. Of course, everything is staged, and we have to question what constitutes reality, of course. . . . *WrestleMania* is only one of those parts of staged realities."

The 1990s pro-wrestling boom ran parallel to other "staged realities," for instance daytime talk shows like *The Jerry Springer Show* and reality show *The Real World*. Like wrestling, few really believed everything happening on *Springer* or *Real World* was completely on the up-and-up. Yet, people watched anyway—at a high rate—and bought in, to an extent, to their staged realities.

WCW and the WWF were part of a greater cultural shift during that era, riding the wave and sometimes even setting the pace of the pseudo-reality entertainment that had been getting more and more prevalent. Those shows tackled controversial topics. Springer producers would rile up their guests, sometimes to the point of (potentially scripted) violence. They were edgier—or trashier—than what television featured previously.

Sociologist Laura Grindstaff, who wrote the 2002 book *The Money Shot: Trash, Class, and the Making of TV Talk Shows*, believes these changes weren't necessarily brought about by consumer need. Network television was stumbling in the 1990s, she said, and cable had expanded to an unprecedented degree. There was a need for consistent, low-cost programming. Talk-show guests and reality-television contestants came much cheaper than actors. So did pro wrestlers.

The idea of the antihero being the protagonist wasn't an especially new one in the entertainment industry. But the nWo hit in such a formative time and was consumed by millions of people every week on a top-rated program in *Nitro*. It wasn't long before shows like *The Sopranos* and *The Wire* and *Breaking Bad* popped up, showing the narrative point of view of not just antiheroes, but actual villains, albeit complicated ones.

Bischoff's product might not have directly led to those hit shows, now cult classics, but the nWo was a viaduct to what was coming next. At the very least, it forced McMahon to change his game plan, growing pro wrestling in the late 1990s to an even more astronomical level led by Austin and The Rock.

"Deep down inside, I'm convinced that had we not made the moves we made with *Nitro*, had we not created the nWo, had we not had the impact on WWE that we did, I'm not sure the [wrestling] business would be around today," Bischoff said.

———

The nWo has been referenced in sports for years, whether it be the NBA, NFL, or college football. In 2019, Northwestern University offensive line coach Kurt Anderson started calling his line the nWo, asking for them to play with the ferocity of Hogan, Hall, and Nash. Even going back to the 1990s, the nWo made a major impression on sports—and not just Rodman and Malone, either.

Several players on the Cincinnati Reds followed wrestling in the 1990s, according to Danny Graves, the team's closer back then and now an ESPN baseball analyst. Graves and his teammates got into it so much that when the Wolfpac split off and opposed nWo Hollywood, the players did the same thing. They chose their side and wore either the red and black or the black and white under their batting-practice jerseys before games. The ringleaders were Graves, Sean Casey, and Dmitri Young, who were giant wrestling fans.

"Half the clubhouse was black [and white], half was Wolfpac, and oh man, we even started doing the [Turkish] wolf, the [hand] symbol that they would do," Graves said. "So we were doing that as our handshakes, and it was phenomenal, man. It was such a good time."

The black and red shirt was, indeed, a fashion statement. So much so that, in 2017, comedian Aziz Ansari wore an nWo Wolfpac sweater while hosting *Saturday Night Live*. Ansari and his brother Aniz, a writer and producer, were walking around New York that week and stumbled upon a thrift store selling vintage wrestling shirts. The two of them were big wrestling fans growing up, especially of the nWo and the Wolfpack, and Aziz thought it would be cool to wear the hoodie on *SNL*.

That same year, influencer Kendall Jenner, of all people, rocked an oversized black and red nWo logo shirt at a Michael Kors show during New York Fashion Week.

Jenner would later date Puerto Rican reggaeton superstar Bad Bunny, one of the world's highest-profile pro-wrestling superfans. He has had Flair in a music video, named a song after Booker T, and referenced countless wrestlers in his lyrics. Once he rocked an nWo T-shirt while clubbing in Miami. Bunny, whose real name is Benito Martínez Ocasio, has even wrestled in several matches for WWE.

Hall slipped and fell at his Georgia home less than a year after the nWo got to give its WWE Hall of Fame induction speech.

The wrestling great broke his hip and was unable to reach his phone to call for help. After no one heard from Hall for a few days, friends called Diamond Dallas Page, who lived in the area and had been trying to help Hall with his substance-abuse issues.

Page found Hall on the floor and took him to a hospital. During surgery, Hall suffered three heart attacks as a result of a blood clot that developed after a hip operation.

Nash got on speaker phone with the other members of The Kliq—Waltman, Michaels, and Levesque—while Hall was in the hospital in critical condition. The call was so they could say goodbye.

"We all talked to him," Nash said. "Or cried is basically all we did."

Hall died on March 14, 2022, at the age of sixty-three. He never won a world championship in wrestling, but his contributions in and out of the ring helped revolutionize the industry.

Nash wrote a poignant tribute to his best friend on Instagram:

"I'm going to lose the one person on this planet I've spent more of my life with than anyone else. My heart is broken and I'm so very fucking sad. I love Scott with all my heart but now I have to prepare my life without him in the present. I've been blessed to have a friend that took me at face value and I him. When we jumped to WCW we didn't care who liked or hated us. We had each other and with the smooth Barry Bloom we changed wrestling both in content and pay for those . . . alot that disliked us. We were the 'Outsiders' but we had each other. Scott always felt he wasn't worthy of the afterlife. Well God please have some gold-plated toothpicks for my brother. My life was enriched with his take on life. He wasn't perfect but as he always said, 'The last perfect person to walk the planet they nailed to a cross.'"

That night, after Hall's death, Hogan gave an emotional speech at his Hogan's Hangout bar and restaurant in Clearwater, Florida. He started it saying, "Hey, yo," a nod to one of Hall's signature phrases, and said Hall taught him "how to be a bad guy."

"He took care of me when I was down and out, and everyone

thought Hulkamania was dead," Hogan said in the speech. "Scott Hall resurrected me. He put me back on the map."

The beef Hall and Nash had with Hogan had long since been cleared up. Bischoff remained close friends with them, too.

Nash said he was contacted by a company out of London in the early 2020s that was doing a documentary about Hogan, and they were going to bring up some of the more negative things about Hogan's past. Nash called Hogan about it before deciding whether or not to cooperate with them.

"Do you know anything about this?" Nash asked Hogan.

"No," Hogan replied.

"Cool, then I'll tell them to fuck off," Nash said.

"Thank you," Hogan responded. "Love you, brother."

"It's as simple as that," Nash said of his relationship with Hogan. "I don't have to be with him twenty-four/seven, but when it comes down to somebody trying to bushwhack him, I got his back, and I know he's got mine."

After all, the nWo?

It really is for life.

Maybe Hall put it best when he was inducted into the WWE Hall of Fame the first time, as Razor Ramon.

"Bad times don't last," Hall said, closing his speech.

"But Bad Guys do."

NOTES

All quotations and information in this book are from interviews and research done by the author, unless otherwise indicated.

CHAPTER 1: THE SPECTACLE OF EXCESS

9 **Hulk Hogan fidgeted:** Scott's Wrestling Collection, "Hulk Hogan on Arsenio Hall Show 1991," YouTube.com, November 18, 2018 (https://www.youtube.com/watch?v=W-RggiPU2xQ&t=206s).

9 **McMahon wanted Hogan to admit:** *Mr. McMahon*, Netflix docuseries, Episode 2, September, 25, 2004 (https://www.netflix.com /title/81048394).

10 **Hogan regretted lying before:** Hulk Hogan with Michael Jan Friedman, *Hollywood Hulk Hogan* (WWE, 2002), 203–8.

11 **In the late 1970s:** Hogan with Friedman, *Hollywood Hulk Hogan*, 39–51.

12 **The elder McMahon thought Bollea looked Irish:** Hogan with Friedman, *Hollywood Hulk Hogan*, 58.

13 **Hogan received a Western Union:** Hogan with Friedman, *Hollywood Hulk Hogan*, 77–92.

15 **A McMahon reached out:** Hogan with Friedman, *Hollywood Hulk Hogan*, 103–7.

15 **Hogan returned to the WWF:** Hogan with Friedman, *Hollywood Hulk Hogan*, 111–15.

17 **Hogan reluctantly agreed:** David Bixenspan, "Hulk Hogan & Mr. T on Hot Properties (with Richard Belzer)," YouTube.com, February 19, 2023 (https://www.youtube.com/watch?v=at1jOAb J7ZA&t).

18 **McMahon invested millions:** Stephanie McMahon on Instagram (https://www.instagram.com/stephaniemcmahon/p/BwA0n ThHrjC/?hl=gu).

19 **Belzer ended up suing:** *Belzer v. Bollea*, April 3, 1990 (https://ca setext.com/case/belzer-v-bollea).

20 **Along with a percentage given to Marvel:** Jeremy Lambert, "Hulk Hogan Explains How He Paid $750,000 to Marvel for 'Hulk Hogan' Name Instead of $35 Million," Fightful.com, July 27, 2023 (https:// www.fightful.com/wrestling/hulk-hogan-explains-how-he-paid -750000-marvel-hulk-hogan-name-instead-35-million).

21 **The WWF claims 93,173:** David Bixenspan, "How Many People Were Actually at WrestleMania III? A Deadspin Investigation," Deadspin.com, March 30, 2018 (https://deadspin.com/how-many -people-were-actually-at-wrestlemania-iii-a-de-1824178481/).

22 **Psychologists have said:** Andrew J. Elliot, "Color and psychological functioning: a review of theoretical and empirical work," *Frontiers in Psychology*, April 5, 2015 (https://pmc.ncbi.nlm.nih.gov/articles/PM C4383146/).

24 **So when McMahon told Hogan that the Ultimate Warrior:** Hogan with Friedman, *Hollywood Hulk Hogan*, 195–200.

26 **Two days before *WrestleMania IX*:** Hogan with Friedman, *Hollywood Hulk Hogan*, 217–19.

28 **"He may have thought that I had turned on him":** Hogan with Friedman, *Hollywood Hulk Hogan*, 203–8.

28 **Hogan's testimony:** Shamarie Knight, "The Hulk Hogan Testimony: Inside the Vince McMahon Steroid Trial," July 14, 2024, Medium .com (https://medium.com/@ShamarieKnight/the-hulk-hogan-test imony-inside-the-vince-mcmahon-steroid-trial-ec9a6b8428b1).

CHAPTER 2: BECAUSE THIS IS WHERE THE BIG BOYS PLAY

30 **In 1993, Bischoff visited Disney:** Eric Bischoff with Jeremy Roberts, *Controversy Creates Cash* (WWE, 2007), 96–98.

32 **Bischoff, a jet-black-haired:** Bischoff with Roberts, *Controversy Creates Cash*, 24–25.

32 **In 1991, Bischoff landed:** Bischoff with Roberts, *Controversy Creates Cash,* 64.

32 ***Torch* reporter Mark Madden reached out to Hank Aaron:** David Bixenspan, "Hank Aaron Sparked Pro Wrestling's First Major Racism Story 25 Years Ago," Deadspin.com, February 16, 2018 (https://deadspin.com/hank-aaron-sparked-pro-wrestlings -first-major-racism-st-1823080138/).

32 **Bischoff, despite feeling like he had no chance:** Bischoff with Roberts, *Controversy Creates Cash,* 83–85.

34 **One day in the summer of 1993:** Hogan with Friedman, *Hollywood Hulk Hogan,* 230.

34 **"Everything in life":** Unreleased portion of Hulk Hogan documentary interview obtained by author (2023).

34 **Journalists Shaun Assael and Mike Mooneyham reported:** Shaun Assael and Mike Mooneyham, *Sex, Lies, and Headlocks: The Real Story of Vince McMahon and the World Wrestling Federation* (Crown, 2002), 134–35.

35 **"Basically, I broke my word":** Unreleased portion of Hulk Hogan documentary interview obtained by author (2023).

35 **Bischoff said Hogan's first contract:** Jeremy Thomas, "Eric Bischoff Reveals Details on Hulk Hogan's Original WCW Contract," 411 Mania.com, April 25, 2019 (https://411mania.com/wrestling/eric -bischoff-reveals-details-hulk-hogans-wcw-contract/).

37 **"This is a business":** Unreleased portion of Hulk Hogan documentary interview obtained by author (2023).

38 **The *Bash at the Beach* pay-per-view buys:** Chris Harrington, "WCW Pay-Per-View Buys," Wrestlenomics.com, March 25, 2020 (https://wrestlenomics.com/resources/wcw-pay-per-view-buys -ppv-buys-ppv-buyrate/).

38 **Hogan vs. Flair II had 4,126,000 households:** Dave Meltzer, "Sept. 5, 1994 Observer Newsletter: Clash with Hogan vs. Flair sets records, most widely-viewed match ever on cable, Summer-Slam disappoints with Taker vs. Taker, famous ECW/NWA double-cross, tons more," *Wrestling Observer Newsletter,* September 5, 1994

(https://members.f4wonline.com/wrestling-observer-newsletter
/sept-5-1994-observer-newsletter-clash-hogan-vs-flair-sets-records
-most/).

39 **Bischoff said Hogan "did a sales job":** Bischoff with Roberts,
Controversy Creates Cash, 142.

43 **"It was a very short and sweet":** Unreleased portion of Hulk
Hogan documentary interview obtained by author (2023).

44 **Hogan met Paul Wight:** WrestleZone, "Paul Wight Wants to Buy
Danny Bonaduce Lunch and Say Thank You," Yahoo Entertainment, January 5, 2023 (https://www.yahoo.com/entertainment
/paul-wight-wants-buy-danny-164652968.html).

47 **When he found out about her release:** Bischoff with Roberts,
Controversy Creates Cash, 188.

48 **"It was a tawdry thing":** James Dixon, *Titan Shattered: Wrestling
with Confidence and Paranoia* (Lulu.com, 2015), 1.

CHAPTER 3: SAY HELLO TO THE BAD GUY

52 **Hall knew an altercation:** ESPN, "The Wrestler," *E:60* documentary, October 19, 2011.

52 **The man, named Rodney Perry Turner:** Sentinel Services, "Bar-
tender Charged in Slaying of Boss," *Orlando Sentinel*, January 16,
1983 (https://www.newspapers.com/article/the-orlando-sentinel
/40604994/?locale=en-US).

53 **Hall was raised in a military family:** ESPN, "The Wrestler."

53 **Hall himself wanted to be a wrestler:** RF Video, Scott Hall Shoot
Interview, 2007.

55 **Hall started having conversations:** Best of the KC Vault, You-
Shoot #33 | Scott Hall, YouTube.com, March 15, 2022 (https://
www.youtube.com/watch?v=FiID9iF2vWI).

55 **"Some guys were higher up":** Title Match Wrestling, "Scott
Hall & Kevin Nash—Full Shoot Interview (2007)," YouTube
.com, 2007 (https://www.youtube.com/watch?v=Bf6TujV_9kQ&
list=PLeEVBrTMHdSP4nzKIvV3oDi31vfRY7pIT&index=3).

59 **"When we did [the Turkish wolf sign]"**: WWE.com, "The 'Too Sweet' History of WWE's Most Iconic Gesture," WWE.com, June 24, 2016 (https://www.wwe.com/article/wwe-too-sweet -hand-gesture-meaning).

59 **Meltzer wrote the following week:** Dave Meltzer, "March 28, 1994 Observer Newsletter: Shawn Michaels ladder match review, Mania X, Tonya Harding AJW, tons more," *Wrestling Observer Newsletter,* March 28, 1994 (https://members.f4wonline.com/wrestling -observer-newsletter/march-28-1994-observer-newsletter-shawn -michaels-ladder-match-review/).

60 **"We almost prided ourselves"**: RF Video, Scott Hall Shoot Interview, 2007.

61 **"It was sort of like the wolfpack"**: Shane Douglas Official, "Shane Douglas on How Scott Hall Made Opponents Look BAD," You Tube.com, October 20, 2023 (https://www.youtube.com/watch?v =IqI2Sr0-rDs).

61 **"[Vince said,] 'What's the deal'"**: Marco Rovere, "Kevin Nash Recalls Vince McMahon Asking to Join the Kliq," WrestlingInc .com, July 14, 2022 (https://www.wrestlinginc.com/news/2022 /07/kevin-nash-recalls-vince-mcmahon-asking-to-join-the-kliq/).

62 **"I said, 'Do I need to improve'"**: RF Video, Scott Hall Shoot Interview, 2007.

62 **"I said, 'I ain't no mathematician'"**: RF Video, Scott Hall Shoot Interview, 2007.

63 **"Vince had you so busy working"**: Best of the KC Vault, "You-Shoot #33 | Scott Hall," YouTube.com," March 15, 2022 (https:// www.youtube.com/watch?v=FiID9iF2vWI).

CHAPTER 4: YOU GIVE THE PEOPLE WHAT THEY WANT

66 **Eight days before Hall:** Dakota Cohen, "Kevin Nash Recalls Smoking Hash with Fellow WWE Hall of Famers," WrestlingInc .com, August 23, 2022 (https://www.wrestlinginc.com/976290 /kevin-nash-recalls-smoking-hash-with-fellow-wwe-hall-of-famers/).

68 **"It just became organic":** Unreleased portion of Kevin Nash documentary interview obtained by author (2023).

68 **Nash grew up in southwest Detroit:** "Biography," KevinNash.co (https://kevinnash.co/biography).

68 **"Early in the game":** Thomas Golianopoulos, "Kevin Nash's Next Angle," Grantland.com, August 7, 2012 (https://grantland.com /features/wrestling-star-kevin-nash-making-headway-hollywood -keeps-night/).

69 **"He grabbed my jersey":** Golianopoulos, "Kevin Nash's Next Angle."

71 **"I saw a guy that was incredibly talented":** Golianopoulos, "Kevin Nash's Next Angle."

71 **Nash agreed:** RF Video, Kevin Nash Shoot Interview, 2007.

72 **"Nash tried to plead his case":** Unreleased portion of Kevin Nash documentary interview obtained by author (2023).

72 **When Hall told Nash the news:** RF Video, Scott Hall Shoot Interview, 2007.

72 **"Now, all of a sudden":** Title Match Wrestling, "How Shawn Michaels & the Kliq Acted to Vince McMahon in WWF," YouTube .com, May 31, 2020 (https://www.youtube.com/watch?v=nAZt-L _7EVQ).

73 **Bruce Prichard:** Marco Rovere, "Bruce Prichard Says Bam Bam Bigelow Believed the Kliq Was Burying Him," WrestlingInc.com, September 11, 2021 (https://www.wrestlinginc.com/news/2021 /09/bruce-prichard-says-bam-bam-bigelow-bought-into-the-hype -that-the-kliq-was-burying-him/).

75 **"I would've cost [Undertaker]":** Title Match Wrestling, "Scott Hall & Kevin Nash—Full Shoot Interview (2007)," YouTube .com, 2007 (https://www.youtube.com/watch?v=Bf6TujV_9kQ &list=PLeEVBrTMHdSP4nzKIvV3oDi31vfRY7pIT&index=3).

76 **"And fucking Taker":** Title Match Wrestling, "Scott Hall & Kevin Nash—Full Shoot Interview (2007)," YouTube.com, 2007 (https://www.youtube.com/watch?v=Bf6TujV_9kQ&list=PLe EVBrTMHdSP4nzKIvV3oDi31vfRY7pIT&index=3).

77 **For the remaining months of 1996:** David Bixenspan and Chris Harrington, "WCW Contract & Payroll Information (1996–2000)" (https://web.archive.org/web/20210305052623/https://sites .google.com/site/chrisharrington/wcw_contracts).

CHAPTER 5: WHO'S THE THIRD MAN?

85 **That episode of *Nitro*:** Dave Meltzer, "June 24, 1996 Wrestling Observer Newsletter: Dick Murdoch bio, one of the best PPVs of all time put on by WCW, Best of the Super Junior tournament, tons more," *Wrestling Observer Newsletter*, June 24, 1996 (https://mem bers.f4wonline.com/wrestling-observer-newsletter/june-24-1996 -wrestling-observer-newsletter-dick-murdoch-bio-one-best/).

89 **"Eric was thinking about putting Sting":** Unreleased portion of Hulk Hogan documentary interview obtained by author (2023).

CHAPTER 6: ARE PEOPLE IN DANGER?

101 **"I got noticed more for wrestling":** John Pozarowski, "Two Man Power Trip Feature Show: Kyle Petty," August 5, 2021(https:// www.podomatic.com/podcasts/tmptow/episodes/2021-08-04 T22_00_00-07_00).

101 **The day of *Bash at the Beach*:** Dave Meltzer, "July 15, 1996 Wres-tling Observer Newsletter: Bash at the Beach 1996 recap, UFC loses big court battle, Warrior suspended from WWF, tons more," *Wrestling Observer Newsletter*, July 15, 1996 (https://members.f4w online.com/wrestling-observer-newsletter/july-15-1996-wrestling -observer-newsletter-bash-beach-1996-recap-ufc/).

109 **"We both were huge [Alfred] Hitchcock fans":** RF Video, Kevin Nash Shoot Interview, 2007.

CHAPTER 7: THAT DIRTY LITTLE FUCKER

116 **"Once we trusted":** Unreleased portion of Hulk Hogan documen-tary interview obtained by author (2023).

116 **Tickets were not sold to *Hog Wild*:** Chris Harrington, "WCW

Pay-Per-View Buys," Wrestlenomics.com, March 25, 2020 (https:// wrestlenomics.com/resources/wcw-pay-per-view-buys-ppv-buys -ppv-buyrate/).

117 **Meltzer also highlighted an issue:** Dave Meltzer, "August 26, 1996 Wrestling Observer Newsletter: WWE considers weekly Saturday Night PPVs, SummerSlam just another show, health problems for big stars, tons more," *Wrestling Observer Newsletter*, August 26, 1996 (https://members.f4wonline.com/wrestling-observer -newsletter/august-26-1996-wrestling-observer-newsletter-wwe -considers-weekly/).

119 **"He just basically sat down":** Unreleased portion of Kevin Nash documentary interview obtained by author (2023).

120 **The bill ended up being around $40,000:** Dave Meltzer, "Sept. 9, 1996 Wrestling Observer Newsletter: Giant joins NWO, Davey Boy falls through, Bret Hart scheduled to return, Warrior lawsuit, tons more," *Wrestling Observer Newsletter*, September 9, 1996 (https://members.f4wonline.com/wrestling-observer-newslet ter/sept-9-1996-wrestling-observer-newsletter-giant-joins-nwo -davey-boy/).

127 **A woman called the WCW offices:** Dave Meltzer, "Nov. 4, 1996 Wrestling Observer Newsletter: Roddy Piper agrees to deal with WCW, Raw moving up one hour, WCW sets another all-time gate record, tons more!," *Wrestling Observer Newsletter*, November 4, 1996 (https://members.f4wonline.com/wrestling-observer-news letter/nov-4-1996-wrestling-observer-newsletter-roddy-piper -agrees-deal-wcw/).

CHAPTER 8: WE'RE STILL THE SHIT

140 **"[Sags is] thinking":** Title Match Wrestling, "Scott Hall—Why Jerry Sags Wanted to Kill Me in WCW," YouTube.com, May 20, 2024 (https://www.youtube.com/watch?v=cQ-B7nHyx_s).

141 **According to the *Orlando Business Journal*:** Alan Byrd, "Wrestler Trades Body Blows with WCW," *Orlando Business Journal*,

May 25, 1998 (https://www.bizjournals.com/orlando/stories /1998/05/25/story4.html).

141 **"Scott was different":** JP Zarka, "Scott Hall, Kevin Nash, and Nasty Boys Fight in Front of Fans," Pro Wrestling Stories, January 10, 2023 (https://prowrestlingstories.com/pro-wrestling -stories/scott-hall-kevin-nash-the-nasty-boys-fight/).

147 **The pay-per-view earned an estimated 345,000 buys:** Chris Harrington, "WCW Pay-Per-View Buys," Wrestlenomics.com, March 25, 2020 (view-source:https://wrestlenomics.com/re sources/wcw-pay-per-view-buys-ppv-buys-ppv-buyrate/).

147 **The best-selling non-WWF wrestling pay-per-view:** Dave Meltzer, "Jan. 6, 1997 Wrestling Observer Newsletter: ECW expected to debut on PPV, original cancellation and Pro Wrestling Torch story, WCW Starrcade, tons more," *Wrestling Observer Newsletter,* January 6, 1997 (https://members.f4wonline.com/wrestling-ob server-newsletter/jan-6-1997-wrestling-observer-newsletter-ecw -expected-debut-ppv/).

148 **His then-wife Linda described it:** Linda Hogan, *Wrestling the Hulk: My Life Against the Ropes* (William Morrow, 2011), 116, 117.

148 **"He was so excited":** Best of the KC Vault, "YouShoot #33 | Scott Hall, YouTube.com," March 15, 2022 (https://www.youtube .com/watch?v=FiID9iF2vWI).

150 **Savage would make $1.9 million:** David Bixenspan and Chris Harrington, "WCW Contract & Payroll Information (1996– 2000)" (https://web.archive.org/web/20210305052623/https:// sites.google.com/site/chrisharrington/wcw_contracts).

155 **"I want trucker women":** *83 Weeks with Eric Bischoff,* podcast, "Episode 38: Souled Out '97," January 14, 2019 (https://podcasts .apple.com/gb/podcast/episode-38-souled-out-97/id1137115 592?i=1000427599040).

156 **Meltzer described the nWo pay-per-view:** Dave Meltzer, "Feb. 3, 1997 Wrestling Observer Newsletter: Jerry Graham passes away, future of NHB in New York in serious jeopardy, Dave Brown quits,

NWO gimmick exposed, more," *Wrestling Observer Newsletter*, February 3, 1997 (https://members.f4wonline.com/wrestling-observer -newsletter/feb-3-1997-wrestling-observer-newsletter-jerry-graham -passes-away/).

162 ***Sports Illustrated* labeled him:** Michael Silver, "Rodman Unchained: The Spurs' No-Holds-Barred Forward Gives New Meaning to the Running Game," *Sports Illustrated*, May 29, 1995 (https://vault.si.com/vault/1995/05/29/rodman-unchained-the -spurs-no-holds-barred-forward-gives-new-meaning-to-the-run ning-game).

164 ***Uncensored* drew an estimated 325,000 buys:** Chris Harrington, "WCW Pay-Per-View Buys," Wrestlenomics.com, March 25, 2020 (https://wrestlenomics.com/resources/wcw-pay-per-view-buys -ppv-buys-ppv-buyrate/).

165 **The WCW house show business was "amazingly hot":** Dave Meltzer, "March 24, 1997 Wrestling Observer Newsletter: Future of MMA takes turn for the worst with PPV censorship, Steve Williams arrested, WCW publicity coup with Dennis Rodman, tons more," *Wrestling Observer Newsletter*, March 24, 1997 (https://members.f4wonline.com/wrestling-observer-newslet ter/march-24-1997-wrestling-observer-newsletter-future-mma -takes-turn/).

165 **Hall had failed a drug test:** Dave Meltzer, "March 31, 1997 Wrestling Observer Newsletter: Scott Hall checks into rehab, WrestleMania 1997 full report, Giant Baba wields his power, tons more," *Wrestling Observer Newsletter*, March 31, 1997 (https://members .f4wonline.com/wrestling-observer-newsletter/march-31-1997 -wrestling-observer-newsletter-scott-hall-checks-rehab/).

167 **Taking place in Philadelphia:** Dave Meltzer, "April 21, 1997 Wrestling Observer Newsletter: ECW PPV historical debut, Ogawa debut, MMA group out of business, more," *Wrestling Observer Newsletter*, April 21, 1997 (https://members.f4wonline.com /wrestling-observer-newsletter/april-21-1997-wrestling-observer -newsletter-ecw-ppv-historical-debut/).

CHAPTER 9: YOU REALLY ARE BATMAN

170 **The whole mess made him furious:** RF Video, Scott Hall Shoot Interview, 2007.

170 **Piper said he charged Nash:** Geries Tadros, "Kevin Nash and Roddy Piper: Their Heated Backstage Fight!," Pro Wrestling Stories, March 3, 2023 (https://prowrestlingstories.com/pro-wres tling-stories/kevin-nash-roddy-piper/).

170 **The *Nitro* in Boston:** Dave Meltzer, "June 16, 1997 Wrestling Observer Newsletter: Dressing room fights in both WWF and WCW, HBK threatens to quit, tons more," *Wrestling Observer Newsletter,* June 16, 1997 (https://members.f4wonline.com/wrestling-ob server-newsletter/june-16-1997-wrestling-observer-newsletter -dressing-room-fights-both/).

175 **Rodman made $750,000:** David Bixenspan and Chris Harrington, "WCW Contract & Payroll Information (1996–2000)" (https://web.archive.org/web/20210305052623/https://sites .google.com/site/chrisharrington/wcw_contracts).

175 ***Bash at the Beach* sold:** Chris Harrington, "WCW Pay-Per-View Buys," Wrestlenomics.com, March 25, 2020 (view-source:https:// wrestlenomics.com/resources/wcw-pay-per-view-buys-ppv-buys -ppv-buyrate/).

175 **Page walked a few doors down:** Diamond Dallas Page on Facebook (https://www.facebook.com/watch/?v=896302308036512).

181 **The attendance and gate ($240,519):** Dave Meltzer, "August 11, 1997 Wrestling Observer Newsletter: SummerSlam 1997 report, Austin tombstone of doom, tons more," *Wrestling Observer Newsletter,* August 11, 1997 (https://members.f4wonline.com/wrestling-observer -newsletter/august-11-1997-wrestling-observer-newsletter-summer slam-1997-report/).

186 **"I didn't drink a dozen beers":** The Four Horsemen Network, "Arn Anderson on confronting Kevin Nash about the nWo parody of the 'My Spot' promo," YouTube.com, October 18, 2019 (https:// www.youtube.com/watch?v=0LDzuX8XUNA).

CHAPTER 10: NO, MAN—IT'S CHRISTMAS

191 **"I don't know if it was the facepaint":** Sting, "The Man They Call Sting," *The Players' Tribune*, March 10, 2022 (https://www.the playerstribune.com/posts/sting-aew-wrestling).

194 *Nitro* **nearly doubled** *Raw*'s **rating:** Dave Meltzer, "Sept. 1, 1997 Wrestling Observer Newsletter: Arn Anderson retires, Steve Austin neck update, All Japan Women future tenuous, more," *Wrestling Observer Newsletter*, September 1, 1997 (https://members.f4won line.com/wrestling-observer-newsletter/sept-1-1997-wrestling -observer-newsletter-arn-anderson-retires-steve/).

194 **Became the most-purchased WCW pay-per-view ever:** Chris Harrington, "WCW Pay-Per-View Buys," Wrestlenomics.com, March 25, 2020 (https://wrestlenomics.com/resources/wcw-pay -per-view-buys-ppv-buys-ppv-buyrate/).

194 *Nitro* **ticket sales were up 892 percent:** Dave Meltzer, "Nov. 3, 1997 Wrestling Observer Newsletter: Halloween Havoc review w/ classic Guerrero-Misterio match, USWA officially dead, Pride 1 review, and much more," *Wrestling Observer Newsletter*, November 3, 1997 (https://members.f4wonline.com/wrestling-observer-news letter/nov-3-1997-wrestling-observer-newsletter-halloween-havoc -review-w/).

195 **A 10 percent ratings decline in** *Monday Night Football*: Dave Meltzer, "Jan 5. 1998 Observer Newsletter: Antonio Inoki retirement imminent, full WCW Starrcade recap, state of MMA," *Wrestling Observer Newsletter*, January 5, 1998 (https://members .f4wonline.com/wrestling-observer-newsletter/jan-5-1998-wres tling-observer-newsletter-antonio-inoki-retirement/).

199 **"There's an Australian guy":** Unreleased portion of Kevin Nash documentary interview obtained by author (2023).

203 **"I just know there were a lot of changes":** K&C Masterpiece, "Sting," 105.3 The Fan, December 12, 2022 (https://omny.fm/shows /kevin-and-cory/sting).

203 **"There has to be some type of out"**: Unreleased portion of Hulk Hogan documentary interview obtained by author (2023).

205 **"I said, 'Bro, I didn't screw you on the finish'"**: Unreleased portion of Hulk Hogan documentary interview obtained by author (2023).

207 **Ticket sales added up to a WCW record $543,000:** Dave Meltzer, "Jan 5. 1998 Observer Newsletter: Antonio Inoki retirement imminent, full WCW Starrcade recap, state of MMA," *Wrestling Observer Newsletter*, January 5, 1998 (https://members.f4wonline.com/wrestling-observer-newsletter/jan-5-1998-wrestling-observer-newsletter-antonio-inoki-retirement/).

CHAPTER 11: THAT WAS THE DOWNFALL OF IT

211 **"Fire our friend"**: Title Match Network, "Scott Hall & Kevin Nash—Full Shoot Interview (2007)," YouTube.com, September 29, 2024 (https://www.youtube.com/watch?v=Bf6TujV_9kQ).

211 **Nash earned a base salary of $1,518,979:** David Bixenspan and Chris Harrington, "WCW Contract & Payroll Information (1996–2000)" (https://web.archive.org/web/20210305052623/https://sites.google.com/site/chrisharrington/wcw_contracts).

212 **Hogan's base salary was $3,788,061:** 1998 Hulk Hogan Contract with WCW (https://www.scribd.com/doc/287131780/1998-Hulk-Hogan-contract-with-WCW).

214 **"That was the downfall of it"**: Title Match Network, "Scott Hall & Kevin Nash—Full Shoot Interview (2007)," YouTube.com, September 29, 2024.

215 **Bischoff asked Hall if he was "going in":** RF Video, Scott Hall Shoot Interview, 2007.

CHAPTER 12: BLEEP BOB COSTAS

224 **Kirk Johnson penned a *New York Times* article:** Kirk Johnson, "Professional Wrestling Cuts Good Guys from the Script," *New York Times*, March 30, 1998 (https://www.nytimes.com/1998

/03/30/sports/professional-wrestling-cuts-good-guys-from-the
-script.html).

224 **"Their heroes that have been popularized in both companies by
doing weekly anti-social behavior":** Dave Meltzer, "Dec. 29, 1997
Observer Newsletter: Near-riots at WWF house shows, Kazushi
Sakuraba becomes a star, nWo Nitro's future in question," *Wrestling
Observer Newsletter,* December 29, 1997 (https://members.f4won
line.com/wrestling-observer-newsletter/dec-29-1997-wrestling
-observer-newsletter-near-riots-wwf-house-shows/).

225 **"He was cleared by the Nevada State Athletic Commission:** New
York *Daily News* staff, "WWE Offers, Tyson Bites Nevada Grap-
ples with Wrestlin' Mike," New York *Daily News,* January 21, 1998
(https://www.nydailynews.com/1998/01/21/wwf-offers-tyson
-bites-nevada-grapples-with-wrestlin-mike/).

225 **"The coronation of Steve Austin":** Dave Meltzer, "April 6, 1998
Observer Newsletter: WWF WrestleMania XIV review," *Wrestling
Observer Newsletter,* April 6, 1998 (https://members.f4wonline.com
/wrestling-observer-newsletter/april-6-1998-wrestling-observer
-newsletter-wrestlemania-xiv-review/).

225 *Raw* **snapped** *Nitro's* **eighty-three-week ratings winning streak:**
Dave Meltzer, "April 20, 1998 Observer Newsletter: Record WWF
Raw ratings, issues between Ric Flair and WCW," *Wrestling Observer
Newsletter,* April 20, 1998 (https://members.f4wonline.com/wres
tling-observer-newsletter/april-20-1998-wrestling-observer-news
letter-raw-record-ratings-flair/).

226 **"We built the Saturn V":** Unreleased portion of Kevin Nash documentary interview obtained by author (2023).

230 **Nash felt that Hall picking Hogan over him:** RF Video, Kevin
Nash Shoot Interview, 2007.

230 **"I wouldn't have tried to wrap my brain around why":** Unreleased portion of Kevin Nash documentary interview obtained by
author (2023).

235 **the WCW records for attendance:** Dave Meltzer, "July 13, 1998
Observer Newsletter: Goldberg wins WCW World title, WWF

Brawl For All begins," *Wrestling Observer Newsletter,* July 30, 1998 (https://members.f4wonline.com/wrestling-observer-newsletter /july-13-1998-wrestling-observer-newsletter-goldberg-wins-wcw -world/).

237 ***Bash at the Beach 1998* sold:** Chris Harrington, "WCW Pay-Per-View Buys," Wrestlenomics.com, March 25, 2020 (https:// wrestlenomics.com/resources/wcw-pay-per-view-buys-ppv-buys -ppv-buyrate/).

237 **"Excuse my French":** Bob Raissman, "The World Is a Stage," New York *Daily News,* July 19, 1998 (https://www.nydailynews.com /1998/07/19/the-world-is-a-stage/).

CHAPTER 13: ONE OF THEM, I KNEW, HAD A GUN

238 **Leno, who averaged around five million viewers per night:** Ryan Faughnder, "Jay Leno's Last 'Tonight Show' Draws Biggest Audience Since 1998," *Los Angeles Times,* February 7, 2014 (https://www .latimes.com/entertainment/envelope/cotown/la-et-ct-ratings-jay -leno-leaves-tonight-show-20140206-story.html).

239 **It was Leno's interview with English actor Hugh Grant:** Lexy Perez, "Jay Leno Looks Back on Famous Hugh Grant 1995 Interview," *The Hollywood Reporter,* June 2, 2023 (https://www.holly woodreporter.com/tv/tv-news/jay-leno-looks-back-hugh-grant -1995-interview-1235506310/).

241 ***The Tonight Show* had nearly fifteen million viewers tune in:** Chris Harnick, "Jay Leno's Final *Tonight Show* Ratings: The Biggest Audience Since 1998," EOnline.com, February 7, 2014 (https:// www.eonline.com/news/508460/jay-leno-s-final-tonight-show -ratings-the-biggest-audience-since-1998).

241 ***The Tonight Show* featuring the nWo's takeover:** Dave Meltzer, "August 10, 1998 Observer Newsletter: Scott Hall arrested, Viewers Choice drops UFC," *Wrestling Observer Newsletter,* August 10, 1998 (https://members.f4wonline.com/wrestling-observer-news letter/august-10-1998-wrestling-observer-newsletter-96877/).

244 **But the pay-per-view numbers were strong again:** Chris Har-

rington, "WCW Pay-Per-View Buys," Wrestlenomics.com, March 25, 2020 (https://wrestlenomics.com/resources/wcw -pay-per-view-buys-ppv-buys-ppv-buyrate/).

248 **He drove drunk often and flipped or rolled several cars:** ESPN, "The Wrestler," *E:60* documentary, October 19, 2011.

248 **"I ain't proud of my behavior":** ESPN, "The Wrestler."

249 **"But it ain't the answer":** ESPN, "The Wrestler."

249 **Hall's ex-wife, Dana Burgio, posted two letters:** Dave Meltzer, "October 19, 1998 Observer Newsletter: PRIDE 4 results, Brian Hildebrand diagnosed with inoperable cancer," Wrestling Observer Newsletter, October 19, 1998 (https://members.f4wonline .com/wrestling-observer-newsletter/october-19-1998-wrestling -observer-newsletter-pride-4-results-brian/).

252 *Nitro* **had what was then the most watched pro-wrestling show in the history of cable:** Dave Meltzer, "September 7, 1998 Observer Newsletter: Ric Flair legal battle with WCW, WWF SummerSlam at MSG," *Wrestling Observer Newsletter*, September 7, 1998 (https://members.f4wonline.com/wrestling-observer-news letter/september-7-1998-ric-flair-legal-battle/).

254 *Starrcade 1998* **did an impressive business number:** Chris Harrington, "WCW Pay-Per-View Buys," Wrestlenomics.com, March 25, 2020 (https://wrestlenomics.com/resources/wcw -pay-per-view-buys-ppv-buys-ppv-buyrate/).

257 **"Makes no sense. Embarrassing":** Unreleased portion of Hulk Hogan documentary interview obtained by author (2023).

CHAPTER 14: I COULD HAVE CALLED HIM PORKY THE PIG

268 **It was ruled by the United States Court of Appeals:** *In Re: Mark Madden* (1998), FindLaw.com, August 6, 1998 (https://caselaw .findlaw.com/court/us-3rd-circuit/1116021.html).

CHAPTER 15: BAD TIMES DON'T LAST, BUT BAD GUYS DO

273 **McMahon had bought WCW:** Andrew Ross Sorkin, "Smackdown! W.W.F. to Buy Wrestling Rival," *New York Times*, March 4, 2001

(https://www.nytimes.com/2001/03/24/business/smackdown
-wwf-to-buy-wrestling-rival.html).

277 **You got four guys that were basically going at Vince:** Marc
Raimondi, "WWE to Honor nWo with Hall of Fame Induction,"
ESPN.com, December 9, 2019 (https://www.espn.com/wwe/story
/_/id/28256144/wwe-honor-nwo-hall-fame-induction).

278 *Time* **magazine did a major story:** James Collins, "Television:
Lords of the Ring," *Time,* June 29, 1998 (https://time.com/archive
/6733029/television-lords-of-the-ring/).

281 **German filmmaker Werner Herzog:** Gabriella Paiella, "Werner
Herzog Cannot Stop Talking About WrestleMania," *GQ,* November 12, 2019 (https://www.gq.com/story/werner-herzog-wrestle
mania).

284 **Hall slipped and fell:** Dave Meltzer, "March 21, 2022 Observer
Newsletter: Death of Scott Hall," *Wrestling Observer Newsletter,*
March 21, 2022 (https://members.f4wonline.com/wrestling-ob
server-newsletter/march-21-2022-observer-newsletter-death
-scott-hall-97817/).

285 **"We all talked to him":** Kliq This, "Kevin Nash on his final moments with Scott Hall," YouTube.com, July 15, 2022 (https://www
.youtube.com/watch?v=MSImPRFq7-A)

285 **"I'm going to lose the one person":** Kevin Nash on Instagram
(https://www.instagram.com/realkevinnash/p/CbEqfqau6zp/).

286 **Nash said he was contacted by a company out of London:** Dante
Richardson, "Kevin Nash Opens Up About Relationship with Hulk
Hogan," ITRWrestling.com, January 9, 2023 (https://itrwrestling
.com/news/kevin-nash-relationship-with-hulk-hogan/).

286 **"Hard work pays off":** WWE, "Scott Hall's WWE Hall of Fame
speech #Short," YouTube.com, March 15, 2022 (https://www.you
tube.com/watch?v=TVnbU0gaveU).

ACKNOWLEDGMENTS

When I was seven years old, I vehemently argued with my uncle Joe, in my parents' Queens, New York, basement that pro wrestling was real. It had to be, I contended, because I saw Jake "The Snake" Roberts' snake, Damian, bite "Macho Man" Randy Savage's arm on television with my own two eyes. How could you fake that?

That was 1991. It was conversations and observations like that one over the last three decades that probably led to the writing of this book.

Many of those discussions in recent years—about characters and storylines and works and shoots and suplexes—have been with my wife, Wendy Arellano. She was alongside me every step of the way, even during a few-month stretch where I watched more than 500 hours of WCW television from the nineties for research. Now that's unconditional love. I couldn't have done any of this without her patience and caring. I wore New World Order socks to our wedding, for chrissakes. But I know our love—like the nWo—is absolutely for life.

I wouldn't be who I am today without my parents, Diane and Louis, and my stepmother, Esther. Amid her swooning at the television whenever Razor Ramon or The Rock came on in the nineties, my mother always pushed me to be my best. Same for my father, who drove me countless times to Blockbuster Video when I was a kid to pick up old wrestling tapes. (I won't tell anyone about the illegal cable box we had that let us watch pay-per-views for free, Dad. . . . Oops.) Esther always made sure I was fueled on arroz con salchichas—and coquito during the holidays. If you know, you know.

And then, of course, there's my younger sister, Marisa, who watched all those hours of wrestling with me as a kid and then willingly (mostly) let me perform the moves on her afterward. Her lower-back issues probably stem from the times she was perilously locked in the Sharpshooter. I've tried to share my love for pro wrestling with her daughters and my nieces, Meadow and Mia. It's come with varying degrees of success. But I have put Meadow in the Sharpshooter. Family tradition.

I also want to thank my closest friends: Esther, Casey, Joe, Zach, Eduardo, Leigh, David, Tivoli, Travis, and Kathleen. I've surely driven you all crazy over the last few decades, but I immensely appreciate you being there for me when I needed you.

This book would not have been possible without my editor, Yahdon Israel, and my literary agent Kirsten Neuhaus. When Yahdon cold emailed me in 2021 and asked if I wanted to write a book about the nWo, I thought for sure it was a phishing scam. Until I googled his name, we spoke on the phone and hit it off right away, with a shared vision of what wrestling is and what this book could be. Kirsten is a rock star and has guided me at every turn, because frankly I had no idea what I was doing in the literary world.

Thanks, also, to all my editors at ESPN who gave me the leeway and patience to write a book while also covering combat sports and then the NFL. Everyone who picked up their phones and agreed to chat with me for this book, I also owe a debt of gratitude.

ACKNOWLEDGMENTS

Lastly, I'd just like to thank the world of professional wrestling as a whole—the wrestlers, managers, producers, agents, ring announcers, commentators, bookers, writers, etc.—who have brought so much entertainment and joy to us fans over the years. When pro wrestling is at its best, there's nothing better.